DEFENDING OXFORDSHIRE

THE MILITARY LANDSCAPE FROM PREHISTORY TO THE PRESENT

MIKE OSBORNE

I0895792

FONTHILL

First published in Great Britain in 2025 by Fonthill
An imprint of
Pen & Sword Books Ltd
Yorkshire – Philadelphia
www.fonthill.media

Copyright © Mike Osborne 2025

ISBN 978-1-78155-914-7

The right of Mike Osborne to be identified as
Author of this work has been asserted by him in accordance
with the Copyright, Designs and Patents Act 1988.

A CIP catalogue record for this book
is available from the British Library.

All rights reserved. No part of this book may be reproduced or
transmitted in any form or by any means, electronic or mechanical
including photocopying, recording or by any information storage and
retrieval system, without permission from the Publisher in writing.

Typeset in Sabon LT 10/13
Typeset by Fonthill
Printed and bound in the UK by CPI Group (UK) Ltd, Croydon, CR0 4YY

MIX
Paper | Supporting
responsible forestry
FSC® C013604

The Publisher's authorised representative in the EU for product
safety is Authorised Rep Compliance Ltd., Ground Floor,
71 Lower Baggot Street, Dublin D02 P593, Ireland.
www.arccompliance.com

For a complete list of Pen & Sword titles please contact
PEN & SWORD BOOKS LIMITED
47 Church Street, Barnsley, South Yorkshire, S70 2AS, England
E-mail: enquiries@pen-and-sword.co.uk
Website: www.pen-and-sword.co.uk

Or

PEN AND SWORD BOOKS
1950 Lawrence Rd, Havertown, PA 19083, USA
E-mail: Uspen-and-sword@casematepublishers.com
Website: www.penandswordbooks.com

Contents

Acknowledgements

As always, there are a number of people to whom I am indebted for their willingness to share information and to make images available. These include the following: Trevor Hancock of Wantage and the Vale & Downland Museum; Joe Gibbs at Edgehill (now Shenington) airfield; Neil Milliner at Bicester Motion; Nick Clarke at the Myers-Briggs Company; Stanley Jenkins for journal articles and personal communications regarding Witney; Phum at Oxford Brookes for access to the ROC control bunker; Miles Young, Warden of New College, Oxford, and his staff; Nigel Dawe of the Ridgeway Military & Aviation Research Group; Sarah Taylor at Rycote Park; Neil Guy of the Castle Studies Group for his generous sharing of images; Judy Dewey of Wallingford Museum and the Wallingford Historical and Archaeological Society; Colin Alexander and Paul Francis for their continuing permission to use their images; and Adrian Armishaw, ever willing to share information and illustrations. I hope I have not missed anyone. As ever, my wife, Pam, has given me support, particularly with our fieldwork expeditions, and at Fonthill Media I have continued to benefit from the professional expertise of Alan, Jay, Josh, and Jamie.

List of Abbreviations

AA	Anti-Aircraft
AAA (AW)	Anti-Aircraft Artillery (Automatic Weapons) US Army, Second World War
AAOR	Anti-Aircraft Operations Room
ACF	Army Cadet Force, successor to TCF
ADGB	Air Defence Great Britain
AERE	Atomic Energy Research Establishment (Harwell)
AFDD	Air Force Distribution Depot (fuel)
AFRD	Air Force Reserve Depot (fuel)
AFS	Auxiliary Fire Service, 1938 and subsumed by new NFS, 1941
AI	Airborne Interception (Radar)
AM (WD)	Air Ministry (Works Department)
ARC	Army Reserve Centre (formerly TA Centre)
ARG	Airfield Research Group
ARP	Air-Raid Precautions
ARS	Air-Raid Shelter
ASU	Aircraft Storage Unit (RAF and MAP)
A/T	Anti-Tank
ATA	Air Transport Auxiliary (civilian ferry pilots)
ATC	Air Training Corps from 1941
ATS	Auxiliary Territorial Service (1938–49, then WRAC)
BAT	Beam or Blind Approach Training
BB	Boys' Brigade
BCF	British Concrete Federation
BEF	British Expeditionary Force
BHQ	Battle Headquarters
CBA	Council for British Archaeology

CCF	Combined Cadet Force (successor to OTC, 1948)
CD	Civil Defence
CEGB	Central Electricity Generating Board
C-in-C	Commander-in-Chief
CLB	Church Lads' Brigade
CO	Commanding Officer
COD	Central Ordnance Depot
CRO/U	Civilian Repair Organisation/Unit (aircraft repairs in the Second World War under MAP)
CSG	Castle Studies Group
CTA	County Territorial Association
DE&S	Defence Equipment and Support Agency from 2007
DFW3	Directorate of Fortifications & Works, Department 3, War Office
DL	Defended Locality
DPs	Displaced Persons (post-Second World War)
DORA	Defence of the Realm Act (emergency legislation)
ECAD	European Civil Affairs Department (US Army)
EMS	Emergency Medical Service
EOD	Explosive Ordnance Disposal (bomb disposal)
(E&R)(S)FTS	(Elementary & Reserve) (Service) Flying Training School
ESR	Essential Service Route
ETOUSA	European Theatre of Operations US Army
FAA	Fleet Air Arm, 1937 hived off from RAF, back into the RN
FAD	Forward Ammunition Depot
FANY	First Aid Nursing Yeomanry
FRIBA	Fellow of the Royal Institute of British Architects
GC&CS	Government Code & Cypher School (Bletchley Park, etc.)
GCI	Ground-Controlled Interception (radar system Second World War onwards)
GDA	Gun-Defended Area (concentration of AA defences)
GEE	RAF radio navigation system in use 1942–70
GHQ	General Headquarters (GHQ Line, GHQ Reserve, etc.)
GL	Gun-laying (radar)
GS	Grammar School
GTS	Glider Training School
GWR	Great Western Railway
Ha	Hectare (2.5 acres)
HAA	Heavy Anti-Aircraft
HGCU	Heavy Glider Conversion Unit (pilot training)
HER	Heritage Environment Record (ex-Sites & Monuments Record)

HF/DF	High-Frequency Direction Finding radio (Huff-Duff)
HG	Home Guard
ISTD	Inter-Service Topographic Department
ITC/PTC	Infantry/Primary Training Centre (Second World War)
JARIC	Joint Air Reconnaissance Intelligence Centre
KRRC	Kings Royal Rifle Corps
LAA	Light Anti-Aircraft
LDV	Local Defence Volunteers, later Home Guard (Second World War)
LG	Landing ground
MAFF	Ministry of Agriculture, Fisheries & Food (post-Second World War)
MAP	Ministry of Aircraft Production (WWII)
MI5, MI6, etc.	Military Intelligence departments
MOD	Ministry of Defence
MOS	Ministry of Supply
MP	Military Police
MT	Motor Transport
MU	Maintenance Unit (RAF)
NATO	North Atlantic Treaty Organisation
NCO	Non-Commissioned Officer
NID	Naval Intelligence Department
NFF	National Filling Factory (First World War munitions plant)
NFS	National Fire Service (Second World War)
NRA	National Rifle Association
OB	Operational Base (Auxiliary Unit secret hideaway)
OBLI	Oxfordshire & Buckinghamshire Light Infantry, 1908–57
OLI	Oxfordshire Light Infantry, 1881–1908
OS	Ordnance Survey (Government mapping agency)
OTB	Officer Training Battalion, First World War
OTC	Officer Training Corps (school or university cadet corps)
OTU	Operational Training Unit (RAF Bomber/Training Commands)
OUAS	Oxford University Air Squadron
OUOTC	Oxford University Officer Training Corps
OURN	Oxford University Royal Naval Unit
(P)AFU	(Pilot) Advanced Flying Unit
PBX	Private Branch (Telephone) Exchange
PIU	Photographic Interpretation Unit
POL	Petrol, Oil & Lubricants (depot or stores)
POW	Prisoner of War
PRU	Photographic Reconnaissance Unit

QARANC	Queen Alexandra's Royal Army Nursing Corps, 1949
QM	Quartermaster (logistics organisation and personnel)
QOOH	Queen's Own Oxfordshire Hussars Yeomanry
RA	Royal Artillery
RAuxAF	Royal Auxiliary Air Force, until 1957
RAF	Royal Air Force (RFC and RNAS from 1 April 1918)
RAFVR	Royal Air Force Volunteer Reserve from 1936
RAMC	Royal Army Medical Corps
(R)AOC	(Royal from 1918) Army Ordnance Corps, until 1993
(R)ASC	(Royal from 1918) Army Service Corps, until 1993
RE	Royal Engineers
REME	Royal Electrical and Mechanical Engineers (formed 1942)
RFA	Royal Field Artillery (until 1924)
RFC	Royal Flying Corps (up to 31 March 1918)
RFCA	Reserve Forces and Cadets Association, successor to CTAs
RGA	Royal Garrison Artillery (until 1924)
RGHQ	Regional Government Headquarters
RHA	Royal Horse Artillery
RHQ	Regimental Headquarters
RLC	Royal Logistic Corps, from 1993 (transport, catering, ordnance units, etc.)
RLG	Relief Landing Ground (flying training)
RNAS	Royal Naval Air Service to 31 March 1918; then RAF's naval branch 1924–37
(R)OC	(Royal from 1941) Observer Corps
RSG	Regional Seat of Government (Cold War bunker)
RVC	Rifle Volunteer Corps (1859–80)
SAA	Small Arms Ammunition
SAC	Strategic Air Command (USAF, post-Second World War)
SCSRD	Station Complement Squadron Reinforcement Depot (included Flak Shacks)
SF	Special Fires (Bombing Decoy—aka 'Starfish')
SHAEF	Supreme HQ Allied Expeditionary Force from 1944 under Eisenhower
SIS	Secret Intelligence Service (aka MI6)
SLG	Satellite Landing-ground (aircraft storage)
SOC	Sector Operations Centre
SOE	Special Operations Executive
SOS	Service of Supply (US Army logistics organisation)
STS	Special Training School (SOE)
TA	Territorial Army (from 1920–39 and 1947–2014)
TAC	Territorial Army Centre (drill hall 1947–2014, see ARC)

tb	temporary brick or half-brick (single brick with buttresses in RAF buildings)
TCF	Territorial Cadet Force, 1908
TDS	Training Depot Station, First World War
TF	Territorial Force, 1908–1918
TNA	The National Archive (formerly Public Record Office, Kew)
TOB	Temporary Office Building (Government offices from 1940)
UED	Universal Equipment Depot (RAF)
u/g	underground
UHF	Ultra High Frequency (radio wavelength)
UKWMO	United Kingdom Warning & Monitoring Organisation
UP	Unrotated Projectile (*see* ZAA)
UTP	Upper Thames Patrol (Home Guard)
USAAC	United States Army Air Corps (until 1941)
USAAF	United States Army Air Force (Second World War from 1941)
USAF(E)	United States Air Force (Europe) post-Second World War
USSTAFE	United States Strategic Tactical Air Force Europe, Second World War
VAD	Voluntary Aid Detachment (First World War medical personnel)
VCH	Victoria County History
VF	Volunteer Force (1860–1908 and 1916–18)
VHF	Very High Frequency (radio wavelength)
VP	Vulnerable Point
VR	Volunteer Regiment (county unit of VTC/VF, 1915–18)
VTC	Volunteer Training Corps, 1914–16 (First World War Home Guard analogue)
WAAC	Women's Auxiliary Army Corps (First World War)
WAAF	Women's Auxiliary Air Force (later WRAF)
WLA	Women's Land Army
WRAC	Women's Royal Army Corps (from 1949–92)
W/T	Wireless telegraphy
YM/WCA	Young Men's/Women's Christian Association
ZAA	AA rocket batteries

Introduction

Oxfordshire commands the Thames Valley, the main east–west route linking London and Wales, and also occupies a key position in the South Midlands astride the route from Southampton to Birmingham and North West England. Key routes have been in use since ancient times, with the extension of the prehistoric trackways known as the Ridgeway and Swan's Way crossing the county to become the Icknield Way as it negotiates the Chilterns. Abingdon marks the meeting point of the tribal lands of the Dobunni, the Catuvellauni, and the Atrebates. Alchester near Banbury is where the Roman Akeman Street, linking Cirencester to St Albans, crosses the Roman road which links the Fosse Way to the south coast through Dorchester-on-Thames. In Saxon times, the city of Oxford itself lay on the very border between Wessex and Mercia. This county, then, clearly contains locations of strategic importance, particularly in relation to northward routes from the potential invasion beaches of Dorset and Hampshire on the south coast, or westward along the Thames Valley. It therefore witnessed conflict between Britons and Romans, Saxons and Danes; between competing claimants to the throne; between kings and rebellious barons; and between the supporters of king and parliament. In 1940, the principal anti-invasion defence line traversed the county along the course of the Thames from Kelmscot to Pangbourne. In two world wars, the training of soldiers and aircrew took place within an environment of munitions production, development, storage, and distribution.

Like many of England's ceremonial counties, Oxfordshire, originally comprising the fourteen Hundreds of Bampton, Banbury, Binfield, Bloxham, Bullingdon, Chadlington, Dorchester, Ewelme, Langtree, Lewknor, Pyrton, Ploughley, Thame, and Wootton, since 1974 has become a significantly larger entity by absorbing the six Berkshire Hundreds of Faringdon, Ganfield, Hormer, Ock, Shrivenham, and Wantage. At the same time, Caversham, formerly in

Oxfordshire, was transferred to Berkshire. This study will examine the county as it stands within its current, post-1974 boundaries.

This is the twelfth volume in a series which began with *Defending Lincolnshire* in 2010. It seeks both to highlight the individual characteristics of the county's military infrastructure, and those elements in the landscape which demonstrate defensive capabilities and continuity. It also seeks to record many of those defensive features at a time when many of them continue to disappear under the plough, through mineral extraction, or housing or commercial development. There are, in the county, some excellent examples of the reuse of redundant military buildings but many more have gone. Nevertheless, many impressive and important structures survive across all historical periods from the prehistoric earthworks of Uffington Castle to the vast hangars of RAF Brize Norton.

Fortunately, relics of conflicts are still coming to light. Prior to construction work on the former RAF Harwell site, Museum of London Archaeologists (MOLA) have unearthed a prototype catapult for launching loaded bombers off a shortened runway. The bomber sat on a circular apron; hooked itself up; and was propelled by compressed air produced by Rolls-Royce engines. This project was begun in 1938 when bomber aircraft such as the Fairey Battle were lighter than those which were to come, and the experiment was not progressed. The idea may, however, have been the genesis of the system which launched Hawker Hurricanes off merchant ships to provide fighter cover for convoys. The pit and trench were subsequently covered by a conventional runway and the excavation has now been backfilled by MOLA.

1

Fortifications in Oxfordshire Prior to the Norman Conquest

This chapter divides this era into three sections examining the prehistoric period: mainly the Iron Age; the Romano-British era; and the times of the Anglo-Saxons and Danes, often misleadingly known as the Dark Ages.

Prehistoric Forts and Defended Settlements

Oxfordshire included within its boundaries the territories of three distinct tribes: the Dobunni who lived north of the Thames and west of the Cherwell, and stretched into Gloucestershire; the Catuvellauni who were north of the Thames and east of the Cherwell, and extended into Hertfordshire; and the Atrebates who were a Belgic tribe which had spread from France and colonised the eastern parts of Hampshire and the western parts of Sussex, as far as Berkshire, south of the Thames. These tribal territories appear to have overlapped around the confluence of the rivers Ock and Thames in Abingdon, due either to fluctuating boundaries or the importance of liminal trading interfaces and focal points of cultural exchange. On the evidence of occupation and coin finds, Dorchester's settlement of Dyke Hills has been put forward as a possible *oppidum*, Belgic in origin and an important tribal centre of the Atrebates.

The Bronze Age in England lasted from 2100–750 BC, and the hilltop enclosures at Rams Hill and Little Wittenham both date from this period. They both show evidence for ramparts, ditches, and palisades, and would later be incorporated into Iron Age hillforts. Rams Hill has been dated as originating in the period 1250–1000 BC with Little Wittenham being slightly younger. Blewburton Hill's earliest palisaded enclosure may also date from the late Bronze Age, but although the white horse at Uffington is assigned a Bronze Age date, the adjacent fort is later. An enclosed settlement at Eynsham has also been dated to the late Bronze Age. Only a very few forts enjoyed such a long lifespan. Sinodun Camp, Castle Hill, Wittenham Clumps, is a roughly heart-shaped enclosure with bank and deep ditch and a single entrance standing on an isolated chalk hill. The rear of the rampart was revetted by a vertical timber fence. The earliest material, from a midden, dates to the late Bronze Age, and a Romano-British settlement with a Roman villa and fifteen roundhouses has been excavated. Lying 200 yards west of the entrance, this site has yielded pottery dating from the first to the fifth century AD. Long occupation, continuing into the Roman period, may account for the continual scouring of the ditch, incrementally producing a massive counterscarp bank, 7 feet (2.2 metres) high and over 30 feet (10 metres) across. At Rams Hill, excavations between 1972 and 1975 uncovered the evolution of a fort dating from the twelfth century BC when an oval area of 2.5 acres (1 ha) was enclosed by a stone-faced rampart inside a chalk-cut ditch pierced by two or three entrances. Before the end of the century, the earlier defences were replaced by a timber-laced rampart and 200 years later, the inner edge of the silted-up ditch provided the base for a double palisade. In the seventh century BC, this inner core was then incorporated into a much larger hillfort of around 8 acres (3.5 ha).

Early Iron Age settlements such as those apparent at Standlake, Dorchester, and Mount Farm consisted of circular huts and enclosures protected by palisaded banks and ditches, most probably intended to protect livestock from predators both human and animal. A middle Iron Age settlement site at Barton, near Oxford, has been found to have been surrounded by double V-shaped ditches up to 5 feet (1.5 metres) deep with an interior bank, deemed by the excavators to be defensive, possibly even part of a linear system. The substantial post-holes of a presumed gate have been shown to have been of unusually sturdy construction, interpreted as providing a higher-than-normal level of protection. Many other ditches enclosing settlements of the middle Iron Age, such as several in the Windrush valley, have been interpreted as boundaries rather than defences.

The future site of Oxford has generated evidence of only intermittent settlement on the gravel banks at the confluence of the Thames and Cherwell, and Salway describes the 'abundance of small, enclosed settlements' in the north of the county, dating from the Iron Age period and continuing into the Roman period. Nevertheless, the county retains plenty of imposing Iron Age hillforts of different types. That class of monument which has the generic 'hillfort' name presents us with several unanswered, probably unanswerable, questions mainly relating to their purpose and use. While some of them occupy potentially defensible positions in the landscape, often enhanced by engineering, it is by no means clear that defence was their primary purpose. Given the investment in labour, the sparsity of signs of occupation suggests other purposes alongside. These could include meeting places for celebrations, rituals, or consultations;

places of refuge for tribespeople and their livestock in times of conflict; secure storage for crop surpluses; status symbols for leaders or clans within the tribe; or fortresses specifically designed to dominate a subject population. All of these purposes may possibly have been valid at different times and in different circumstances. Most of Oxfordshire's hillforts are located on the higher ground of the county's north-west, with several situated along the Ridgeway. Few occupy obvious defensive positions and therefore must rely on wholly artificial defences rather than being built on carefully selected positions of natural strength. English Heritage's Wessex Hillforts Project includes Uffington and Segsbury as typical of the region's forts occupying easily defended locations but emphasises Alfred's Castle as an anomaly, unusually sited on lower-lying land and included for that reason. Although Oxfordshire's hillforts such as Ilbury or Cassington Big Ring have mostly been damaged by ploughing, quarrying, or gravel-extraction, plenty of details survive to point to the general principles underlying their location and construction even if their purpose often remains unclear. All these hillforts can be characterised as falling into four distinct categories.

Uffington Castle: the rampart and ditch of this hillfort near the Ridgeway.

Sinodun Camp: the rampart, ditch, and particularly impressive counterscarp.

Dorchester Dyke Hills: the banks enclosing the *oppidum*. Originally classified as a promontory fort with rivers on three sides, it is now seen as a large valley fort.

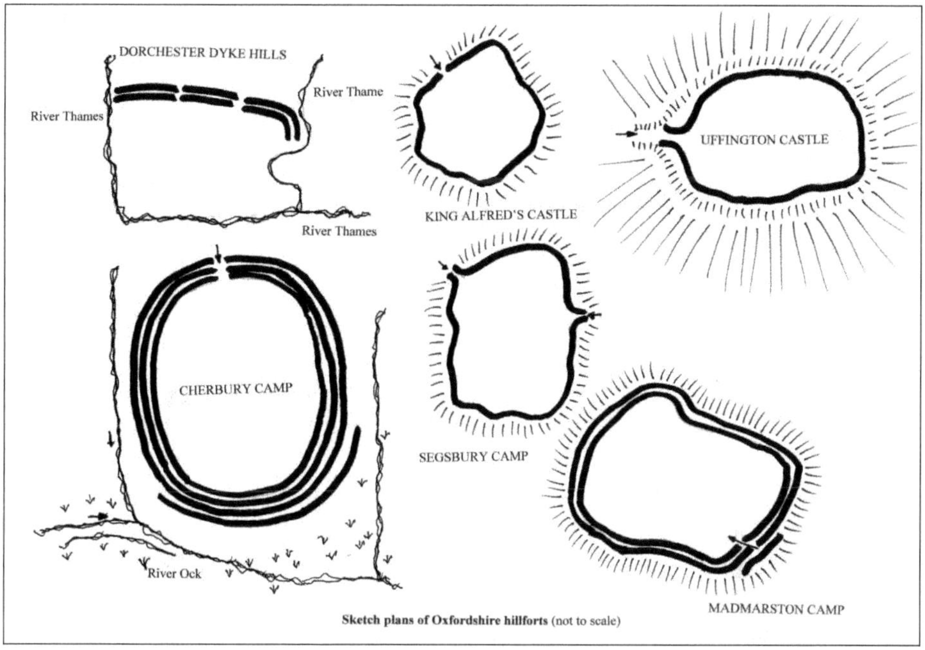

Sketch plans of six prehistoric Oxfordshire forts (not to scale).

Contour Forts

Some forts occupied the summits of hills, and their defences followed the humps and bumps and are therefore known as 'contour forts'. Madmarston Hill Camp, Swalcliffe; Segsbury Camp or Letcombe Castle; Alfred's Castle; and Uffington Castle on White Horse Hill are examples of such forts. Segsbury/Letcombe is a univallate hillfort of around 25 acres (10 ha) alongside the Ridgeway, classified as a partial contour fort on the edge of a scarp, and found to have been in intermittent use between the sixth and second centuries BC. The rampart—which is 16 feet (5 metres) higher than ground level in places, showing signs of different types of construction including timber framing—was faced with sarsen stones like the neighbouring Uffington and Alfred's Castle, with a possible revetment behind the rampart. An entrance on the east had an out-turned rampart and a horn-work, and a very wide ditch surrounded the whole fort, with a pronounced outer counterscarp bank. Evidence of roundhouses, however, showed no great density of occupation. Uffington Castle on White Horse Hill is a hillfort with elements dating from the earliest Iron Age. It measures 240 by 170 yards (220 by 160 metres) and is surrounded by a rampart, composed of timber bracing and chalk rubble, its inner face lined with sarsen stones and a ditch. The entrance on the west takes the form of a causeway where the inner rampart's ends turn outwards to meet a heightened counterscarp bank on both sides of the entrance. There appears to be a second, blocked entrance at the eastern end of the fort, also indicated by heightened counterscarp and inward turning rampart. A silver coin of the Dubonni was found inside the camp but only sparse evidence for occupation. Uffington exhibits more signs of use, generally burials, in times later than the Iron Age and its defences were slighted in the Roman period. Alfred's Castle, above Ashbury, is a small, irregularly hexagonal, hillfort, occupying a late Bronze Age landscape of ditched enclosures. The fort, itself, measuring 150 yards (136 metres) across, is univallate with a rampart faced with sarsen revetments as at its neighbours. The original south-eastern entrance is defended by outworks whereby a hollow way enters through a second outer bank, forming a triangle on the eastern side of the entrance. There being no corresponding feature on the western side, this has been interpreted as an earlier barrow, incorporated into the defences. Badbury Hill is a roughly circular Iron Age hillfort known as Badbury Camp standing on an elevated site. Chastleton (Barrow or Burrow) Camp is located on a hilltop site and defended by a single, steep-sided, stone-faced rubble wall 13 feet (4 metres) high externally, its internal rampart revetted with laid polygonal limestone blocks, some of them up to 4 to 6 feet (1.2 to 1.8 metres) in length but lacking any evidence for a ditch. Madmarston Hill Camp, Swalcliffe, is a contour fort defended by two ramparts but a single ditch on the north-east and east with double ramparts of piled clay, strengthened by quantities of glutinous grey clay, and two ditches on the south and south-west, with a third, outer counterscarp bank, enclosing an oval area of 7 acres (2.8 ha), occupied for 200 years from the first century BC. An entrance on the southern side was screened by a mound, while the entrance passage, represented by a layer of stones, 11 feet (3.4 metres) across, pierced the rampart at an oblique angle and the post-holes of a possible gate were found. The ditch was 30 feet (9 metres) across and 10 feet (3 metres) deep. The rampart was not revetted but held together by its hardened clay capping, and there were indications that a timber framework had been laid to hold the clay as it was being laid down. On the north side, traces of postholes underlying the rampart suggest an earlier palisaded rampart. Optimum use was made of the natural slope with the result that it was unnecessary for ramparts to be unduly high.

Promontory Forts

'Promontory forts' were built on spurs of land which generally benefitted from having drops on three sides with the fourth side, the direction of approach, protected by ramparts and ditches with defended entrances. Hardwell Camp, Compton Beauchamp, is a promontory fort combining contour features with a naturally strong position at the head of two small valleys to enhance its defensibility. A central area, roughly 650 feet (200 metres) square, is defended across its south side by a turf and stone rubble rampart with an entrance and a further, outer bank with a ditch 50 feet (16 metres) wide. On the north, two projecting spurs are defended by low ramparts along their top edges. The inner slopes of the valleys have been adapted by scarping further to improve the defences. Binditch or Bozedown Camp, Whitchurch, of 58 acres (22 ha) has univallate defences and stands on the edge of a plateau which falls away to the Thames. A V-shaped ditch 10 feet (3 metres) deep with traces of a counterscarp bank has been excavated. Not strictly a promontory fort, use is nevertheless made of an elevated site with a steep drop on one side.

Plateau Forts

Standing in often elevated, but flat locations, 'plateau forts' are surrounded by land at the same level as themselves and therefore have none of the benefits of sheer drops or natural glacis defences. Idbury Camp is a small, roughly circular, univallate fort of 9 acres (3.5 ha) standing in a prominent position on a plateau with fine views over the Cotswolds. The Roundabout at Lyneham is an Iron Age plateau fort with a single bank and ditch enclosing 4.5 acres (1.8 ha), but largely destroyed through ploughing. A cross-section of the rampart showed large stone slabs forming a revetment on both inner and outer faces. The presence of large stones laid along the summit of the bank may indicate a paved rampart walk. Tadmarton Heath Camp is a roughly circular, bivallate plateau fort of around 5 acres (2 ha). The inner rampart had an outer revetment wall of stone, 5 feet (1.5 metres) high and 2 feet (61 cm) thick. Castle Bank, Shutford, is an almost square enclosure covering 5 acres (2 ha), bounded by a ditch and a stream with the surrounding land falling away only slightly. It is ambivalently described by Sutton as having 'nothing obviously un-hill-fort-like about it', a reference to its unusually sharp corners, perhaps. Castle Grove Camp, Checkendon, in Wyfold Wood, is an irregularly oval, univallate fort of around 5 acres (2 ha), whose rampart is composed of piled gravel with a gap where ponds and swampy land provide protection. The south-west entrance has been described as 'oblique', presumably meaning an entrance passage incorporating a dogleg or an angled approach facilitating covering fire from the wall walk.

Valley Forts

Marsh-forts, or 'valley forts', are coming to be seen as a separate monument category, analogous to hillforts but built on low-lying land. Oxfordshire contains a number of examples: Dyke Hills, Dorchester; Cassington Big Ring; Cherbury Camp; Burroway; and Abingdon Vineyard, all dating to the later period of the Iron Age, and all appearing more likely to have included settlements. Dyke Hills has bivallate defences enclosing an area of 114 acres (45 ha) formed by a bend in the Thames and its confluence with the River Thame. The 975-yard-long (900-metre-long) bank, apparently built up in successive phases, rises to 10 feet (3 metres) above the interior and may have had an original entrance on its eastern side. Between this inner rampart and a higher outer bank is a ditch, generally thought to have contained water and this may have been intended to link the Thame and the Thames. Unusually, there is evidence for high levels of occupation signified by roundhouses and large finds of coins. Abingdon's Vineyard is also classified as a valley fort and was surrounded on two sides by massive double or triple wet ditches with the Thames on the other two sides, the area enclosed being around 33 acres (13 ha). Two main ditches, varyingly 23 feet (7 metres) and 32 feet (10 metres) apart, were apparently in use at the same time and may have been supplemented by a third ditch in places. The site was already well established as a trading centre prior to its continued existence into the Roman period. Cassington Mill Big Ring has been destroyed by gravel extraction but formerly was a valley fort occupying a site of 32 acres (13 ha) at the confluence of the Evenlode and the Thames. Excavation has suggested that part of the defences consisted of a massive gravel bank with pilings on both inner and outer faces. Its use appears to have spanned 1,000 years from 800 BC into the Roman period. Cherbury Camp, of 25 acres (10 ha), is now seen as lying on an apparently vulnerable, low knoll, but was once surrounded on all sides by streams and marshes, recognised by millions of upturned snail-shells, with the only viable access by a narrow neck of land on the north-east, thus creating an effective defensive situation. This is the only example of a multivallate hillfort in Oxfordshire with three, and in places four, concentric ramparts and ditches best seen on the north-west, broken by gaps on three sides but only that on the north-east, leading from Race Farm, regarded as an original entrance with a metalled surface leading to a cobbled street. The fort dates from early in the first century BC and shows no more than slight traces of occupation.

Design and Construction of Hillforts

The primary defensive feature of all these forts was the combination of rampart and ditch. Ramparts could be single, or univallate, as are most of Oxfordshire's, or multivallate, with concentric rings of defences such as at Begbrooke. In almost all cases, the material forming the rampart was won from the surrounding ditch, but in some cases, scarping was used to improve on natural slopes. Knoll Bury Camp at Chadlington is a fairly typical rectangular univallate fort with sides of 500 and 300 feet (154 and 92 metres). It had a steep-sided rampart built of piled earth and stone rubble behind a dry-stone revetment of large limestone slabs. All earthworks are liable to be affected by slide or erosion and this problem was tackled in two ways. The front face of a rampart might be revetted as at Alfred's Castle; on the inner face as at Uffington; or on both faces as at Lyneham and Chastleton. These revetments might be of timber as at Blewburton Hill and Sinodun or, more commonly, of stone, in the form of slabs laid either vertically or layered horizontally as a wall. The rampart itself, composed of earth, turf, clay, gravel, chalk rubble, or limestone blocks might be braced by timbers, either vertical posts or lateral cross beams as at Blewburton. Evidence for timber-laced box ramparts has been found at Uffington, Madmarston, and Segsbury. A similar method is for timber gabions, filled with rubble and other material, to form the core of the rampart. The rampart at Alfred's Castle is anchored on rows of sarsen blocks running parallel to the ditch, five deep, giving a width of 5 feet (1.5 metres). Cherbury's innermost rampart was revetted by a wall of at least ten to twelve courses of well-laid thin oolite slabs. At Cassington Mill, the gravel rampart was held together by timber piles.

A fort's ramparts were usually surmounted by a timber palisade, often carried over the gate passage, and most commonly furnished with a wall walk—that at Lyneham, apparently, being paved with stone slabs. Ditches around low-lying forts could be wet as at Cherbury and Dorchester, but forts at higher levels could use scarping to accentuate their depth or contrive a counterscarp as at Hardwell Camp. Ditches would primarily provide the material for the rampart whose height they effectively doubled but this was not always straightforward. At Alfred's Castle, the V-shaped ditch, 10 feet (3 metres) deep, had to be cut into the bedrock.

A hillfort's most vulnerable point was its entrance. Where the lie of the land permitted, this would be via a sunken approach dominated by the defences of the rampart. The western entrance passage at Uffington stretches for 52 feet (16 metres) through the ramparts, which are in-turned, and the counterscarp heightened. Entry points could be protected by extra external banks as at Segsbury or formed into a dogleg as at Checkendon. Cherbury's entrance passage was lined by walls of coursed oolite slabs similar to those forming the rampart's retaining walls, with postholes 4 feet (1.2 metres) deep at its inner end to hold robust gateposts with shallower holes adjacent to hold their supports. Access to Madmarston is via an obliquely set entrance. At Blewburton, its double gates, set either end of an entrance corridor, was backed by a ditch in the interior of the fort, perhaps an early form of the retrenchment employed by the besieged in the Civil War. Early hillforts defended their entrances with timber gatehouses but the development of assault techniques involving fire and stone missiles saw a move toward projecting, stone-lined gate passages which presented a target less vulnerable to fire or demolition.

Evidence for the occupation of prehistoric hillforts is patchy and entirely lacking on some sites. While there are sketchy signs of structures at Uffington, pottery, loom weights, and animal bone point to some occupation, although there were long periods of time when it was deserted. Despite the occasional appearance of food storage pits such as those at Blewburton Hill, there is no evidence that Oxfordshire's hillforts performed a major role in the storage and distribution of food surpluses seen elsewhere in England. Although it could be argued that insufficient excavation of hillfort interiors has been carried out, the available evidence points to a low level of any prolonged occupation. Alfred's Castle, incorporated into a villa estate and yielding evidence of a Romano-British building of chalk blocks measuring 40 by 80 feet (12 by 25 metres), also produced coins and other artefacts of the third century AD. Only at the low-lying sites of Dorchester and Abingdon, which remained in use for longer, has further evidence for denser and longer levels of occupation been found.

Some forts offer evidence of actual conflict. Blewburton Hill's first period of occupation was in the fourth century BC when a group of circular huts and grain storage pits was surrounded by a palisade. The next phase was marked by the construction of a bank and ditch where both faces of the rampart were revetted in timber and separated from the V-shaped ditch by a berm and accessed on the west by an entrance 37 feet (11.5 metres) wide, probably around 300 BC, after which the defences deteriorated. Sometime in the first century BC, the ditch was recut, and the resultant spoil was added to the rampart; the entrance was narrowed to 25 feet (7.7 metres) and the flanking rampart revetted with drystone walling. Before AD 50, the fort was destroyed, with humans suffering violent deaths; animals being crushed by the collapse of the rampart; and the defences of the gateway being burnt. Responsibility for this destruction may lie with the Romans, the Catuvellauni who took over the area around AD 25, or the Belgae. Burroway is a small, roughly circular, univallate valley-fort of 5 acres (2 ha) on the Thames floodplain with a rampart of timber corduroy displaying evidence of burning. Bladon Heath, Round Castle, Begbrooke, is a small multivallate hillfort with two concentric oval ramparts constructed of stone rubble and originally between 13 and 23 feet (4 and 7 metres) wide, surrounded by a ditch, around 23 feet (7 metres) across, and this site, too, shows evidence of burning. Finds at Madmarston included some slingshot, but whether they were ever used in anger is impossible to discover.

Oxfordshire's forts range in size from Eynsham Park Camp or Alfred's Castle, both of under 4 acres (1.5 ha) to Bozedown Camp's 58 acres (22 ha) and the even more extensive Dyke Hills, Dorchester, with an area of 114 acres (45 ha). Not all forts necessarily had strong defences but may still have formed part of a wider defence system. Lyneham, Chastleton, Idbury, and Tadmarton belong to a small group of univallate camps in the eastern Cotswolds distinguished by their small size, circular form, and lack of natural defences. Lyneham Camp and Idbury, 4 miles (6.5 km) apart, are intervisible, which might suggest that they formed part of a warning system using beacons.

Linear Dykes

The multiplicity of dykes in the county, many of which have traditionally become known generically as 'Grims Ditch', have hence been interpreted as forming a cohesive whole larger than the sum of their several parts. This has led to claims that the South Oxfordshire 'section', running from the Thames near Wallingford, eastwards toward the Chilterns, relates to other 'sections' which run parallel to the Icknield Way along the Chilterns. While it may be convenient to assign the known dykes to a particular time in history and to give them a common purpose, it would appear that different construction methods, contradictory alignments, and doubtful historical references render such conclusions unsafe. The South Oxfordshire Grims Ditch was probably prehistoric, possibly marking a tribal boundary facing south, or simply changes in the landscape. Aves Ditch is an Iron Age ditch, 1.25 miles (2 km) in length, facing west between Bicester and the River Cherwell.

The North Oxfordshire Grims Ditch, between Woodstock and Charlbury, consists of a roughly circular series of discontinuous banks, in several locations, seen as concentric lines of dyke, with external ditches. Apparently covering 80 square kilometres, and pre-Roman in origin, it is far too large for an *oppidum* and, furthermore, there are no signs of settlement within. Following investigations, speculation that the dykes were defensive—either as manned obstructions to a Roman invasion or as unmanned barriers to disrupt Roman mopping up operations—has largely been discounted. The dykes' most likely purpose was political, acting as boundaries with clearly defined gaps to regulate the access of people and goods. Had defensive motives underlain the earliest of the dykes, then they were superseded by this later function. The dykes consisted of banks formed by the spoil from the ditches and possibly revetted with turves, but there is no evidence for the palisades one might expect on earthworks primarily intended as fortifications.

Grims Ditch at Ditchley consists of a single bank 20 feet (6 metres) wide and 6 feet (1.8 metres) in height, and a V-sectioned ditch 20 feet (6 metres) wide and 6 feet (1.8 metres) deep. It extends 1.5 miles (2.4 km) east–north-east, and then 2.5 miles (4 km) south–south-east to the top of Blenheim Great Park. It possibly represents the territorial boundary of an Iron Age tribe in the first century AD expanding westwards. A further stretch of dyke, also known as Grims Ditch, runs in an easterly direction from Wallingford along the line of the Ridgeway nearly 6 miles (10 km) past Nuffield toward Nettlebed. Around 3 miles (5 km) to the north, south of Britwell Salome, a short length of dyke runs between the Ridgeway and the Icknield Way which converge a little way to the north. Aves Ditch, north of Kirtlington, a 2.5-mile-long (4-km-long) earthwork running north–north-east with the ditch on its west side, has been identified as an Iron Age boundary ditch which would see reuse in the Anglo-Saxon period. Only a short distance east of the River Cherwell, it plausibly follows the boundary between the Dobunni to the west and the Catuvellauni to the east. Although it appears to spring from Akeman Street, it has been found by excavation not to be a Roman road.

To the west of Moulsford and just above the Ridgeway, there are at least three short lengths of dyke named the Devils Ditch and (yet again) Grims Ditch. Further lengths are marked on the OS map following the line of the Ridgeway westwards as far as a point level with Wantage. These may be the remnants of a south-facing boundary dyke, parts of which have been erased, or may be the complete, but discontinuous, lengths of a longer boundary like Offa's Dyke on the Welsh border. It may be significant that the line follows the ancient trackway of the Ridgeway/Icknield Way, below the crest of the Downs; forms current, but long-established, parish boundaries; and marks the post-1974 boundary between Oxfordshire and Berkshire.

Roman Fortifications and Roads

There appears to be no evidence for resistance to the Roman invasion, but several Iron Age sites did remain in occupation into the Roman era. Abingdon continued to operate as an Iron Age defended settlement or *oppidum*, but over time, outgrew its boundaries and parts of its ditches had been deliberately backfilled by the second century AD. Several Roman masonry buildings have been discovered in the town which appears to have thrived into the fourth century. Hardwell hillfort, a rectangular enclosure between Uffington and Woolstone Hill, is surrounded by a shallow ditch and Roman sherds have been found, suggesting the possibility that it remained in occupation as a Romano-British settlement.

Oxfordshire is traversed by two major Roman roads with Alchester standing at their junction. The first is a south–north route originating in Silchester (*Calleva Atrebatum*) in Berkshire and running through Dorchester-on-Thames, across Otmoor, crossing the River Ray at Fencott and reaching the Akeman Street crossroads at Alchester. It then ran on to meet Watling Street at Towcester (*Lactodurum*) in Northamptonshire. The other, Akeman Street, is an east–west road running from Watling Street at St Albans (*Verulamium*) in Hertfordshire, to Cirencester (*Corinium*) in Gloucestershire. Another road appears to link Alchester to the Fosse Way north-west of Banbury, and a road whose course remains uncertain appears to run along the county's southern boundary. At a point south of Dorchester-on-Thames on the Roman road to Silchester, the two prehistoric trackways—the Ridgeway and the Icknield Way—meet. Wantage where the A417 Reading to Cirencester road crosses that from Hungerford to Oxford, now the A338, has been described as standing on the Portway which had originated as an ancient trackway, its use continuing into Roman times, and running from Silchester to Old Sarum in Wiltshire. Wantage was a small Roman settlement serving the agricultural hinterlands and lying near to the road linking

Alchester to Ermin Street near Lambourn. A further Roman settlement, nearer to the Ridgeway, has been discovered near Letcombe Bassett. A second Portway, which may also have its origins in prehistory, ran from Wallingford past Oxford, probably crossing the River Ray at Islip and Akeman Street above Kirtlington before heading past the Heyfords into Northamptonshire.

Roman Alchester began life around the middle of the first century AD as a legionary fortress for the Second Augusta legion and a supply base during Vespasian's westward campaign, located on the boundary between the Dobunni and the Catuvellauni tribes. This was a convenient location near to the Fosse Way which for a while marked the Roman frontier. The fort was the usual playing card shape in proportion, but with squarer corners rather than the more usual rounded ones and was surrounded by a V-shaped ditch inside outer ditches. However, there appear to have been no ditches on its western side where the annexe was soon to be added. This western annexe is thought to have contained a parade ground, and the whole complex covers up to 37 acres (15 ha). The timber gateposts of the annexe's entrance, dated by dendrochronology to AD 44–45, suggest that the main fort had been established even earlier and thus very soon after the Claudian invasion. The fort served its purpose over two decades until the legion had moved on into south Wales and the West Country, probably by AD 68. The discovery of the smashed tombstone of a veteran Roman soldier, incorporated in the later stone town wall near the fort's west gate, has been interpreted as confirmation that the Alchester fort was headquarters for a while of Vespasian, who would go on to become emperor in AD 69, ruling until his death ten years later. Historic England's listing includes a temporary camp and training ground on a separate site which may pre-date the fort.

After the soldiers had moved on, the fortress developed into a walled town of 45 acres (18 ha), roughly square with sides of around 350 yards (325 metres) and laid out to a grid pattern. The defences consisted of a rampart of gravel and sand, almost 23 feet (7 metres) wide, faced by an 8-foot-thick (2.4-metre-thick) stone wall on pitched limestone footings. The two may possibly have been contemporary but it is more likely that the stone wall was added to the earlier rampart in the third century as was the case at many similar smaller Roman towns. Internal towers have been unearthed at the north-east and south-east corners and it is likely that there was such a tower at each of the other two corners. Unlike many other similar small towns, there appear to have been no added external bastions dating from the later years of Roman occupation. There was a ditch on three sides with a natural brook on the fourth, south side. The fact that no pottery uncovered during the 1974 excavation was later than the middle of the second century provides a reasonably accurate date for these defences, and any ditches which pre-date these defences are likely to have been for drainage. By the fifth century, the stone was being robbed for building in new settlements such as Bicester. In the later Roman period, the Thames–

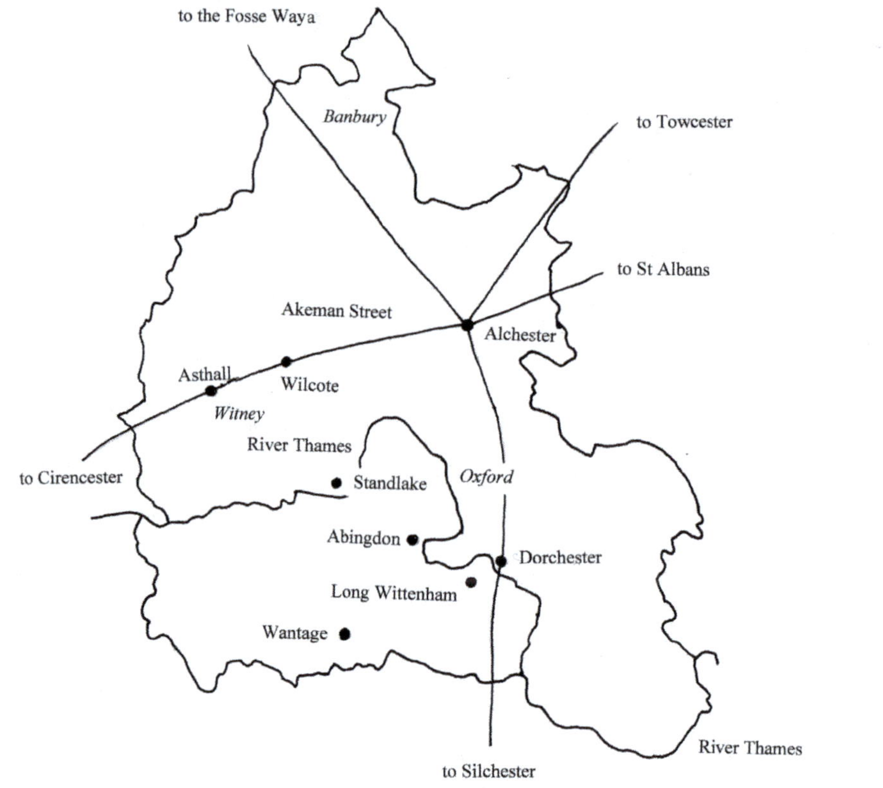

A sketch map of Roman Oxfordshire showing roads and settlements

Above: A sketch map of Roman Oxfordshire showing roads and settlements.

Left: A reconstruction of the gateway of an early Roman fort such as that at Alchester; photographed at The Lunt near Coventry.

Cherwell line marks a conjectural boundary between the provinces of Britannia, midway between Cirencester to the west and St Albans to the east. Alchester has been suggested as a suitable location for local civil administrative functionaries acting in support of the military.

Dorchester-on-Thames was a Roman town, half the size of Alchester, built where the north–south road from Alchester to Silchester crosses the Thames. A rectangular area measuring 375 by 175 yards (350 by 160 metres) was surrounded by an earth rampart enclosing 13.5 acres (5.5 ha), bounded by double ditches. The outer ditch measured 50 feet (15 metres) across and 5 feet (1.5 metres) deep and the inner ditch was 15 feet (4.6 metres) wide and 4 feet (1.2 metres) deep. Both ditches have been proven to have been permanently wet, possibly fed by the adjacent River Thame. The rampart was around 45 feet (14 metres) thick and sloped up from the interior to the rampart walk on top of the wall. This wall had been set into the front face of the rampart, possibly in the first half of the second century, and sunk several feet (*c.* 70–80 cm) into the natural gravel with a narrow berm between it and the inner ditch. It was 9 feet (2.75 metres) thick at the base and would have stood around 15 feet (4.6 metres) high. There were gates to the north and south for the Roman road, but these have not been definitively located, although possible causeways have been tentatively identified—two on the longer west wall and one on the south. Inscriptions point to the town constituting a customs post, staffed by military personnel, controlling the crossing of the Thames, with a garrison of Germanic troops in the fourth century, possibly equipped with artillery in the shape of *ballistae*. Dyke Hills, the Iron Age promontory fort, served as a Roman cemetery and it was finds associated with burials there which indicated a Germanic connection.

Asthall, on Akeman Street, was where the road crossed the River Windrush, first by a ford approached by a raised causeway, and later by a timber bridge. It would almost certainly have been a military post in the early days of conquest and developed as a small town with both timber and stone roadside structures. It may have retained a small military presence carrying out administrative functions. Wilcote was a Roman settlement shown by a spread of remains along Akeman Street and its local name 'Wicham', indicating a Roman site, appears in an Anglo-Saxon charter. Traces of a Roman linear village settlement have been found at Long Wittenham (SU549936). The Roman road linking Alchester and Dorchester-on-Thames passed 3 miles to the east of present-day Oxford through Headington. Evidence for extensive pottery manufacture in east Oxford has been found alongside this road but represents only scattered rural settlement, a factor confirmed by Roman remains from what is now urban Oxford. A strong case can be made for the existence of a Roman fort near to Standlake, a nodal point where the road running south-east from Asthall crosses the Thames near its confluence with the Windrush. Despite the existence of Roman settlements around Standlake throughout the first two centuries of Roman rule, there is no apparent evidence to support a military presence.

Among the many other candidates for the location of Boudica's defeat, an analysis of terrain features set beside the topographical information in the account of Tacitus has put forward Tidmarsh as a possibility. This proposal would place Boudica's rampaging army, fresh from its complete obliteration of Colchester, London, and St Albans on track into Oxfordshire and on to Cirencester and Gloucester. As we know, the Britons were held by the army of Suetonius and, according to Tacitus, annihilated, saving the day for Rome and allowing the peace-loving Romano-British farmers of Oxfordshire to sleep at night.

Anglo-Saxon Oxfordshire

Several sites afford chinks of light into what are often referred to as the Dark Ages, representing either a carry-over from Iron Age to Anglo-Saxon occupation or continuity between Romano-British and Anglo-Saxon use. Barton Court Farm near Abingdon was continuously occupied from Neolithic times through the Romano-British era and into the sixth century, latterly, as the centre of what had previously been a villa estate. The villa had systematically been demolished during the final quarter of the fourth century, but seven sunken buildings and a pair with timber frames had subsequently been constructed. While little is known of the social organisation in operation at this time, high status artefacts in the shape of jewellery have been uncovered at Wantage and at Barton Court. A prominent barrow, alongside Akeman Street at Asthall, unusually built with a drystone retaining wall, was excavated and dated to the turn of the sixth century. It contained charred human and animal bones along with fragments of a ceramic Merovingian bottle and a Byzantine metalwork bowl and other metal objects such as strap ends. Such high-status objects suggest that trade with the continent was continuing, and important individuals were experiencing sophisticated lifestyles. A settled sub-Roman community at Dorchester is just one of a number of sites exhibiting signs of continued or renewed use. These include a possible Iron Age rampart and ditch at Binsey which may have been reused in the early Anglo-Saxon period; Segsbury Camp, thought to have been occupied after the Romans had left *Britannia*; and the Roman settlement of Wilcote astride Akeman Street, reoccupied for over 100 years, starting during the seventh century. However, not all examples of continuity are so immediately obvious: the boundaries of the Roman estate of Ditchley have been shown to align almost exactly with those of the later parish, and Long Wittenham shows evidence of continuity of occupation. On the other hand, the early Saxon village at New Wintles Farm, Eynsham, found to contain 'substantial' huts dating from the sixth to eighth centuries, with a surrounding trench for a 'stout' palisade, and ditches, apparently occupies a virgin site. The Tribal Hidage is an eleventh-century document, its contents traceable back to the seventh or eighth centuries, with a suggested origin in Mercia in 627. It details territories on the basis of their capacity to render required amounts of produce, taxation in kind, to a higher authority. At this time, the hide was composed of the number of households necessary to produce this specified amount of produce, and therefore differed from place to place, the extent of each hide determined by how productive the land was and how effectively it was managed. Charlbury, its name suggesting a fortified place, lay at the centre of a discrete area of 300 hides within the kingdom of the Middle Angles and may have been known as 'Faerpinga'.

The area of the Ridgeway, or central section of the Icknield Way, is associated with the struggle between the Britons and the incoming Saxons, and then, in turn, the Saxons and the Danish invaders. The legendary Battle of Mount Badon, or Mons Badonicus, fought by the probably mythical King Arthur early in the sixth century, probably in 516, is widely held to have been fought above Badbury, at Liddington Castle where the Icknield Way turns east towards Uffington, although a strong case has been made for Badbury Rings in Dorset (but only weakly for Badbury Hill outside Faringdon). The Britons had then been decisively defeated in 556 at Barbury Castle, a little further to the south-west in Wiltshire, but still on the Ridgeway. The Anglo-Saxon advance, thus, was ultimately unstoppable and Benson is listed as one of four royal towns captured from the Britons by Cuthwulf in 571. Another battle was fought in 584 at *Feonleag/Fethelee*, thought to be Stoke Lyne near Bicester. Here, the West Saxon King Cutha inflicted heavy casualties on Britons resisting his advance. South-east of Wantage lies a Bronze Age barrow known as Cwichelm's Barrow and now as Scutchamer Knob. This is remembered as the location for both a victory for the West Saxons led by King Cwichelm over the Britons who lost over 2,000 dead in 614, and Cwichelm's own defeat and death in 636 at the hands of Edwin of Northumbria. It is also thought to be the site of a beacon or signal fire, lit to alert the locals to a hostile incursion by the Danes, and summoning them to turn out in defence of their lands. In 752, the West Saxon King Cuthred fought a battle against the Mercians led by Aethelbald. The battle took place at Burford, in a field still known as Battle-Edge alongside Sheep Street. Cuthred put his Mercian overlord to flight and, according to legend, captured the Mercians' golden dragon standard. This may have been an echo of the universal symbol of Roman power but has been traditionally attributed as the *rebus* of Uther Pendragon of Arthurian legend.

The Thames Valley has been identified as an area where aspiring Anglo-Saxon tribal leaders built high-status settlements centred on complexes of timber halls surrounded by sunken huts or *grubenhäuser* used as weaving sheds or workshops. Long Wittenham, where there had previously been a Romano-British village, has yielded up the remains of what appears to be such an Anglo-Saxon high-status hall complex. This consists of three timber halls constructed on beams laid horizontally in trenches, supporting vertical posts carrying gabled roofs. A fourth hall, some distance away, measures 50 by 20 feet (16 by 7 metres). One excavated building measuring 36 by 20 feet (11 by 6 metres) has been reconstructed on its footprint. The oak for posts and trusses came from Blenheim; walls were constructed of hazel wattle panels daubed with clay and dung; and the roof was thatched with straw over an insulating layer of turf. Around sixty further *grubenhäuser* have been identified by aerial survey, with animal bones recovered from the site being dated to the seventh century. Many graves have also been discovered of which some belonged to what are presumed to be Germanic mercenaries, buried with their swords and shields. Further such sites are known at Benson and at Sutton Courtenay/Drayton, where a large rectangular hall, 100 feet (30 metres) long (SU487938) with a smaller building overlaying a sixth-century sunken building, were both loosely dated to the seventh to ninth centuries. As the largest such hall yet found, this has been proposed as a royal palace, with over thirty Saxon houses around a large open space. Eynsham and its surrounding settlements have been included in Professor Blair's proposed examples of the use of a grid based on the possibly Anglian short perch (15 feet/4.57 metres) as an aid to laying out building plots. As we have seen, the county's linear dykes are likely to have originated in prehistoric times, but the Streatley Ditches are thought to date from the fifth or sixth centuries and have been suggested as being part of those dykes controlling access to the Ridgeway to the west.

As the northernmost part of Wessex, the county would become both a fortified frontier and a battleground. The battle of Aescesdune, in which King Alfred achieved a great victory over the Danes, was fought in 871 but its location has never been fixed with any certainty. There have been numerous claims for Ashdown, below Alfred's Castle, to have been the location but, given that the name 'Ashdown' was generally applied to the whole of the Berkshire Downs, alternative locations become plausible. Although an attempted association with the Uffington White Horse is likely to be spurious, a link to Waylands Smithy, a neolithic chambered tomb standing high above Ashbury may have a better claim. A further hypothesis places the battle some 20 miles (30 km) to the east between Kingstanding Hill and Lowbury Hill, both lying alongside the Ridgeway. The story goes that the Danes had sailed their longships up the Thames to Goring and had then begun a march along the Ridgeway heading for Wantage. The Saxon army, led by King Ethelred, Alfred's elder brother, had fled in disarray from their recent defeat near Reading and had gathered in the fortified town of Wallingford to re-group, prior to establishing a camp behind the defences of the Iron Age hillfort on Blewburton Hill, lying a little to the north of the Ridgeway, the expected route of the Danish army into the heart of Wessex. Not wishing to lose an opportunity to cut off the Danish advance, Alfred took half the army on ahead and engaged the enemy, holding them until his brother might arrive with the rest of the Saxon troops to complete the victory. It was reported at the time that two Norse kings and four jarls were killed along with thousands of their men, an unlikely total given the strength of the Saxon army was reckoned not to exceed 1,000 men. The remnants of the Danish army retreated to their base at Englefield near Reading, a feat more possibly accomplished from here than the longer trek from suggested sites much further to the west. Both oral tradition and local placenames reinforce this identification of the battle site. King Ethelred died that same year, to be succeeded by Alfred. While this had been a famous victory which raised Saxon morale, it would be a further seven years before Alfred could be confident in the security of the Anglo-Saxon kingdom of Wessex. Local tradition has it that during Edward the Elder's campaign against the Danes, a battle was fought in 914 to the north-east of Banbury leading to the probably spurious local name of Danes Moor. A further local legend, much embroidered, concerns an assault by the men of Uffington Castle on a Danish encampment in the nearby Cherbury camp. This is said to have subsequently led to a Danish victory in a battle fought at a location between Charney Bassett and Buckland, its site memorialised in the name 'Gainfield'.

The Burhs of Anglo-Saxon Wessex and Mercia

The defensive strategy of Alfred and his son Edward the Elder in Wessex, and his daughter and son-in-law in Mercia, was based on the fortified town or *burh*. The *burh* was surrounded by ditches and earth banks surmounted by timber palisades, with timber towers at the angles, and accessed via gates under further timber watchtowers. In the event of an emergency, the walls would be manned by men from the *burh* itself and from the surrounding villages, the extent of the defences being determined by the number of hides of land available to generate the required manpower. Wallingford was rated at 2,400 hides whereas Oxford, occupying a much smaller area, was assessed at 1,300–1,500 hides. Wallingford has also been identified as an important link in the chain of beacons which formed a signalling system along the Thames valley to facilitate the mobilisation of the *fyrd*, the citizen army obliged to turn out in times of danger.

Wallingford was founded as a *burh* on a site previously only minimally occupied. It was one of the two largest of Alfred's thirty-three *burhs* as recorded in the Burghal Hidage, equal in size to Winchester. It was roughly rectangular, covering 107 acres (43 ha) and measuring 760 by 540 yards (700 by 500 metres). It was probably constructed in 878–9 and refurbished and strengthened in the 890s, possibly with a mint operating from the ninth century. Later figures inferred from the Domesday survey suggest an urban population of 1,500 to 2,000 in the town itself, with at least a comparable number in the immediate hinterland. It has been suggested that its layout represents a conscious attempt to replicate the grid of streets characteristic of Roman towns in an effort to enhance a visible civic status and to promote Alfred's vision of urban development. Wallingford's houses and other structures never covered much more than two-thirds of the enclosed area, and it may be that space was earmarked for the assembly of troops and their associated encampments and dumps of stores and forage. Despite the strength of its defences, Wallingford was reported in the *Anglo-Saxon Chronicle* to have been burnt down in 1006 by the Danish host which then set off along the Ridgeway, managing to avoid the ill-omened Cwichelm's (or Cuckhamsley) Barrow and escaping via the coast to the south of Winchester.

Although there is as yet no evidence to suggest the idea of an earlier Mercian bridgehead on its southern frontier, an Anglo-Saxon *burh* is recorded at Oxford in the Burghal Hidage. Its defences would have closely resembled those of Wallingford and other *burhs* with a rampart of earth, rubble and turves with an intermittent retaining wall and an outer ditch. It appears likely on the archaeological and topographical evidence that the original *burh* of the later ninth century received the addition of an eastern extension early in the tenth century, rather than the next century as had originally been accepted. This addition might explain the misalignment of the northern and southern circuits of walls necessitating the kinks visible in the plan but does not detract from the regular street pattern. It would also account for the discovery of a stone wall on the line of the eastern end of the primary *burh*. Such stone walls, added to the earth and turf rampart have been uncovered on other stretches of the *burh* walls such as near St Michael's Tower. It has been suggested that the primary *burh* defences of earth and turf were constructed in 878–9 and strengthened with a stone wall in the 890s, although the stone walls have also been assigned to a reworking of the defences following the burning of the town in 1009 and Swein's attack in 1013 when the town capitulated without offering more than token resistance. The extension can be attributed to Edward the Elder, Alfred's son, between 911, when eastern Mercia, including Oxford and London, was annexed by Wessex, with a campaign against the Danes being instigated, and his death in 924. Whatever their date, the stone walls must have been substantial on the eastern circuit as they apparently sufficed until replaced on the same line in the early 1200s. Traces of a roadway near the Carfax, composed of two layers of rounded stones or cobbles, over a bed of loam laid on the natural gravel, are likely to be Saxon. St George's Tower, later to be incorporated into the castle, and St Michael's Tower both date from pre-Conquest times, suggesting that Oxford's pre-Conquest defences were stronger than the majority of their contemporaries. Saxon halls and associated structures have been excavated on the castle site, possibly a royal complex, and there may have been other walled enclaves within the defended area, allocated to individual thegns who might build a hall and, perhaps, a church. Once a unified nation began to evolve, Oxford ceased to be a frontier town but assumed another importance as a trading and administrative centre astride road and river highways. But this status did not help the town to avoid future troubles.

Above left: Oxford: St Michael's Tower dates from Saxon times and appears to have formed part of the *burh* defences at its North Gate.

Above right: Oxford: St George's Tower was built in the first half of the eleventh century to defend the city's West Gate. It was then integrated into the Norman castle.

Excavations at Oxford's castle site have revealed something of the construction of the *burh* defences. The rampart, around 50 feet (15 metres) wide, was composed of gravel, earth, and clay dug out of the surrounding ditch, with layers of turf interpolated for stability. This was topped by a timber palisade, which would subsequently be fronted by a stone wall. Like the hillforts before them, this construction represented a formidable investment in labour, and it has been estimated that Wallingford's defences might have required the expenditure of 120,000 man-hours, alternatively expressed as 500 labourers working for a month, and appearing to be a gross underestimate. Oxford's circuit was roughly the same as Cricklade's where it has been estimated that 43,230 cubic yards (34,000 cubic metres) of material were shifted by 1,000 men working for four months. Reports in the *Anglo-Saxon Chronicle* of *burhs* going up in a month under the eyes of the king, as is claimed in the cases of Edward the Elder at Bedford in 915, and at Buckingham in 918, may need to be taken with a pinch of salt.

Other settlements in the county dating from the Saxon period include Abingdon, Bicester, and Wantage. As well as the foundation of a monastery there in the seventh century, there is an argument for Abingdon's market being founded in the tenth century in an area known as the 'Bury', a site possibly connected to the Iron Age settlement or to an Anglo-Saxon high-status manor. At Bicester, the discovery of five rectangular timber halls spanning the late tenth to early twelfth centuries; sunken-featured huts; and traces of an enclosing bank around the Minster church, along with the 'Bury End' placename, raise the possibility of a defended settlement. Wantage developed around a Saxon royal palace where Alfred was born in 849.

The hunting lodge on Andersey Island at Culham was used by Offa and continued in use by William I and William II. Although it was described as a 'fortres' by Leland, no Anglo-Saxon remains have ever been found there. Anglo-Saxon thegnal residences with their enclosures, accessed by a gate and containing a hall and belltower, would not have differed greatly from the ringworks the Normans would build in the eleventh and twelfth centuries. The earthwork bank and ditch that would later become the outer bailey of Deddington Castle has been dated to late Saxon times and may represent such a thegnal fortified residence. The Laws of Alfred prescribed that an enemy's dwelling had to be blockaded for seven days before the defences could, lawfully, be breached. In all probability, a useful mechanism for cooling hot-headed subjects in what is often, and possibly erroneously, reckoned to be a violent society. An enclosure at Binsey, surrounded by what appears to be a defensive revetted rampart and a ditch containing Anglo-Saxon material, has been linked to St Frideswide, an eighth-century abbess, and known as Thornbury. The still discernible oval island appears to have had a rectilinear moated enclosure, later added around the Norman chapel and well. The results of excavations led to the conclusion that the site might well represent reuse in Anglo-Saxon times of an earlier, possibly Iron Age, valley fort in an area and at a time of known expansion.

Anglo-Saxon Tower-Naves and Churches with West Towers

Qualifications for enjoying the status of thegn included holding a defensible gate, implying the existence of an enclosure; a hall; a chapel; and a tower. Michael Shapland has identified what he calls tower-naves, which were free-standing multi-functional structures serving as belfries, watchtowers, refuges, beacons, focal points for mustering troops, private chapels, and, possibly most significantly, symbols of power and prestige, contributing to a process of nuclear settlement. He has found thirty-five of these structures nationally and fully five of them lie in Oxfordshire, all of them lordly or manorial in origin. The earliest was the circular, apsidal, turriform rotunda at Abingdon Abbey built by King Eadred between 946 and 955 as a royal chapel cum watchtower and which collapsed when the abbey was rebuilt by a Norman abbot. In Oxford, the tower of St Michael's dating from the first half of the eleventh century was integrated into the defences of the *burh*'s north gate and the slightly later St George's Tower performed a similar function at the west gate. The tower at St Matthew's church at Langford dates from after the Conquest but was built by a Saxon lord, Aelfsige of Faringdon, who incorporated both Saxon and Romanesque architectural features. It would have met the criteria for the role of watchtower and those towers with flat roofs might also have served as beacon sites. The tower at Holy Rood, Woodeaton has been found by excavation to have replaced an earlier timber tower and was dated to the eleventh century. All these five examples were ecclesiastical but initiated by secular authorities and, by the end of the twelfth century, to accommodate congregations, naves had been added to all of them. Their relationship to Anglo-Saxon churches with western towers such as Bampton, Caversfield, or North Leigh has yet to be determined. Bampton's central tower with its possibly originally external stair-turret, may have started out as the west tower of the Saxon church and it must be noted that the enclosure surrounding Bampton's church was temporarily refortified by Matilda during the fighting of the Anarchy. Caversfield, with a tenth-century ground-floor stage to its west tower, has manorial origins and the west tower at North Leigh was once a central tower of *c.* 1050. Some such towers may initially have been of timber, a feature echoed by the pilaster strips symbolically applied to some Anglo-Saxon stone towers, but others were more than substantial. Shapland points out that St George's Tower at Oxford, later to have a nave added and to be incorporated into the castle, is a contemporary of the early keep at Langeais (Indre-et-Loire) and shares its significant construction investment of 83,000 workdays. A part-excavated stone structure within the enclosure of Middleton Stoney, apparently standing on Saxon foundations, and underlying the motte with its collapsed stone keep, has been classified as a Saxon aristocratic residence, and may represent a further example of a tower-nave. The earliest earthwork enclosure at Deddington Castle has been shown to date from the Anglo-Saxon period. Also included in a list of excavated Anglo-Saxon lordly residences is Cogges, near Witney. The estate was one of several in Oxfordshire later held by one Wadard who appears in the Bayeux Tapestry on horseback and was a tenant of Odo of Bayeux. Excavations uncovered post-holes and trenches which suggested that an earlier timber hall complex, dated to the mid-tenth century, probably preceded the late Saxon manor which had been made over as a priory by 1103. Masonry in the west wall of the adjacent church appears to be Anglo-Saxon in origin displaying the 'pillow-stone' quoins, characteristic of the Anglo-Saxon style and suggesting that the church might have been contemporary with the earlier manor.

The lower stages of the west tower of Caversfield church date from Saxon times.

Conflict with the Danes

The St Brice's Day massacre of 1002 was ordered by the ill-advised King Aethelred in response to warnings that he was about to be killed by his Danish subjects. In Oxford, the Danish citizens fled into St Frideswide's Church, the forerunner of Christ Church Cathedral, which was then burnt to the ground, with all therein perishing. The graves of three dozen young men were uncovered at St John's College in 2008, an examination of whose remains revealed evidence of healed wounds from previous conflicts, suggesting they were Viking warriors who had died in a conflagration around the right time. It is likely that any such massacre was not widespread but confined to towns such as Oxford which lay on the edge of the Danelaw. In 1006, a Danish army was rampaging through Wessex and the last Saxon defenders awaited their coming at Scutchamer Knob for the final showdown. But that battle would ultimately be fought further to the south-west, near the pre-historic circle of Avebury. The Danes soon got their revenge for the St Brice's Day massacre when Oxford was sacked by a Danish army in 1009 and submitted to Sweyn of Denmark four years later. Still occupying a psychological boundary between Wessex and Mercia, Oxford was the setting for unsuccessful attempts to establish a concerted resistance to Cnut. King Aethelred summoned his thegns to Oxford, but the ealdorman Eadric of Mercia lured the two most important from the Five Boroughs into his chamber and had them killed. The next two years saw the death of Aethelred; continued, but fruitless, resistance by his son Edmund; and the ultimate success of Cnut who came to Oxford to negotiate a peace and to confirm the old traditional laws for his new kingdom. In 1035, after Cnut's death, it was in Oxford that the succession was decided. Scutchamer Knob, scene of such turmoil, would subsequently become a place of meeting for both shire and Hundred. As the battle of Hastings heralded yet another regime change, the Anglo-Saxon leaders made their final submission to William I at Wallingford, prior to his coronation on Christmas Day, 1066.

2

Oxfordshire in the Middle Ages, 1050–1500

For knightly families, medieval times could be dangerous, rewarding, and challenging. This is neatly exemplified by the adventures of the four Harcourt brothers who accompanied William I in his invasion of 1066. Their successors would establish what would become a prominent Oxfordshire family, while some would return to Normandy. Those who remained in England were initially granted lands in Leicestershire, but in 1191, Robert de Harcourt inherited land at Stanton from his father-in-law, and this became Stanton Harcourt. With a foot in both French and English camps, the Harcourts fought to preserve their lands in Normandy by siding with whichever side could offer them the greater benefit. In 1234, a misunderstanding around the Norman branch saw the Harcourt lands seized and then returned. More problems followed when their English lands were again temporarily seized due to the misplaced support of Sir William Harcourt for Simon de Montfort, who counted John Harcourt of the Norman branch of the family among his friends. Following an adjudication by the French king which went against him, and which deprived him of his Norman lands, Geoffroy de Harcourt changed sides to become a prominent leader of the English army in France in 1346. He was commissioned by Edward III to lay waste the Normandy countryside with a picked force of men-at-arms and archers. He was a member of the Black Prince's bodyguard at the battle of Crécy where his brother, Jean IV, Compte d'Harcourt, was killed fighting on the French side. Remorse prompted Geoffroy to return to the French fold, relinquishing his English lands, but in 1355, Jean V was seized by Philip VI of France, accused, along with three others, of some heinous but unspecified crime, probably the murder two years previously of a royal favourite, and all four were summarily beheaded. Geoffrey's nephew's execution and threats to his own safety pushed him back into Edward III's camp, and in an unsuccessful attempt to ambush French troops in Normandy in 1356, he found himself cornered. Given his history of changing sides and knowing what his fate would be, he refused to surrender and was cut down. Back in England, Sir Thomas was custodian of Oxford Castle in 1376. Harcourt knights held the manor of Stanton Harcourt throughout the medieval period with only the occasional hiccup, and they continued to retain their lands, upgrading their manor house throughout the fifteenth century, but enjoying mixed fortunes. Sir Robert, steward of Oxford University and sheriff of four counties including Oxfordshire, was killed fighting in a feud with the Staffords in 1470. His son, Sir John, having fought for Edward IV in France, was outlawed in 1483 for backing Buckingham's rebellion against Richard III, dying the following year, while his son, another Sir Robert, was standard-bearer to Henry Tudor at the battle of Bosworth in 1485.

Norman Castles

As an apparent continuation of the Anglo-Saxon tower-nave we saw in the previous chapter, Shapland suggests that Norman monastic proprietors added 'great western towers', very often wider than their attached naves, onto their churches. He cites seventeen examples, of which two are from Oxfordshire: Bampton, built by the bishop of Exeter in the mid-twelfth century; and Cumnor, built by the abbot of Abingdon some fifty years earlier. Although the Bampton tower is now central, it is likely that, with its stair turret, it once stood at the west end of an earlier church. After the Conquest, most Norman castles generally consisted of earthworks, conforming to one of two common types: the motte and bailey or the ringwork and bailey. The latter was basically similar to earlier Saxon thegnal residences. It would consist of an inner raised platform carrying a hall, a chapel, and other domestic buildings, encircled by a rampart, palisade and ditch, accessed via a timber gate-tower with a timber bridge over a moat. A larger, outer enclosure would have held stables, barns, forge, and dwellings for the lord's retainers. The motte, on the other hand, was a large earthen mound raised from the spoil of its surrounding ditch. It usually carried a timber tower and was often accessed via a flying bridge. The bailey would contain all the domestic buildings which allowed the castle to function as judicial, administrative, residential, and military centre. The motte tended to be applied in urban settings such as Oxford and Wallingford where it was necessary to dominate the townspeople. Some of these early earthwork castles would be rebuilt partially or entirely in masonry over the succeeding two centuries, while others would be allowed to erode into shapeless humps and bumps.

By 1066, Oxford had grown to be the sixth largest town in England but would soon face setbacks with half of its properties inactive by the Domesday accounting but, nevertheless, still boasting a population 4,000–5,000 strong. Guarding the route from London to Gloucester and South Wales, Oxford became the site for one of the Conqueror's urban castles, intended to overawe the population and, while built outside the line of the *burh* defences, may still have caused the demolition of existing dwellings. By the early 1100s, it was the base for a sheriff administering two counties, also serving as an arsenal storing weapons, siege engines, and other munitions. By this time, Oxford Castle consisted of a large motte topped by a timber tower; the pre-Conquest St George's Tower attached to a church whose crypt was probably constructed around 1074; and a bailey with either timber or stone defences with a western gateway between the motte and St George's Tower. This bailey would likely have contained a hall and other domestic buildings. The motte was built up of stepped layers of sand and gravel, capped by layers of clay affording the motte time to stabilise sufficiently to carry a stone tower eventually. In the meantime, a timber wall around the top of the motte, with pentices built up against its inside, may have prefigured the later decagonal stone shell keep. During the Anarchy, it was regarded as of sufficient importance for specific provision to be made for its handover to Henry II on Stephen's death in 1154. The Norman castle at Wallingford, occupying the north-east corner of the *burh* enclosure, was built as early as 1071 on a mainly unoccupied site next to the river. It consisted of a motte, measuring nearly 200 feet (60 metres) around the base and 45 feet (13.5 metres) high, plus the depth of the surrounding ditch. The motte has been dated by the Round Mounds Project to the mid- to late eleventh or the early twelfth centuries and is likely to have initially carried a timber tower. A bailey would have had a palisade and ditch with a fortified gate tower, surrounded by wet ditches integrating the earlier *burh* defences as an outer layer. However, there

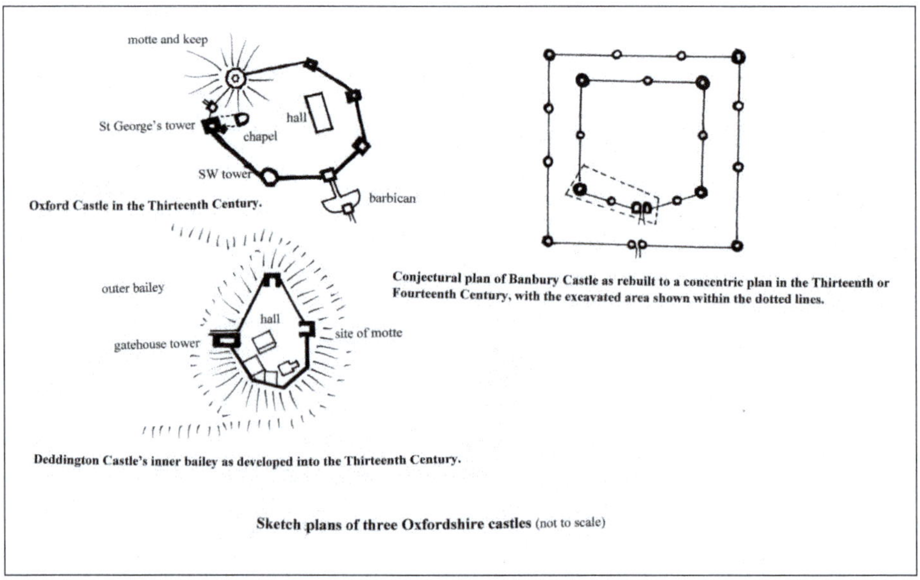

Oxford Castle in the Thirteenth Century.

Conjectural plan of Banbury Castle as rebuilt to a concentric plan in the Thirteenth or Fourteenth Century, with the excavated area shown within the dotted lines.

Deddington Castle's inner bailey as developed into the Thirteenth Century.

Sketch plans of three Oxfordshire castles (not to scale)

Sketch plans of three Oxfordshire masonry castles.

is evidence to show that masonry was already present by 1135 with more to follow in the next few years.

Immediately following the Conquest, newly built castles reflected the strategic importance of the county. As well as Oxford and Wallingford, castles were built at Deddington, Chipping Norton, and Mixbury. Chipping Norton, an early post-Conquest ringwork between two baileys, was later walled in stone and used as a hunting lodge by the Fitzalans of Clun in the thirteenth century. Deddington Castle was held by Bishop Odo of Bayeux, half-brother to William I, who held 307 hides of lands in Oxfordshire constituting his second largest estate, some 18 per cent of his total holdings, and Deddington may have been Odo's caput for those of his estates spread across Oxfordshire and Buckinghamshire. The castle developed an earlier Anglo-Saxon enclosure by constructing a motte at one end astride the earlier rampart. This was soon subsumed into an inner bailey which would contain a small L-shaped stone-built hall. In the first half of the twelfth century, this lozenge-shaped inner bailey was walled in stone and the motte was replaced by an open-backed tower. Over the next century, this inner bailey acquired a tower at the northern apex; a gatehouse on the west for accessing the outer bailey; and a complex of buildings including a chapel, a hall, and a solar along with other domestic buildings, all occupying the south-western quadrant of the inner bailey. At Beaumont Castle, Mixbury, held by Roger d'Ivry in 1086, the earthworks appear to be a rampart and ditch enclosing timber buildings, possibly on a low platform, although a mound 16 feet (5 metres) in height stands astride the near-circular bailey rampart which is surrounded by a ditch up to 16 feet (5 metres) deep. During the 1950s, unstructured 'excavations' uncovered what was probably a stone-lined well in one corner of the enclosure. Fitzharry's House at Abingdon was a motte with a small bailey, surrounded by wet moats. It was mentioned in 1247 when it was acquired by the abbey but probably dates from the late eleventh century, and was held of Abingdon Abbey by a Norman named Oin or Owen, who came over with William I. He was one of thirty knights fulfilling a requirement, made by the Conqueror between 1071 and 1084, to provide knight service to the abbey. Replaced by a manor house in the thirteenth century, the structure on the motte, either stone or, more likely, of timber, was recorded as remaining defensible. By 1247, Hugh Fitz-Harry, the current holder, was under pressure from the abbey, being painted as a 'heavy oppressor and unjust extortioner both of his neighbours and strangers'. Succumbing to these indictments and finding it impossible to withstand the abbey's attempts forcibly to evict him, Hugh agreed to cut his losses and join the Templars on Crusade. After one final, unsuccessful attempt to thwart the abbey, he gave in to what amounted to a compulsory purchase.

Throughout the twelfth century, particularly during the years of unrest known as the 'Anarchy', castles were built by lords and prelates alike. A castle was being built at Banbury by Alexander, bishop of Lincoln (1123–48), and was still unfinished in 1139, possibly the rationale for Stephen allowing it to remain in his possession while his other castles were confiscated. Excavations in 1972 uncovered a rectangular stone building measuring 14.5 by 36 feet (4.5 by 11 metres) and dating from the early twelfth century. At a similar time, bishops of Winchester, including Henry de Blois, brother of King Stephen, were building half a dozen palaces or castles to defend their extensive estates. One of these estates was centred on Witney and a strongly fortified structure was built as its administrative centre. It consisted of a square walled and moated compound enclosing a substantial solar tower or keep, along with an aisled hall, detached kitchen, chapel, and other buildings. The enclosure was accessed via a square, two-storey gate tower, loopholed and battlemented, with a range of lodgings attached on its west side. The solar tower, standing on its excavated and now exposed undercroft, measured 36 by 20 feet (11.5 by 6 metres) internally with massive walls almost 10 feet (3 metres) thick, and was constructed of fine ashlar masonry of the highest standard. Shortly after its completion, a substantial, square stone pier was added into the undercroft to support the upper floors. Attached to the tower's north wall was a domestic range with a fireplace, and a garderobe block was added to its eastern face. For some inexplicable reason, later in the twelfth century, large amounts of soil were dumped around the tower up to first-floor level. Despite the odd royal visit and the bishops' own visitations, use of the building declined, but only in the 1750s was it finally demolished to be substituted by a new house, itself replaced by the present Mount House in 1905.

The excavated basement of the solar tower at the bishop of Winchester's palace at Witney, showing the thick walls and the massive central pillar supporting the upper floors.

Alongside such substantial constructions, many castles were of an only temporary nature, predominantly of earth and timber, and with only minimal masonry. Ascott under Wychwood lays claim to three such structures. At Ascott D'Oilly, earthworks of a motte and bailey castle may date from *c.* 1130 when Robert d'Oilly established the chapel which may have stood within his castle. The motte was composed of clay, piled up around the base of a stone tower 35 feet (10.7 metres) square, with walls which were 8 feet (2.4 metres) thick with ashlar quoins. This was planted, for stability, on the original ground level and may have been accessed via an external wooden stair. A survey of the earthworks identified a small inner bailey and a large outer enclosure which might have pre-dated the castle. The castle was most probably destroyed in 1176 after the Assize of Northampton. The later manor house retains some masonry dating to the thirteenth century and may represent its successor. The earthworks of the second castle at Ascott Earl lie 910 yards (840 metres) to the south-west and consist of a flattened motte with a kidney-shaped bailey. The third structure, a possible motte and bailey site on the banks of the Evenlode about 400 yards (370 metres) to the north-east, may be either a precursor to one of the other two, or a castle of even shorter duration, raised for a specific purpose during a conflict such as the Anarchy. Of flimsy construction, and described as amateur by its excavators in 1939, a motte and bailey of the early twelfth century at Hinton Waldrist, consisting of a ditched enclosure and a low motte, was subsequently adapted as an ornamental garden feature. Middleton Stoney is an earthwork castle first mentioned in 1215 but likely to have been in existence from around 1140. Its destruction was ordered by King John in 1216 and nothing more is heard of it subsequently. What appeared to have been a motte, constructed of laid layers of limestone, quarried from the surrounding ditch, has now been interpreted as a collapsed stone tower but not, as had been the case at Ascot D'Oilly, encased in a motte. A square bailey, defined by an earthwork bank, surmounted by a stone wall, and ditch, lies to the west of the motte, but the eastern enclosure, thought to have been the bailey with three sides remaining and abutting the motte, may be a later enclosure. Swerford is a motte of stone and earth, 60 feet (18 metres) across at the summit and 13 feet (4 metres) high. Its kidney-shaped bailey is surrounded by a stone rampart 16 feet (5 metres) across and 10 feet (3 metres) high. Part of the surrounding ditch has been destroyed by the enlargement of the churchyard. There are foundations of stone buildings in the bailey with an entrance opposite the ford and a second bailey in the form of a platform with neither bank nor ditch. Pottery finds point to a construction date at the time of the Anarchy. The earl of Chester built a ringwork, an oval enclosure 100 yards (91 metres) in diameter, surrounded by a shallow ditch at Ardley. It was attacked in 1136 but the attackers were beaten off. The castle was destroyed after 1154 but traces of buildings are said to remain. As well as new and existing castles, the Anarchy saw standing buildings being adapted to the needs of conflict. Radcot Bridge is an important crossing-point of the Thames. In 2008, local archaeologists invited TV Channel 4's *Time Team* to investigate what they thought might be a stone keep, established in 1141 in inaccessible marshland. Alongside finds from many periods and later damage caused by the superimposition of a seventeenth-century Civil War fort, the footings of a square tower with walls 13 feet (4 metres) thick, similar in size to St George's Tower at Oxford Castle, was located, but reckoned to have lasted no later than the end of century. It had initially had a central pillar, but this had been superseded by a cross-wall. There appeared to have been a gatehouse and chapel plus other buildings all mangled by the trenches of the later fort. The Gatehouse website has suggested that it could have been a domestic house, over-engineered by builders unfamiliar with flint masonry, and temporarily fortified by Matilda, who may have been responsible for strengthening the tower with the cross-wall. The large oval Anglo-Saxon enclosure with its ditch and bank, surrounding Bampton Church, formerly a Saxon minster, was refurbished by Matilda as a temporary fortified camp in 1141–2, excavation revealing evidence that the ditch had been re-cut around that date. The solid Saxon church tower was also brought into play as a central strongpoint offering commanding height.

The 'Anarchy' 1135–1154

William the Conqueror's three sons had spent the years since their father's death in fighting for control of the kingdom of England and the dukedom of Normandy. After William II, known as 'Rufus', was killed while hunting in the New Forest, it was the youngest brother, Henry, educated partly by the Benedictines at Abingdon, who opportunistically seized the throne. Despite siring two dozen natural progeny—one would become a monk at Abingdon and the mother of another would marry Robert D'Oyly, son of Oxford Castle's constable—he had only a single legitimate male. Unfortunately, this potential William III was drowned crossing the Channel in the *White Ship*, and Henry I was forced to settle the succession on Matilda, his daughter, sometimes known as 'Maud'. She was the widow of the Holy Roman Emperor, hence her title of 'empress' and her subsequent marriage to Geoffrey of Anjou, explained her 'Angevin' affiliation. Despite the solemn agreement of the nobility to this arrangement, on Henry's death, his nephew, Stephen, contested the succession, and declared himself king in 1135, supported by many who had sworn to respect Matilda's accession. When she crossed the Channel in 1139 to assert her rights, a civil war, generally known as the 'Anarchy', flared up between supporters of the two factions. In Oxford, Stephen had arrested Roger, bishop of Salisbury, and his nephew, Alexander, bishop of Lincoln, for permitting their followers to brawl with those of Alan of Brittany, an inflammatory action seen by some as little more than a pretext for curbing their power and seizing their castles. In 1141, however, Robert D'Oilly, governor of Oxford Castle, declared for Matilda and a year later, Stephen arrived in the autumn with an army to claim his own. The town quickly fell and was burnt, but the castle held out for three months. Robert of Gloucester, Matilda's half-brother and chief supporter, attempted to relieve the siege by enticing Stephen away. He promised those he was besieging in Wareham Castle (Dorset) that if they could persuade Stephen to relieve them, a respite would be granted. But Stephen refused to take the bait. Matilda, who had been in residence in Oxford throughout the siege, was forced to escape before its inevitable fall. This was the famous occasion when, wrapped in a white cloak, her flight across the frozen Thames and her arrival at Abingdon became the stuff of legend. Under its new governor, William de Chesney, Oxford would remain a base for operations against Matilda's forces by Stephen and his son Eustace. After those nineteen winters when it was reported in the *Anglo-Saxon Chronicle* that Christ and his saints slept, Oxford finally provided the setting for the peace agreement between Stephen and his nephew, Matilda's son, who would succeed as Henry II. Two mounds, 'Jews Mount' and 'Mount Pelham', are said to have been raised as possible siege castles during either the siege of 1142 or that of 1216 in the Barons' War, but this is only one of many explanations for their existence.

Wallingford was held for Matilda and controlled the Thames Valley to the west of Windsor (Berkshire), but was besieged three times in 1139, 1146, and 1152–3. The castle had expanded since its first building, with a stone shell keep on the motte and stone walls defending its inner and outer baileys, with partially wet moats, fed by the nearby Thames, adding to its strength. The sieges are famous for the use of siege castles—temporary fieldworks designed to blockade the invested fortress against supplies, reinforcements, or relief, and as jumping off points for assaults. They probably resembled miniature versions of the earth and timber forts of the time. In the first siege of 1139, Matilda's garrison was blockaded by two royal forts. The horseshoe-shaped structure, labelled on OS maps as 'Stephen's Mount', stood on the east bank of the Thames at Crowmarsh Gifford and controlled the bridge. The other lay to the west of the town. The collapse of the 1139 siege was ascribed by a contemporary chronicler to the desecration of a church as the basis for one of these siegeworks, but the relief column led by Miles of Gloucester may also have contributed. In 1140, Stephen's chief steward was imprisoned in the castle, only being released on the surrender of his castle and lands at Shirburn. For the second siege in 1146, the defenders had constructed bridge-head defences on the east bank, countered, once again, by the Crowmarsh Gifford fort. Matilda had retreated to France in 1148 leaving her son, the future Henry II, to advance their interests. Stephen laid siege again to Wallingford in July 1152–3, reducing the bridgehead defences, raising a second fort on the east bank to support the existing one at Crowmarsh Gifford covering the approach to the bridge, which he is said to have captured. The Crowmarsh Gifford site has now been built over, but an 80-foot-wide (25-metre-wide) defensive ditch, whose spoil was used to construct an oval platform, around 160 by 115 feet (50 by 35 metres), forming an entrenched camp, was uncovered prior to development works in 2011. The ditch had subsequently been backfilled within a short space of time—probably around twenty-five years. Other contemporary ditches excavated at the same time may represent either further defensive works on the east bank, or channels to bring water from the river to fill the moat. Three possible sites for further siege castles have also been identified to the west of the town at a distance suitable for the purposes of blockade, but not close enough for assault. The first is at Brightwell (SU578907) near St Agatha's church where the earthworks of a moat survive. The second possible siege castle (SU562884) stands between South Moreton Manor and the railway, and only the north-east corner of a third stands across the railway from St Mary's church at Cholsey (SU585868). It is quite possible that one of these three sites was occupied during the first siege but not all these three western siege works would have been necessarily active or even occupied at the same time. A further site listed at South Moreton (SU558880) is a damaged or, more probably, an unfinished motte on the bank of the Mill Brook near the church. This castle was only mentioned in 1220 but appears to date from the years of the Anarchy and offers a fourth possibility as a siege castle. The town was relieved from its final siege when Henry arrived to confront Stephen and invest the bridgehead. The resultant negotiations, made easier by the unexpected death of Stephen's son, saw Henry accepted as Stephen's successor. Henry II held a council in 1155 in the town and granted Wallingford generous conditions in a charter in recognition of the town's support for his mother in the civil war. In 1176, Henry II at the Assize of Northampton ordered all those castles erected during the Anarchy, and specifically those held against his mother's Angevin cause, to be levelled.

Although it has been pointed out that military action was intermittent and localised, its random and unpredictable nature caused unsettled conditions across the entire country for the whole period of nearly twenty years. One explanation of why the term 'anarchy' was adopted was the scope for brigandage afforded by the power vacuum caused by competing leaders and a lack of central authority. Violence could be actual, or it could be potential involving extortion. Despite being bribed to leave Abingdon Abbey's property alone, the constable of Wallingford Castle still plundered the abbey's grange at Culham. Existing in constant fear, it took only the sighting of a few riders in mail coats to spook a whole village. These criminal activities ran alongside the more conventional military operations of the war. In 1145, Robert of Gloucester, Matilda's half-brother and chief supporter, began building a castle at Faringdon, thereby securing communications between Gloucester and Wallingford. It was quickly attacked by Stephen, and it surrendered before help might arrive. The assault by Stephen in 1145, employing stone-throwing catapults and sustained arrow-fire to subdue the defenders, forced a hurried and surreptitious surrender and the destruction of the castle. Excavated in 1935 when a folly tower was being constructed, it was shown to have been built with clay revetments and drystone foundations. It has recently been suggested that Faringdon's castle lay elsewhere and that the twelfth-century earthworks on Faringdon Clump or Folly Hill represent a siege work, a structure erected for purely military use and seen as an ephemeral work serving a distinct and singular function in a particular context.

The common perception at the time, therefore, was of a country subject to lawlessness and chaos. Rob Liddiard has, nevertheless, pointed out that most castles never saw any military action. Even including the Civil Wars of the seventeenth century, the total for England is given as just under 640 instances of assaults or sieges. Hulme has counted 162 such incidents at 106 separate sites in England during the Anarchy: around a quarter of the total for the seven centuries. Oxfordshire can lay claim to at least five of these concerning castles, with two further instances for towns, during this time.

The Development of Oxfordshire's Early Castles

Many of those castles which survived Henry II's cull developed into strong fortresses over the next two centuries. Sometime in the thirteenth or fourteenth centuries, the original castle at Banbury was completely remodelled in concentric form with a five-sided inner ward surrounded by a ditch within a rectangular outer enclosure, itself also ditched. There was an outer gatehouse with twin towers, curtain walls with corner towers, a chapel which had gone out of use after 1340, and a prison in use from 1276 until the sixteenth century. One circular corner tower, 17.5 feet (5.4 metres) in diameter, has been traced, bonded into a stone curtain wall 5 feet (1.5 metres) thick, with a slightly smaller interval tower between it and the gatehouse. One of the gate towers was square fronted but with a round back so may have been modified from an original round tower. It stood 13 feet (4 metres) from its partner to which it was joined by a cross-wall. The whole was surrounded by ditches, triple in places, with an earlier stone building buried in the outer bank. The castle would see action in the Civil War but has totally vanished from sight.

From his outright acquisition of Wallingford Castle in 1230, Richard, earl of Cornwall, Henry III's brother, had transformed it into a 'concentric, show-fortress' covering 30 acres (12 ha). He was clearly regarded as an expert when it came to fortification as he was asked by his brother to advise on improvements to the royal castles of Dover in 1243 and Oxford in 1255. A reconstruction drawing of Wallingford shows a shell-keep with a high tower; three concentric walls with square, round, and open-backed towers; wet moats with one side along the riverbank; gardens and orchards; halls, chapel and other domestic buildings ranged along the curtains; a gatehouse complex near the bridge over the Thames; and further twin-towered gatehouses on the landward side. Discovery in 2010 of a possibly thirteenth-century wharf, which may have been an unloading point for building materials for the castle and then become a high-status entry point, could have been accessed by a Water Gate. The extensive baileys, unusually extending over the town's North Gate, contained numerous halls, religious foundations, and domestic buildings making the castle one of the largest in the kingdom. At some point in his building work, probably before 1250, Richard cut into the motte to erect a large rectangular tower house set astride the wall of the inner bailey. On his death in 1272, the castle passed to his son, Edmund, but then reverted to the crown. In the 1360s, the Black Prince, celebrating his famous victories on the continent, had a new hall, kitchen, and prison built, along with a room in which pleas might be heard. He also carried out repairs and improvements to his own apartments, the chapel, and the great tower. The castle was a residence for Henry V's widow and for Henry VI, becoming predominantly a prison in the 1430s. Only extensive earthworks and odd fragments of masonry now remain.

At Oxford, the tower on the motte is most likely to have begun as a timber construction, later replaced in stone. Chambers were built around the inside of the ten-sided shell wall leaving an open space in the centre from which was accessed a hexagonal well chamber buried deep in the motte and thought to date from 1173 or thereabouts. From the outside, the keep would have looked like the solid tower depicted in various manuscripts and maps. Five or six circular, rectangular, and polygonal stone towers, curtain walls, and two gatehouses replaced the timber palisades of the bailey. The apparently circular base of the south-west tower survives as the foundation of a later prison building. Faulkes de Breaute demolished a church which compromised the defences and built the barbican to the East Gate after the siege of 1216. The presence of at least two medieval stone buildings have been confirmed by excavation, one of which is presumed to have been the main hall measuring around 40 feet (13 metres) in width and which may have continued in use as the Sessions House. The other, cut into the rampart in the southern part of the bailey was represented by cellars measuring 26 by 13 feet (8 by 4 metres) with an adjacent garderobe pit. Accounts record maintenance costs through the next two centuries under Edward I and his son, but by the early 1400s, much of the castle was in a state of near collapse and only a prison, constructed in 1420, and the Exchequer were considered habitable. Ruin was complete at the end of the Civil War when, in 1652, the castle was slighted.

Built by Henry I, the royal Beaumont Palace was a walled enclosure with a strong gatehouse situated outside Oxford's North Gate. It comprised an aisled hall, a kitchen, and a chapel. Improvements were made over the years including a new chapel and queen's chamber connected by a pentice, and new stables.

Right: Oxford Castle: the rounded base of the south-west tower built into a later prison building. One view of the tower from the late 1700s depicts the tower as polygonal, a half-hexagon externally, which may have represented the upper storeys.

Below: Wallingford Castle: a photograph of the reconstruction model of the castle. (*Judy Dewey and Wallingford Museum*)

It was the birthplace of Richard I and John, but Edward I was the last king to maintain the buildings. Materials were being removed to patch up the castle in 1308 and in 1318, it was handed over to the Carmelite friars. Fragments of Norman masonry present in properties on Woodstock Road in the early 1800s were presumed to have come from the palace. Woodstock Palace, originating as a hunting lodge in the forest of Wychwood and used by Aethelred II from late in the tenth century, became one of Henry I's favourite royal palaces and an important centre of his spreading bureaucracy from around 1110. Perched on a small hill on the banks of the River Glyme and ringed by a 7-mile-long (11-km-long) wall of Cotswold stone which enclosed a hunting park and a menagerie of exotic beasts, the palace was approached by a causeway which was raised up between fishponds and was securely walled with several of its buildings sporting crenelations, if only for ornamental effect. By the reign of Henry II, the palace included a large, aisled hall, at one end of which was the king's high chamber, accessed from the courtyard by a flight of stone steps, later encased in a porch, with the queen's chamber below. At least two chapels, one of them circular or semi-circular, were in use, that of the queen being connected to the chamber-block by a covered passage. Also within the walls were chambers for the royal household, stables, a smithy, and detached kitchens. The only known plan, dating from the time of Blenheim Palace's landscaping, shows a compact block of domestic buildings ranged around a courtyard. A short distance to the west of the palace lay Everswell, a detached compound accessed by a drawbridge across the Glyme and containing a natural spring which fed ponds. This structure has been identified as enclosing Rosamund's Tower and garden, traditionally associated with Henry II, as well as a cloister, chapel, and royal chambers connected by a passage, much of this built by Henry III to provide a rural retreat from the formality of the court. Woodstock, birthplace in 1330 of both Edward III's first child, Edward, the Black Prince, and his fifth surviving son, Thomas, in 1355, was maintained and improved throughout the centuries with a new, embattled tower being added by Edward IV. By the time of Princess Elizabeth's imprisonment there in 1554, only the gatehouse would have been habitable, and the remains of both the palace and its annexe were demolished when Blenheim's parklands were landscaped. As we have seen, however, many of the county's early castles had never been developed; had fallen into disrepair; or had been ordered destroyed by Henry II or John.

Further Barons' Wars and Power Struggles

The new reign of the Plantagenet King Henry II may have brought general peace to the country, but disputes continued to arise. The abbey of Abingdon had been granted extensive market privileges by Edward the Confessor and confirmed by Henry I, but in 1164, the traders of Oxford and Wallingford, feeling disadvantaged by Abingdon's powerful monopolies, and led by the royal constable of Wallingford Castle, marched on Abingdon. They were routed by the abbey's retainers and the resultant court case confirmed the abbey's dominant position. Prior to the rebellion in 1173–4 of Henry, the young king, against his father Henry II, £60 had been spent on strengthening Wallingford Castle, traditionally the property of the king's eldest son and Oxford, a royal castle, was put into a state of armed preparedness. The rebellion of young Henry, his mother, and brothers fizzled out after eighteen months of scattered actions on both sides of the Channel. By 1185, Oxford Castle had become a royal prison. While his brother, Richard I, was away on Crusade, John took the opportunity to seize Wallingford Castle, but it was retaken by Richard's allies and given to the queen dowager, Eleanor of Aquitaine, in 1193. On being crowned six years later, John repossessed it despite his mother living on for a further five years.

Oxford would feature prominently in the negotiations surrounding the challenges to King John mounted by many of his barons and supported by the French crown. John held meetings of parliament and state councils in Oxford on several occasions after 1204, and in 1210 the barons were instructed to attend unarmed as the king felt threatened. John met the barons there again in July 1215 to try to find solutions to the impasse but refused to attend a pre-arranged meeting the next month as they were held to be in arms against him and he, once more, feared for his safety. The king's mercenary captains were ordered to strengthen Oxford's defences along with those of all the other royal castles and the sheriff of Berkshire was ordered by King John to mobilise a workforce to prepare Wallingford for a siege in 1215 in case Windsor fell to the rebels. Oxford was besieged by the rebels in 1216 when it was relieved on behalf of King John by one of his notorious mercenary leaders. In 1216, Wallingford was strongly garrisoned and provisioned for a siege and later in the year, John progressed through Burford, Oxford, and Wallingford, gathering up troops as he went, prior to his final campaign. Following John's death, his mercenaries sought to secure their position by strengthening further such strongholds as Oxford Castle, now being held against the lawful king, but once Henry III was in a position to consolidate his power, he summoned his supporters to Oxford to discuss the royalist plan of action.

However, the power struggle between monarch and baronage, initiated by the signing of Magna Carta but far from resolved, still had a long way to travel. Grasping the opportunity of a supplicant king seeking to raise finance, in 1258, a cabal of barons led by Simon de Montfort, used the occasion of a parliament, convened at Oxford's Dominican friary, to create a body of constitutional reforms, the Provisions of Oxford, which were intended to force King Henry III to increase the involvement of the country's nobility in the process of government. They proposed the establishment of a council of twenty-four, half nominated by the crown and half by the baronage; a fifteen-member Privy Council, with nine of them appointed by the barons; the summoning of three parliaments each year; baronial oversight of royal appointments; and the custody of royal castles and control of local administration. One of the dozen representing the king's interest was Aymer de Valence, bishop of Winchester, whose nephew would build Bampton Castle. One of those fifteen appointed to the Privy Council was the staunch royalist Sir James Audley whose son would become lord of Stratton Audley and father of the Sir James who we will find fighting at Poitiers. These provisions were further extended the next year in the Provisions of Westminster but thrown out by Henry in 1261, an action leading to the Barons' War of 1263–67. Oxford was caught in the middle of this conflict between Henry III and the barons led by de Montfort as the advantage swung backwards and forwards. De Montfort was greatly influenced by Robert Grosseteste, bishop of Lincoln, and drew support from several other Oxford educated churchmen including Adam Marsh and Bishop Stephen Berksted of Chichester. The moneylender, David of Oxford, also figured early on in de Montfort's fifty-year-long struggle to gain his wife's dowry from her brother, Henry III. The town was fined by Henry III's son, the Lord Edward, for supporting the enemies of his father, but continued to play host to parliaments which sought to strengthen the barons' position and in 1261 was the rallying point for the barons' rebellion against Henry III. The town also witnessed violent town *versus* gown riots. The abbot of Abingdon was accused of sending money and troops to de Montfort at Windsor. Rather disingenuously the abbot defended his actions by saying he thought the request, accompanied by dire threats, had come from the king and that de Montfort must have forged the royal seal.

Oxford was again an assembly point in 1264, this time for the king's summons of the feudal host prior to the campaign which led to his defeat and capture at Lewes. While the king was notionally free but under de Montfort's control, his son Edward, brother, Richard of Cornwall, along with his sons, Henry of Almain and Edmund, were all held hostage in Wallingford Castle under the care of de Montfort's wife, Eleanor, Richard's sister. Supporters of Edward with 300 horsemen stormed the castle but were dissuaded from penetrating the inner bailey by threats to release the heir to the throne to them via mangonel. The hostages were then transferred to the more secure castle of Kenilworth in Warwickshire. Right up to his defeat and death at Evesham, de Montfort maintained a garrison of foreign mercenaries in Wallingford, as he did at both Dover and Windsor, emphasising the castle's perceived importance. Only this victory for Henry III, his son the Lord Edward, and his supporters led to the final annulment of the Provisions in 1266.

Along with conflict at the national level, local disagreements could escalate and get out of hand. In 1293–4, a disputed provision of the prebend, or estate income, of Thame saw supporters of the papal candidate attempting to depose the protégé of the bishop of Lincoln. The resultant fight, involving 200 armed men attacking the church, saw priests celebrating mass being showered with arrows; a blockade of the church; the destruction of a bridge; and obstruction of the highway. Excommunication of those supporting the papal Provisor by the bishop of Lincoln swiftly followed. This might be seen as an ominous precursor of the century to come.

The Order of Knights Templar had accumulated rich estates in Oxfordshire, administered from their HQ in the preceptory of Sandford-on-Thames which had taken over from the Temple Cowley site in 1240. Here, in an extensive, walled compound with high status structures and farm buildings, lived the grand master, precentor, constable, and eight knights, served by large numbers of lay brothers who worked the land. Templar properties operated as revenue-producing commercial concerns to underwrite the order's crusading activities in the Holy Land. In 1308, in a cynical move to seize their lands and wealth, in collusion with the French King Philip IV, Edward I suppressed the order, citing the behaviour of the knights—sacrilege, witchcraft, and worse—as justification. The preceptories' officers were arrested, interrogated, probably tortured, or, at the very least, threatened with torture, and their 'confessions' were taken as proof of their beastliness. At Sandford, William Sautre, the precentor and thus at the centre of the house's business for the previous twenty years, gave evidence, calling on his colleagues to support his protestations of innocence. The conclusions had been reached long before any investigation was initiated and, once royal debts to the Templars had been wiped out, their properties were summarily transferred to the Knights of St John of Jerusalem, the Hospitallers. While many of the order's leaders in France were executed as heretics, most English Templars reconciled themselves with the church, leaving only the exceptional individual condemned to spend the rest of his life in prison.

Weak or unpopular kingship bred lawlessness and the reign of Edward II saw attempts to enlist the town's support for several causes. Thomas of Lancaster, cousin to Edward II, was instrumental in the persecution of Piers Gaveston, the king's favourite, who had been granted the earldom of Cornwall, previously intended for one of Edward I's younger sons, along with Wallingford Castle, traditionally held by the heir apparent. Here, in December 1307, was held a great tournament to celebrate Gaveston's marriage to Margaret de Clare, sister of the wealthy and influential earl of Gloucester. Over 200 knights attended the tournament, but the defeat and humiliation of the established nobility by the young blades of a gloating Gaveston, apparently egged on by a doting king, stoked the growing enmity toward the king's beloved 'brother-in-arms'. This antipathy forced Gaveston into exile, and on his unsanctioned return, he was detained by a group of lords which included the earl of Pembroke, who wished to negotiate a settlement with the king. Meanwhile, Gaveston was lodged for safekeeping, at Deddington, probably in Castle House, under Pembroke's protection. However, he was seized from there by the earl of Warwick, his nemesis, and killed. Since he had been ex-communicated, his body could not be given a Christian burial but was rescued by Dominicans from Oxford to await a decent burial. Aymer de Valence had succeeded to the earldom of Pembroke in the same year of Edward II's accession to the throne and had supported Thomas of Lancaster in his opposition to Gaveston, but this dishonourable abduction from protective custody at Deddington, prompted him to abandon the rebels. Too late to prevent Gaveston's savage execution at the hands of Warwick, he had sought help from the University of Oxford to salvage his honour by affording Gaveston a fair trial, but an affronted Pembroke shifted his allegiance to Edward. He next tried to broker a peace between the king and Thomas of Lancaster but, in the end, would be one of those condemning Lancaster to death. Wishing to cement his influence at court, he sought to establish a power base in the Thames Valley, between his lands in South Wales and Kent, and received a licence to crenellate Bampton Castle in 1315. Unappreciated as a peacemaker and unable to compete with the king's new favourites, the Despensers, father and son, he was soon marginalised, bankrupted, and reduced to carrying out minor diplomatic tasks for the king, dying in Picardy in 1324.

The Despensers, who had become Edward's next set of favoured retainers, were equally unpopular as Gaveston, and Thomas of Lancaster led another rebellion but was defeated at the battle of Boroughbridge in Yorkshire in 1322. Hugh Audley of Stratton Audley, one of Thomas of Lancaster's supporters surrendered before the battle of Boroughbridge but was incarcerated in Wallingford Castle where he died four years later. Robert de Ardern, with manors at Wickham and Drayton, appointed as keeper of Banbury Castle by Edward II, raised the men of Oxfordshire to fight in the royal force which would put down the rebellion. After the battle, a tribunal composed of those very men the old nobility sought to eject convicted Thomas of Lancaster of treason and he was executed. This was not to be the end of the matter and the Marcher lords, led by Roger Mortimer, rebelled against Edward and his Despenser favourites but were defeated and Mortimer was imprisoned. After his escape to France, he joined up with Edward's queen, Isabella, daughter of the French king. In 1326, Isabella and Mortimer invaded England with the intention of deposing Edward II and putting her son, the fourteen-year-old Henry on his father's throne. Although the men of Oxfordshire were once again called out to counter the queen's forces, there was little effective resistance as most of the country's leaders were sympathetic to her and her main support, Roger Mortimer, who despoiled the Despensers' property including their six Oxfordshire manors. All the rebels converged on Oxford where Isabella lodged in the Carmelite friary and Mortimer went to Oseney Abbey. The bishop of Hereford preached them a sermon comparing Despenser to the snake in Genesis. Mortimer's father had studied at Oxford, and Mortimer himself would build a cabal of Oxford-educated prelates, including Orleton of Hereford and Burghersh of Lincoln, as he gathered support against the king and his hated favourite. It was to England's larger towns such as Oxford which all these actors looked for popular support, and in-fighting between the resultant factions caused significant disruption to the town's affairs. Finally, the Despensers were taken and executed, and Edward II was deposed and reported as murdered in Berkeley Castle in Gloucestershire. After the king's reported death, an imposter claiming to be the son of Edward I was swiftly disposed of. Wallingford, scene of so many upheavals and plots, had been returned to royal ownership and was now a royal arsenal, inventoried in 1327 in a stock-take of the various sizes of crossbows and other weapons; its manufacturing capability; and the storage of disassembled siege engines for deployment as needed.

William de Monte Acuto (Montacute/Montague) had been granted licence to crenellate his house of Cassington by Edward II in 1317. Viewed by the king's opponents as an over-enthusiastic supporter of his monarch, he was sent abroad as an administrator in Aquitaine where he died in 1319. His son, also William, was born at Cassington around 1302, fought alongside Edward II and was knighted in 1326. However, he acted for the young Edward III during his minority and was heavily involved in the overthrow of Isabella and Mortimer, benefitting from the young king's consequent gratitude. He was employed by Edward III as a soldier and a diplomat and created 1st earl of Salisbury but died from injuries received in a tournament in 1344. Sir Robert de Grey fought for Edward I in Wales and his son, John de Grey, fought for Edward III in Scotland and Flanders, being rewarded with a barony. He fought at Crécy in 1346 and on his return, he was granted a licence to crenellate Greys Court, his house at Rotherfield. He became one of the original twenty-six knights of the garter and later returned to France for the campaign of 1356. Another of that original band was Sir Hugh Courtenay who was given the manor of Nuneham by his father in 1341. James Audley had become tenant of the manor of Stratton Audley by marriage in 1244 and had built the castle there by 1263. His son had an illegitimate son who, as a courageous and successful captain in Edward III's French wars, was rewarded by being created another of the initial knights of the garter. He accompanied the expedition to France led by the Black Prince and was lauded as the hero of their victory over the French at Poitiers in 1356. He was appointed seneschal of Aquitaine and died of sickness after the siege of La-Roche-sur-Yon, south of Nantes, in 1369.

After Edward III ascended the throne, Robert de Ardern was granted licence to fortify his houses of Wickham and Drayton with stone walls and crenellations. Both he and his neighbour, William de Montague, were also pardoned for all murders, etc., itself an indication of the deplorable state of things and the continuation of lawlessness and violence: the Audley manor house at Stratton Audley was broken into and goods removed in 1335, and in 1336, Ralph de

Chasteleyn was killed in a fight with the de Noyers of Churchill. His son, Gilbert, inherited the manor and was granted a licence to crenellate in 1347. Both are incidents typical of the period. With the onset of the Hundred Years' War, dangers would come from home and abroad. In 1378, in view of a continued threat of invasion by the French, the mayor and bailiffs of Oxford, together with the three dozen wealthiest burghers, were ordered to repair the city walls, an injunction extended to many towns and castles in southern England. In 1381, although Oxfordshire was for the most part untouched by the Peasants' Revolt, a clerical poll tax collector had been attacked in the county in April 1380, and the town decided to respond to external threats by widening the town ditch. The reign of Richard II was characterised by further conflicts of one kind or another. Five powerful nobles including the king's uncle, Thomas of Woodstock, duke of Gloucester and constable of England, along with Henry Bolingbroke, the future Henry IV, attempted to challenge the king's unpopular favourites. Having raised an armed rebellion, they defeated a royal army, led by de Vere, earl of Oxford, at the battle of Radcot Bridge, in 1387. With the bridges held against him, and another rebel army behind him, de Vere abandoned the fight and escaped, leaving his armour scattered behind him. Many of his men perished in the river and its surrounding marshes. Following the battle, the lords' victorious army paraded through Oxford to march on London and impose their dominance on the king, mercilessly purging his supporters. When Richard regained the upper hand, he had his uncle Thomas of Woodstock arrested and imprisoned in Calais, during which time he was murdered.

Historians have described the fourteenth century as everything from difficult to calamitous. Oxford, in 1334, was the ninth wealthiest town in England, but disasters such as the famine of the Little Ice Age of 1315–17 and the Great Plague of 1348–9 affected everyday life, with crop yields in the surrounding villages falling by 50 per cent, populations halved, and by 1349 the national economy contracting by a quarter. Some villages such as Tusmore and Tilgarsley were completely abandoned as no tenants could be found to replace those who had died. Ever present, but exacerbated by such problems, conflict between town and gown would continue to break out throughout the century, spilling over into unrestrained violence, culminating in the three-day riot which began in Oxford on St Scholastica's Day in February 1355. This saw townsfolk armed with knives and bows killing and maiming scores of scholars and led to punishments and penances which saw the University finally come out on top. Oxfordshire would see the first recorded instance of the violence which escalated into the Peasants' or Great Revolt of 1381. Despatched by the dean of Bicester to collect Poll Tax contributions from the clergy who felt just as burdened as everyone else, William Payable (an early example of lazy careers advice) was attacked and severely beaten before he had collected any money, suggesting that robbery was not the object. In April 1381, those responsible, never identified, were excommunicated, a sentence broadcast throughout the county's churches every Sunday. Edmund Stonor—son of a former chief justice, and himself a former sheriff of Hertfordshire and a Poll Tax commissioner, despite being mainly based in Oxfordshire—was threatened with extreme violence by men from Puttenham while watching his papers being burned and one of his servants murdered. Seven townsmen of Abingdon were arrested for being party to the rebellion. Following Richard II's revocation of the promises extracted under duress, his commissioners would brook no delay in their pursuit of anyone implicated in the rebellion, and the sheriff of Oxfordshire was ordered to pull in anyone who had previously been bailed, however legal their actions might have been at the time.

As the century drew to a close, violence continued to be endemic. In 1391, Sir John Lovell was initiating legal proceedings against malicious folk who prevented him reaching his house at Minster Lovell. Oseney Abbey was in dispute with Oxford's burgesses in 1415 over the issue of local taxation when canons of the abbey forcibly seized the borough collector and a bailiff. This led to violent retaliation by the townsfolk involving the seizure of valuable property of the abbey including the abbot's horses. The dispute appeared to have been resolved by 1419 but soon resumed over a boundary dispute which dragged on for years more. In 1416, the abbot of Abingdon was forced to institute legal proceedings against Sir John Drayton of Nuneham after he had erected a fortalice on abbey land and his men had fired on the vicar of Culham and his parishioners, preventing them from beating the bounds. Once again, a weak king had overseen the erosion of central authority allowing lawlessness to spread.

Lollardy was a religious movement based on the teachings of John Wycliffe of Oxford University which demanded the reform of a corrupt and misdirected Roman church, and in 1381, twelve learned doctors of the university had pronounced his theses not only unorthodox but heretical. Despite, or maybe because of, this condemnation, his ideas continued to gain support, especially locally. A revolt in 1413 petered out when its leaders, 200 or so of them, were condemned and hanged or burned at the stake. In 1431, a further such revolt involving Lollards from Faringdon, Buscot, and villages around Oxford was centred on Drayton, near Abingdon. Intending to destroy Abingdon Abbey, representing everything they saw as iniquitous and corrupt, the rebel army, said to number as many as 20,000 was intercepted and crushed by the duke of Gloucester, who captured their leader, one William Perkins, or William Mandeville, but who went under the name of 'Jack Sharp'. He was conveyed to London for execution by hanging, drawing, and quartering, with his parts displayed in Oxford and Abingdon, the heartland of his support. James Fiennes, Lord Saye and Sele, served the weak and unpopular Henry VI as lord high treasurer of England and, along with his son-in-law, he was beheaded by the mob during Jack Cade's rebellion in 1450. Broughton Castle would pass to the Fiennes family by marriage in 1457. His son, William Fiennes, now lord of Broughton, continued to support the Lancastrian cause and was killed at the battle of Barnet in 1471, fighting for Henry VI.

This conflict between the houses of York and Lancaster would bring further disruption to the lives of both rich and poor across the country. Richard, duke of York, father of the future Edward IV and Richard III, led the opposition to Henry VI. In 1452, he wrote a letter which documented his aspirations to become heir to Henry VI and sought support for these ambitions in Oxford. Interpreted as an incitement to rebellion against the lawful king, it was forwarded to the Privy Council. However, it would be a further eight years before Richard finally raised his standard at Abingdon on what he thought would be his triumphal march on London in the autumn of 1460. Meanwhile, Queen Margaret had visited Abingdon to lobby for the abbey's support for her Lancastrian cause. She was accompanied by Thomas Courtenay, earl of Devon, a previous supporter of York but, following disagreements, now firmly in the Lancastrian camp. While at the abbey, Devon suddenly died, and although poisoning was suspected, nothing was ever proved. Like the Fiennes, other local families were touched by the wars. Within two generations of their ownership, Stratton Audley castle had passed from the Audleys to Humphrey, earl of Stafford, created duke of Buckingham by Henry VI. Betrayed by the treachery of Grey of Ruthin, he was killed leading the Lancastrian army in 1460 at the battle of Northampton. The manor then passed to the 2nd duke, who was an enthusiastic supporter of Richard III in his claim to the throne. In 1483, unwilling to admit his apparent involvement in the suspicious disappearance of Edward IV's two sons, he attracted many Yorkists, loyal to Edward V, and plotted with Margaret Tudor, in an attempt to raise a rebellion. Lord Lovell, initially constable of Wallingford Castle and by this time Richard III's lord chamberlain, gathered his forces at Banbury prior to marching westwards, unnecessarily as it turned out, to crush the rebels. Adverse weather conditions and bad timing contributed to the precipitate collapse of his rebellion; Buckingham was taken prisoner and was swiftly executed without trial.

In 1469, populist risings in the north of the country, purporting to be instigated by one 'Robin of Redesdale' and ostensibly a reaction to the king's Woodville in-laws' abuse of power, had given the earl of Warwick both the motivation and the opportunity to attack Edward IV. As Warwick's forces marched north to link up with the rebels, the earls of Devon and Pembroke were instructed by the king to advance east from their bases to intercept them. Contemporary accounts relate that a squabble over their troops' quarters in Banbury led to the earl of Devon withdrawing his third of the Yorkist army, possibly only as far as Deddington Castle. This left the earl of Pembroke, leading a much-reduced force which would suffer ignominious defeat at the ensuing battle of Edgecote or Danes Moor at the hands of Warwick's rebel army. Although the phantom Robin of Redesdale was reported as being killed in the battle, Pembroke's army was routed, and its leaders duly executed. Although the king was arrested and his in-laws beheaded, there was little support for Warwick, and Edward was soon released. Two years later, Banbury was once more an assembly point for forces led by the duke of Clarence, marching to support his brother, Edward IV, at the battle of Barnet. The Wars of the Roses were unusual in that there were frequent pitched battles; few if any sieges; and, symptomatic of the bitterness of civil war, given that execution rather than ransom was the preferred option of the victors on both sides, the deaths of half of the nobility of England and a significant proportion of the country's gentry.

John Sant, the mitred abbot of Abingdon Abbey, was a staunch Yorkist supporter who was posted abroad to negotiate treaties and to act as Edward IV's ambassador to Rome. As well as papal *nuncio*, he was joint president of the Benedictine order. After the battle of Bosworth, opposition to Henry VII continued and following the unsuccessful rebellion of John de la Pole, earl of Lincoln, defeated at the battle of Stoke, outside Newark in Nottinghamshire, in 1487, Humphrey and Thomas Stafford claimed sanctuary at Culham, a manor of Abingdon Abbey. Sadly for them, Abingdon was not accepted as a sanctuary for treason, but only for debt and felony. Thomas Stafford was dragged out to be hanged, drawn, and quartered. Other friends of Abbot Sant included Edward Franke, who was finally beheaded in 1489 and Francis, 1st Viscount Lovell, of Minster Lovell near Witney. Lovell, chief butler to the king and constable of Wallingford Castle, was one of the three notorious supporters of Richard III, shamed in the popular rhyme: 'the cat (Catesby), the rat (Ratcliffe) and the dog Lovell'. After the battle of Bosworth, Lovell escaped to Flanders where he lay low, but returned to fight for de la Pole at Stoke when, after Lincoln's defeat, he was last seen swimming his horse across the Trent and was presumed to have drowned. The abbot himself was accused of providing material and spiritual assistance to Lincoln's supporters but, more seriously, was also indicted for plotting to present an imposter as the Yorkist earl of Warwick, imprisoned in the Tower of London by Henry VII. Only payment of a very large fine freed him to continue as abbot of Abingdon until his death in 1496. The body, presented to the populace as the freed earl, was actually Lambert Simnel, first masquerading as one of Edward IV's sons, the princes in the tower, and only later as Edward of Warwick. Based on no more than a vague physical resemblance to the Plantagenets, Simnel, the son of an Oxford joiner, was put forward by a local priest as a rallying point for latent Yorkist supporters. Despite the real Warwick being paraded in public, Simnel continued to attract strong support and only the defeat at Stoke would end his adventure. The priest was incarcerated for life in the bishop's prison, probably the Bocardo, accessed via St Michael's Tower by Oxford's North Gate. Simnel, however, as no more than a pawn and a dupe, was taken into the royal kitchens as a scullion, later becoming royal falconer. As an inconvenient last male survivor of the Plantagenet line, Warwick was eventually executed in 1499.

Later Medieval Castles in Oxfordshire

A new generation of fortified dwellings began to appear in the fourteenth century. These generally contained more comfortable living quarters but often continued to employ the vocabulary of fortification. Their primary purpose was less defensive and more domestic but nevertheless remained blatant expressions of lordly power. Many of the nobility during the later Middle Ages fought for their king against Scotland, in Wales and in France. Those taking part in the great victories of the Hundred Years' War such as Crécy or Agincourt might accrue great wealth through plunder or the ransoming of important prisoners. Sometimes, they might invest this wealth in a tangible monument to their success such as a castle or a church. Their castles, at this time, very often took the form of a quadrangular court with a tower at each corner; often moated; accessed via a gatehouse defended by a drawbridge and portcullis. Domestic buildings, including a hall, private apartments, chapel, and service buildings, were ranged around the inside of the walls. An outer court might contain barns, stables, and workshops. The dividing lines between castles, fortified manor houses, and strong houses are very narrow. Neither is the existence of a licence to crenellate any real guide as to the defensive capacity of a medieval dwelling. The grant of such a licence was seen as a mark of royal favour, much as a minor decoration might be seen in modern times. It appears not to have ever been mandatory to apply for one, but a successful grant was seen to confer bragging rights. More licences may have been granted during the reigns of weak or unpopular kings, meaning either that a king needed to buy support by dispensing royal favour, or that the recipients felt so insecure that they felt it necessary to fortify their homes. Such licences were granted during the reign of Edward II for Camoys Court at Chiselhampton, Cassington, Bampton, and Stanton Wyard. At Camoys Court, licensed to Richard de Luches in 1318, the fourteenth-century solar block survives in the later farmhouse within its moat. Cassington's moat, measuring 200 by 130 feet (60 by 40 metres) survives as a ditch 80 feet (25 metres) wide and 7 feet (2 metres) deep, but nothing remains of Stanton Wyard, a separate manor in the village of Stanton Harcourt, now vanished. The licence was granted to John Wyard, a man-at-arms in the service of Roger Mortimer. Wyard was clearly useful to his employer as he was appointed a royal sergeant-at-arms in a position to observe the goings on around the young prince, the future Edward III, reporting back to his true master anything suspicious. Mortimer granted him both the manor itself, previously owned by his uncle, Roger Mortimer of Chirk in Denbighshire, and the licence to crenellate for services rendered in October 1327, the month after Edward II's reported death. One of the fourteen charges subsequently brought against Mortimer, and which led to his execution, related specifically to his use of Wyard as a spy in the royal court. This may not have been the most heinous crime in Edward III's determined indictment of Mortimer, but it was nevertheless considered sufficiently reprehensible to be included.

The licence issued by Edward II to Aymer de Valence, earl of Pembroke, was for his new-build castle at Bampton in 1315. It was commenced to a quadrangular design with a round tower at each corner and a projecting rectangular gatehouse in the middle of its west side. Midway each side of the gatehouse was a bartizan at battlement level. The gatehouse, the only surviving element, with its two-bay vault, extends back into the courtyard and has a turret containing a spiral stair at its south-west corner. The gate arch is now blocked, and the gatehouse itself now forms part of a house known as Ham Court. Pembroke died in 1324 so it is impossible to know how much of the build was achieved in his lifetime. Examination of design features such as mouldings and windows, suggests that the gatehouse, the castle's only significant survival, might not have been completed until nearer to 1330. Somerton was one of the manors of Odo of Bayeux but by the middle of the thirteenth century, it had passed to Walter de Grey, archbishop of York. The de Greys built a castle which, in 1295, was described as being ranged around a courtyard with fishponds, dovecote, and gardens, only vaguely traceable in fields north-east of the church. Stratton Audley Castle was in occupation in the late 1200s. All that remains is the rectangular moat in Court Close, measuring 290 by 310 feet (90 by 95 metres). Slight evidence of masonry has been found on site, most probably representing a hall complex. It was the birthplace around 1291 of Hugh Audley who married Gaveston's widow, Margaret de Clare, a niece of Edward II and a co-heiress to the estates of Gilbert de Clare, killed at Bannockburn, thereby becoming the earl of Gloucester and yet one more opponent of the Despensers. A manor house was first mentioned at Watlington in *c.* 1250, but a licence to crenellate was only issued to Nicholas de la Beche in 1338. He was constable of the Tower of London and charged with guarding the royal princesses in their parents' absence. In disgrace for neglecting these duties, he was then posted to administer Gascony and was occupied in both diplomacy and warfare in France. In 1442, the house was occupied by a king's sergeant. Cogges lies near a ford across the River Windrush on an ancient trackway which runs up through Witney. It was an Anglo-Saxon manorial complex repurposed, before 1103, as a priory, parts of which survive in the rectory. A new fortified manor house or castle was then established next door inside the double, partially water-filled moats, which surround two roughly equal four-sided islands, whose western sides abut the river. A castle here figures in local tradition, memorialised in the name 'Castle Yard'. The moated southern island features foundations of buildings, including a pair of parallel walls 23 feet (7 metres) apart which were uncovered by grave-digging in the expanded churchyard, so this is possibly evidence for the transition from an earthwork castle to a moated manor. A second manor house was built, probably by Archbishop Walter de Grey in 1241–2 with a stone chamber block in 1250–80, within a walled enclosure, which is encased in

Bampton Castle: the former gatehouse of this fourteenth-century castle, later converted into a house known as Ham Court.

Above left: The Great Tower of Greys Court at Rotherfield Greys.

Above right: The octagonal south-east tower of Greys Court at Rotherfield Greys. The apparently similar south-west tower dates from 200 years later.

the standing manor house, now Cogges Manor Farm. The two manors operated independently until they were combined by the de Greys.

The Grey family had owned the manor of Rotherfield since the Conquest. John de Grey, 2nd Lord Grey of Rotherfield from 1338, was a councillor and steward of the royal household. He received a licence for his house at Rotherfield in 1346 and 1348 and it is likely that a masonry castle already existed which de Grey transformed into a quadrangular castle with a tower at each corner. The ruins of a square north-east tower stand along with the square great tower of four storeys, both of which may pre-date Grey's licence. The great tower's lower courses may have been the end wall of a twelfth-century chamber, projecting into the courtyard and the curtain wall to its south is also of an early date. The south-east tower is octagonal, capped with a pyramidal roof, of three storeys, and has been dated to de Grey's time, possibly as one of a pair of gatehouse towers. The apparently similar south-west tower, however, is an addition of 1587, built by a later occupier to restore symmetry to the castle's footprint. It has been noted that in times of drought the parch marks of gatehouses to north and south are visible. The present residence, particularly in its kitchen, retains some medieval features and a jettied timber-framed range, containing services and lodgings, is the work of William Lovell who married the castle's heiress in 1422.

Warin de Lisle, 2nd Baron de Lisle, inherited his father's manor of Kingston Lisle near Wantage. He fought in France for much of the time between 1359 and 1378 but also held office in his local county. In 1377, he was granted a licence to crenellate Shirburn Castle near Watlington on a previously occupied but by now decayed site. This new quadrangular castle had a circular, three-storey tower at each corner, a square gatehouse, also of three storeys in the west wall, and sits in a wide wet moat, almost a lake. Two-storied buildings lined the interior leaving a rectangular courtyard in the centre. An almost total rebuilding in the eighteenth century involving new two- and three-storey ranges and remodelled towers leaves questions of the castle's serious military intent unanswered, although arrow-loops are still discernible in the upper storey of the gatehouse tower, but the current drawbridge is a fanciful reconstruction. Only this unusual gatehouse, which lay flush in the middle of the range rather than projecting, and the lower stages of two of the corner towers can be felt definitively to date from the 1370s. The castle occupies a square plinth of stone and brick, lapped by the waters of the moat. It is built of a mix of masonry, both dressed and rubble, and brick, much of which is being revealed as the eighteenth-century render drops off.

Two licences were issued to one Richard English by Edward III. The first, in 1356, was for a house in Newnham Murren, lying on the east bank of the Thames, south of Crowmarsh Gifford, marked by the twelfth- to thirteenth-century St Mary's church. The site of Upholcombe at Great Holcombe, licensed to him in 1360, may lie south of Newington House where the remains, consisting of glazed ridge tiles and decorated floor tiles, of a high-status medieval building have been located.

Above left: Shirburn Castle within its moat. (*Neil Guy*)

Above right: Broughton Castle: the gatehouse and bridge over the moat.

Broughton Castle is a moated fortified manor with a bridge and gatehouse, only licensed to Thomas Wykeham in 1406, when the curtain walls, at least one mural tower, and gatehouse were built, although the lower stage of the gatehouse may be earlier. An earlier house, dating to the first half of the thirteenth century is likely to have been incorporated into an ambitious rebuilding begun around 1290 and this rebuild may have been financed from the spoils of war as Sir John de Broughton II was one of Edward I's key captains. Following further expansion in 1331, a private chapel was licensed to Sir John de Broughton III. After 1377, the castle passed through the Wykeham family to Margaret who married Sir William Fiennes, 2nd Lord Saye and Sele. In 1450, his father, treasurer of England and a staunch supporter of Henry VI, had been killed by the mob during the rebellion of Jack Cade, and Sir William was killed at the battle of Barnet in 1471, fighting for Edward IV on the Yorkist side. The sale of land and other grand houses financed the remodelling of Broughton as an Elizabethan country house from 1528 and continued the house's complex building history. A number of features such as drawbars, turnpike stair, and guard chambers suggest that fifteenth-century modifications to the house's layout indicated a desire to create a suite of chambers which were not only private, but were also defensible, described by Gordon-Slade as 'an independent tower-house to the east of the hall'.

Moated Sites, Fortified Manor Houses, and Strong Houses

While the more important or prominent lords were building castles, the minor squirearchy often simply dug a moat around their more modest houses. This might discourage wandering thieves or discharged soldiers from pilferage or worse. A moat would also provide a supply of fish, a means of drainage and a water supply. Over 100 moated sites are recorded in post-1974 Oxfordshire, with just six scheduled as ancient monuments and only a few excavated. As might be expected, they occur more frequently on the clay lands of the Oxford Clay Vale extending through the Upper Thames Valley into north-east Oxfordshire with a lesser concentration on the London Clay of the Lower Thames Valley. Half of Oxfordshire's moated sites were within the bounds of existing villages with a further quarter on deserted village sites with the majority of these representing manorial sites. Occasional so-called empty moats, such as that around an orchard at Kidlington, will have been dug to protect a cash crop such as orchards, vegetable gardens, or beehives, but most will have contained houses, farms, and service buildings, with many of those exhibiting continuous occupation to the present. Moats were most commonly square or rectangular but others, such as the irregularly pentagonal moat at Barford St John, were laid out to conform to the lie of the land. Some moats were dry or only intermittently wet, draining surplus water, but others might involve ambitious engineering works such as a dam, to contrive permanently wet moats.

Throughout the medieval period, purely domestic and overtly defensible establishments share many features: great halls at Appleton Manor, Cogges, Broughton, and Minster Lovell; and solars at Thame Park, Minster Lovell, and Camoys Court where an annexe contains a garderobe. A first-floor, defensible hall was more usually preferred in Norman times to the unusual ground-floor, stone-built hall, dated to 1192, at Sutton Courtenay. Later great halls built by the abbot of Abingdon at Cumnor and his 'Abbey' at Sutton Courtenay, with less apparent need for defence, would be lofty, single-storey edifices. Castle House, Deddington, acquired in 1353 by the dean of Windsor, contains a first-floor chapel, while Pope's Tower at Stanton Harcourt has a vaulted chapel on the ground floor, but the chapels at both Thame Park and Stonor are detached. The gatehouse at New College, designed for Bishop William of Wykeham by William Wynford in the 1380s, consists of a square tower of three storeys with a higher stair turret at one corner. A similar gatehouse was built at All Souls' College, some fifty years later. Minster Lovell's south-west tower and Pope's Tower have both been likened to the original inner gatehouse of Magdalen College, now known as Founder's Tower. Perhaps all three, roughly contemporaneous, shared the same architect, William Orchard, as Sir Robert Harcourt was high steward of Oxford University from 1446–71. The three-storey Abbot's Tower at Thame Park, built around 1530, was residential with a solar and a bedroom above. In new domestic arrangements, retainers, family, and guests would be accommodated in lodgings such as the attic 'barracks' at Broughton, or the Long Gallery for monastic officials at Abingdon with its two fireplaces, but more often were ranged around courtyards. These have parallels with the fourteenth- and fifteenth-century lodgings for scholars at Worcester, All Souls', Merton, and New Colleges in Oxford.

Some sites, usually associated with moats, could be very grand and contain obvious defensive features. Stanton Harcourt was a semi-fortified manor house to the west of the churchyard. It was surrounded by a battlemented wall and consisted of a domestic range with hall, chapel, a fourteenth-century detached stone kitchen with a pyramidal roof renewed in 1485, and the north-east tower of 1460–71, known as Pope's Tower, standing around 40 feet (12 metres) high. The whole ensemble, ranged around a courtyard, dated from the middle years of the fifteenth century. Farm buildings occupied an outer courtyard where stables and a gatehouse, added in 1540, have now together been converted into a dwelling. The bulk of the medieval house was demolished after 1750 when the family moved to a new house at Nuneham Courtenay. In 1422, William, Baron Lovell and Holand, had married the heiress to Rotherfield's Greys Court. He was engaged in the wars in France until 1431 when he returned to Oxfordshire and decided to replace the existing hall and farm buildings at Minster Lovell with a new manor house, built between 1431 and 1442. William's house was constructed around three sides of a quadrangle with the fourth side closed by a buttressed wall along the bank of the River Windrush, intended to prevent flooding. It is entered through a vaulted gatehouse adjoining the chapel which fronts a large hall and a first-floor solar. The east range contains a kitchen and stables, with service rooms occupying the west wing, at whose corner stands the battlemented south-west tower, added in 1487. This was of four storeys and was accessed at first-floor level, by an external stair. The upper floors were reached by a spiral stair housed in an octagonal turret in the angle of the west wing. A wide passage through the east wing may represent the original main entrance. The house was occupied until around 1730 but had been largely demolished or robbed of stone by 1750 and now presents as picturesque ruins.

These two examples of semi-fortified houses above, retain significant standing remains but others, once equally substantial, have left fewer traces. Wytham Abbey was built in 1459 with a three-storey gatehouse tower and two courtyards, but its drastic remodelling of 1809 managed to preserve only its west side with an oriel window and the gateway with more oriels and a polygonal stair turret. Beckley Park Lodge's concentric triple moats represent a hunting lodge (labelled as a 'palace' on the OS map) of Richard, earl of Cornwall, built in 1227 as the centrepiece of a 300-acre (120 has) walled deer park. It was in regular royal use in 1300 and consisted of a hall, chambers, stables, and service buildings and was refurbished from 1376 for Edward III. The present grand house, still set

Above left: Stanton Harcourt: the fifteenth-century Pope's Tower, supposedly containing the poet's writing room.

Above right: Minster Lovell: the south-west tower with its octagonal stair-turret accessing the upper two floors.

Above: Minster Lovell: the chapel with the hall behind it and the vaulted gateway tunnel on the left.

Left: Wytham Abbey: the three-storey gatehouse tower of this two-courtyard house, built in 1459, and drastically remodelled in 1809.

within the moats, was built by Lord Williams of Thame around 1550. Barentin's Manor, Chalgrove, has been more thoroughly excavated than most similar sites. It consisted of two islands, raised by the spoil from its thirteenth-century moats, 33 feet (10 metres) wide and 5 feet (1.5 metres) deep. The larger platform, surrounded by an earthen bank, held a three-bay stone-built hall with detached kitchen, chapel, and barns around a walled courtyard accessed by a gatehouse. Additional buildings were added throughout the thirteenth and fourteenth centuries, but the site had been abandoned and largely demolished by the 1480s. Appleton Manor stands in a three-sided dry moat and consists of a two and a half-bay hall and a two-storey service block, dating from the early 1300s, with a second moat at nearby Tubney Manor Farm. Manor Farm, Kingham, stands on a rectangular platform with possible foundations of buildings, within three sides of a moat, presumably the house for which Gilbert Chasteleyn received licence to crenellate in 1347. The moated Holton House, known as Halle Place in 1461, supersedes a moat 300 yards (280 metres) to the south-east once held by Richard of Cornwall. Foundations in its south-west corner indicate buildings dating from 1450 with continual alterations right up to its 1805 demolition. The moat measures 160 by 175 feet (50 by 54 metres) with its sides supported by stone revetments. There are two access points on the north-west and the south-east corners with timber bridges on stone piers. The width of the moat is 75 feet (23 metres) on the north-west; 50 feet (15 metres) on the south-east; 25 feet (7.5 metres) on the south-west, with a dam to the north-east, 80 feet (25 metres) across. Close to Manor Farm in Islip and excavated in 2007 lies the rectangular moat built by William of Curlington, abbot of Westminster in the fourteenth century. A small excavation has uncovered evidence of recut ditches and of a possible stone wall aligned to a ditch and other masonry foundation remains robbed out for the successor house perhaps. The moat was set within other earthworks representing abandoned house platforms. The moated Phillis Court in Henley-on-Thames dated back to 1301 and would feature in the Civil War. At Copcourt Manor near Lewknor, the VCH records the 'medieval stone bastion' which represents one end of a drawbridge across the moat, now crossed by three eighteenth-century bridges. When it was first mentioned in 1244, Merton College's manor at Cuxham consisted of a stone solar over a cellar within a small spring-fed moat. It was acquired by Walter de Merton to fund his college in Oxford in 1264. By the fourteenth century, it had outgrown its restricted moat which now contained only the core buildings. The majority of the buildings, now having had their thatch substituted by tiles, lay within an outer cob wall entered through a gatehouse.

In the second half of the fifteenth century and even into the sixteenth, although houses such as Yelford were timber-framed and thoroughly domestic, others were still being built using the language of medieval power. Ewelme Palace was built for the Chaucer family and, following his marriage to Alice Chaucer, enlarged *c.* 1440 by de la Pole, earl of Suffolk, with work only interrupted by his assassination in 1450. An inner moated courtyard contained a house with a hall, chapel, lodgings for retainers, and a guest wing, while service buildings occupied an outer court entered by a two-storey gatehouse. While associated church, school, and alms-houses survive, the palace has left few traces. Rycote is a fourteenth-century house remodelled early in the sixteenth century as a courtyard house, built in brick, with turrets at the corners and two large towers flanking the entrance. It was built by Sir John Heron, Henry VIII's treasurer, who was a commissioner for the dissolution of the monasteries and seized the best of the church lands, including Thame Abbey, for himself. It was destroyed in 1745 but for one octagonal corner turret which survives. Hanwell is another courtyard house, begun around 1490 by Henry VII's cofferer, William Cope, who died in 1503. It had four corner towers, three storeys high, with higher octagonal turrets, of which that at the south-west corner still stands. Built in fashionable brick, it has quoins and parapet copings of stone. Brick was also used for the square early fifteenth-century tower of the chapel at Stonor, and the residential long gallery at Abingdon Abbey. In 1537, Cuddington Manor, later built over by the Brownes, consisted of a hall, measuring 24 by 18 feet (7.5 by 5.5 metres) with ten chambers and services on the south side of a courtyard which measured 140 by 100 feet (43 by 30 metres). On the east was a barn and to the west a kitchen, well, and stabling for six horses. The north was enclosed by a sturdy stone wall and a gatehouse. For many *arriviste* Tudor gentry, it remained important to be seen to be keeping up appearances by assuming implied pedigrees.

Town Defences

The defences of Roman Alchester and the ninth- and tenth-century Saxon *burhs* of Oxford and Wallingford were all clearly meant as a response to genuine threats. Towns in medieval England very often used physical markers primarily as boundaries relating to jurisdiction or trade. Abingdon town ditch, in part following the course of the Iron Age defences, probably had significance only as a boundary rather than fulfilling any defensive purpose. At Henley-on-Thames, a town ditch is marked on the 1898 OS map but was probably a sewer being used as a boundary marker. There are vague references from 1397 but no physical, firm documentary, or archaeological evidence for a defensive feature. Woodstock was granted murage in 1322—that is, permission to levy tolls for financing defences—but no traces of such constructions remain, if they ever existed. There were, however, bars on several roads into town, barriers to monitor the arrival of incoming goods and produce for market. Similarly, in Banbury, there was a North Bar and a southern St John's Bar, both destroyed by 1817, along with three other gates all of them built in the twelfth century by the bishop of Lincoln. A bridge gate has been mentioned as the East Bar by the bridge over

Above: The surviving angle turret at Rycote Park. (*Neil Guy*)

Right: Hanwell: the single remaining corner tower, one of the original four.

the Cherwell, but there is no evidence for a fortified gate on the bridge itself. All these bars were, in effect, customs posts, protecting the commercial interests of the town but also useful as a way of excluding undesirables. The two exceptions were Oxford and Wallingford, where serious town defences were maintained.

The mid-eleventh-century tower of St Michael's church had dominated the northern entrance to Oxford through the Saxon *burh* defences, which had comprised a turf rampart with a stone revetment. The medieval wall was built some 15 yards (14 metres) to its north, early in the thirteenth century, when the Saxon ditch was infilled, partly to accommodate the new walls, the outer one of which, in places, occupied the site of this ditch. It has been suggested that the tower of St Michael's once actually constituted the gate itself, with a dog-leg passage traversing the ground floor of the tower which was embedded in the rampart. Recorded as far back as Domesday Book are householders with responsibilities for the upkeep of the walls, a shift from the old burghal hidage system, where it was the rural communities who shared obligations to maintain the *burh*'s defences. In the 1220s, the sheriff had attempted to enforce the old system on householders, but this responsibility was in process of being passed to the town authorities who would take on the cost of construction and maintenance, with the town's occupants being responsible for manning the walls. This new system relied on murage grants which constituted permission to levy local taxes for the purpose of financing town defences. Payment was collected at the town gates from those entering for commercial reasons and was levied on livestock and goods arriving by road or river. Such grants were made for Oxford in 1227, in 1257, and in 1263, each one lasting for five years and would continue up to the end of the next century. In 1233, the king granted the town timber for use as joists in the town walls and this may have come from the abbot of Abingdon who had supplied wood for the piles needed for the construction of the walls. In 1244, the Greyfriars were allowed to expand their friary across the wall but were required to replace the demolished section. Records show both receipts and expenditure relating to the walls throughout the period between 1306 and 1460. As we have seen, the turbulence of the Peasants' Revolt caused the burghers of Oxford to strengthen their defences by widening the town ditch and in June 1381 the Commonalty of Oxford was granted a licence to crenellate their town walls. However, this was later revoked.

Oxford's medieval walls roughly followed the line of the rectangular enclosure formed by the earlier circuit. The wall is crenellated and stands to a height of 25 feet (7.7 metres), surmounted by a wall-walk. In 1263, the town was permitted to add at least twenty-one bastions to its walls, and the best surviving section is in the north-east corner at New College, where the open-backed, half-round bastions may be seen each side of the angle bastion. The northern wall had been fronted by a second, outer wall, an arrangement unique in Britain, and most likely constructed between 1280 and 1300, a murage grant for four years being made in 1285. But by 1387, bastions were being let out as workshops or dwellings and the spaces inside the walls had been built over. Much of the outer wall is long demolished. There were bastions on both walls, equipped with arrow-loops and forming a continuous wall-walk. Bastion 11, surviving in the gardens of New College, contains a single type 'A', inverted keyhole gunport. This is more or less identical to others found in known contemporary structures, including some associated with William of Wykeham, who had bought the land adjacent to the walls for the building of New College and had agreed to be responsible for the upkeep of the walls. One bastion was replaced by the college's belltower in 1400 and another was pierced by an entrance in the eighteenth century. A long stretch of the southern wall with a single semi-circular bastion appears to survive below Merton College and turns the corner to form the buttressed wall of the college garden. Medieval Oxford was accessed by five gates and at least one postern. The Bocardo Gate in the north may have incorporated the tower of St Michael's, previously an integral part of the defences. The East Gate was recorded during the reign of Edward III as consisting of two round towers with chains and stout doors. This had disappeared by 1578 when a square tower was shown on a map of the city. Littlegate consisted of an arch for carts and a narrower one for pedestrians. A postern gate in the north-east corner led into the wet moat and appears to have been related to fishing rights. All the gates had been demolished by 1772.

Oxford city walls: a mural tower in New College grounds. (*With the permission of the Warden & Scholars of New College, Oxford*)

Left: Oxford city walls: an early keyhole gunport in a mural tower in New College grounds. (*With the permission of the Warden & Scholars of New College, Oxford*)

Below: Oxford city walls: the interior of a mural tower in New College. (*Author's collection*)

Wallingford had retained its *burh* walls with the north-east corner of the enclosure occupied by the castle. Assaults and sieges from the time of the Anarchy to the Civil War failed to discriminate between town and castle, treating the combined fortifications as an entity. Town gates of stone had been constructed, the North Gate in *c.* 1250, but the extension of the castle under Richard of Cornwall in 1275–1300 caused its demolition and burial, though the defences were kept up with gateways at cardinal points and a fortified bridgehead across the Thames.

Ecclesiastical Defensible Buildings

Most monastic precincts were surrounded by walls and accessed by gateways. Whether this was primarily to exclude outsiders or to confine the members of the religious community is open to question. One part of Godstow Abbey, built in the mid-thirteenth century on what was effectively an island between streams running into the river, was surrounded by a massive enclosure wall, 4 feet (1.25 metres) thick. A plan of 1666 shows a two-storey gatehouse with a room over a gate passage with a folding gate, standing in line with the bridge and linked by an embattled wall to the tower of the church. This was the main access from the Wolvercote–Wytham road and the gatehouse had carriage and pedestrian arches giving entry to the outer court. Earthworks around the abbey include a moated area (SP487090). At Oseney Abbey, the extensive site was surrounded by a precinct wall with a gatehouse on Oseney Lane into the great court, and a water gate on the river frontage, possibly represented by the timber-framed structure, possibly of fifteenth-century date, with a stone, four-centred arch, typical of the time, in an attached wall, on Mill Street. In Oxford, the Cistercian St Bernard's monastery, now St John's College, has a mid-fifteenth-century gate tower of three storeys with two-storey ranges each side and a four-centred arch filling the entire width internally and externally. The gateway is ornamented with an oriel window and niches for statues. Near the terminus of the Oxford Canal, a short length of wall with an archway represents the only remaining trace of the thirteenth-century Cistercian Rewley Abbey (SP506064). The eighteenth-century Thame Park, built around the remains of the Cistercian abbey, incorporates, at the end of the South Wing, the abbot's lodging, built after 1530 and comprising an almost free-standing, three-storey embattled tower with a solar on the first floor, and now incorporated into Thame Park. Thame Abbey had been founded in 1140, furnished with a gatehouse and adjacent chapel for the use of travellers. There also remain a thirteenth-fourteenth century range and a two-storey hall block of *c.* 1500. Following a visit by Edward III, and riots in 1327 during which the townspeople looted the abbey and burned legal documents, the abbot of Abingdon Abbey was granted a licence to crenellate the abbey's gates and walls, the hospital of St John and the church of St Nicholas within the precinct, to mitigate further attacks. However, throughout the 1360s, the town sought unsuccessfully to wrest control of the market from the abbey. The abbey's late fifteenth-century gatehouse has two original archways. The Porter's Lodge built into the south side became a police station in the nineteenth century, but it was removed in 1965 to provide a third archway. The room over the arch was a prison until 1812 and then converted into a meeting room in 1826. At Eynsham, a moat, dug in the late eleventh to mid-twelfth century, and occupying a platform composed of the spoil, was absorbed into the abbey precinct in the early thirteenth century. In 1344, Eynsham Abbey found itself threatened by an armed gathering, reputed to number 1,500 during a leadership dispute, and also suffered a violent attack by the retainers of Sir Robert Harcourt in 1503. The medieval gatehouse of Bicester Priory has been converted into a dwelling as Old Place Yard House at the east end of the parish church. Dorchester Abbey lay outside the defences of the Roman town, with its own precinct stretching as far as the river. The abbey guesthouse, once a school and now a museum, with a blocked four-centred archway in its rear wall, adjoined the northern cloister along the access road which led from the gatehouse on the High Street, a site later occupied by a post office. But for odd architectural fragments, dotted around the village, all traces of the abbey itself: cloister, gatehouse, and precincts have completely disappeared. Castle House, Deddington, retaining the lower two floors of a thick-walled, tower-like structure dating from the thirteenth century and a chapel from the same date, was the rectorial manor house, once a prison for Piers Gaveston.

The preceptories of the military orders, the Templars and the Hospitallers, comprised estates which were often indistinguishable from either secular moated sites or monastic granges. Temple Cowley was a preceptory of the Knights Templar, which received grants of land from Matilda, Stephen's consort, and from William Marshall. At their Sandford-on-Thames preceptory, fragments of the thirteenth-century chapel survive in a barn at Temple Farm. A moated site remains at Friars Court, Clanfield, but no medieval buildings remain of the preceptory of the Knights Hospitaller. Stoke Grange Farm at Stoke Talmage, was formerly a moated grange belonging to Thame Abbey. The Prebendal House at Thame, whose thirteenth-century solar survives in later buildings, was recorded in 1234 with a moat on three sides and the Thames on the fourth, within a possible precinct wall and gatehouse.

The external face of Abingdon Abbey's Great Gateway.

Oxford: the gatehouse of St Bernard's monastery, subsequently St John's College.

Castle House, Deddington contains the lower storeys of a medieval tower-house, once the prison of Piers Gaveston from which he was abducted and executed. The current occupier reports a secret chamber, possibly a priest's hole.

3

Oxfordshire in Tudor, Stuart, and Georgian Times, 1500–1840

After the turmoil of the Wars of the Roses, Henry VII had brought in legislation, the Statutes Against Unlawful Retainers, to outlaw the private armies hitherto maintained by magnates. Edward Stafford, duke of Buckingham, lord of Stratton Audley, had constructed an enormous palace at Thornbury in Gloucestershire, incorporating all the outward signs of a fortress with lodgings for his liveried retainers in an outer courtyard. Although he managed to survive Henry VII's reign, he would be executed by a suspicious Henry VIII in 1521. The demise of private armies saw a return to levying the citizen militia of previous times. The Certificates for the Militia Return for both Oxfordshire and Berkshire of 25 April 1539 are, unfortunately, missing the numbers, and the abstracts for 1588, the year of the Spanish Armada, are only slightly more helpful. Just over 4,500 men, levied from the fourteen Oxfordshire Hundreds, are listed as 'Ablemen', that is able-bodied, aged sixteen to sixty, usually classified as either archers or bill-men, but, of those, only 1,164 are recorded as being armed and, by implication, reckoned as having been trained. Details of available weaponry would also normally be recorded. Berkshire raised 3,000 men across the whole county with one-third of them deemed trained. The Statute of Winchester of 1285 had laid down individuals' obligations to hold specific weapons, but this was repealed by Queen Mary in 1553 on the grounds that those weapons were now largely obsolete. The substitute requirements were for gentlemen with an income of over £100 *per annum* to retain horses suitable for six heavy and ten light cavalrymen; thirty bows plus arrows; forty pikes; twenty bills; three complete sets of armour; and forty steel bonnets. Those lesser mortals, but still worth £10 *per annum*, were required to provide a pike, a bow, and a hackbut—a type of primitive firearm. Some counties including Oxfordshire assiduously recorded a roll of personnel along with their weapons and accoutrements. In 1539, in Stanton St John, the gentleman, Kelham John, worth £10 in land, was equipped as a foot soldier with a harness (a breastplate or suchlike), a bill (a spear with an axe-blade and a spike), a sword, and a dagger. His neighbour, Edward Ffrenche, worth 20 marks (£13 13*s* 4*d*) in goods, was also a foot soldier with similar equipment. Nobody could avoid making a contribution. In 1543, eleven men in Stanton St John, whose combined wealth totalled just 26 marks (£17 13*s* 4*d*), were ordered to equip an archer with arms and armour. The mark was a unit of value rather than of currency, amounting to two-thirds of a pound sterling: 13 shillings (13/-) and fourpence (4*d*), around £300 in current purchasing power, but three weeks' wages for a skilled tradesman. Within each Hundred, individual parishes were required to retain communal collections of armour, often stored in the church, but this requirement appears to have slipped. In 1522 in the Shrivenham Hundred, only two parishes held such equipment and the whole county altogether could find only 100 sets of armour. The 1588 Oxfordshire abstract specifically lists only thirty 'pioners' or foot-soldiers; thirty 'launces' or heavy cavalry; 150 'lightorse' or light cavalry; and forty 'petronelles' or cavalrymen armed with pistols braced against their chests (French: *poitrine*). This force would be led by Lord Norris, the lord lieutenant of Oxfordshire. Prior to the Dissolution, monasteries had been liable to supply troops from their tenantry. The abbeys of Abingdon and Eynsham had obligations but, perhaps understandably, Oseney, as a nunnery, was excused. In 1522, four of the abbot of Abingdon's manors produced a total of 117 tenants, but, of these, only thirty-five could be pronounced as able. The muster commissioners were empowered to levy men for service anywhere the crown so ordered. A network of beacons, presumably located as successors to their Anglo-Saxon precursors, was maintained for warnings of invasion. Beacon Hill, Swinford, rises to 430 feet (133 metres) and was the site of a beacon, which would be lit in 1588 as warning of the Spanish Armada. Beacon Hill, Lewknor, most probably represents another site and other such long-established sites across the county would have been reused, just as many of the original sites were refurnished for the silver jubilee of Queen Elizabeth II in 1977.

In 1545, during an invasion scare, the men of Oxfordshire were levied by Sir John Brome to go to Portsmouth to defend against the invaders. In both the 1545 and 1558 muster organisation, Oxfordshire would only be required to be mobilised in defence of the southern half of the country. Moreover, while they had been required in 1543 to serve in Flanders, in 1545, they were omitted from the force despatched to Boulogne to defend the Calais Pale and also avoided service in Ireland. Given the royal preference for recruiting other than agricultural labourers, towns were also included in the levy, and Oxford was among the ten boroughs ordered to send contingents to the king's army in 1514, and one of the seven directed to provide levies in 1544 for service in France. It may have been singled out for special attention on two counts: its size in population terms and its status as a university town. The key to raising and leading these levies was the appointment of experienced and competent captains. One such was Sir Adrian Fortescue, resident at his wife's house of Stonor Park. He recruited from his own manors such as Henley, serving the country for periods totalling over twelve months across ten years of campaigns in France and Flanders, fighting alongside Henry VIII in the middle-ward or battle, the central part of the royal army between the vanguard and the rear-guard. In 1536, he raised troops from his manors of Watcombe and Sotwell for the force suppressing the Pilgrimage of Grace. Ever willing to reward loyalty, Henry VIII, alongside whom Sir Adrian had been created a Garter Knight in 1503, had him interrogated at Woodstock. He was then arrested, imprisoned for two years, and then released. When he refused to take the Oath of Supremacy, he was charged with treason, and beheaded without trial on Tower Hill, aged sixty-two. His servants were hanged, drawn, and quartered at Tyburn. His crime, for which he and his household paid with their lives, was the treason of being related to his cousin, Anne Boleyn, and of failing to support Henry's new English church. He was closely connected with the Dominicans in Oxford and was selected as a Knight of Devotion of the Order of St John of Jerusalem and beatified as a martyr in 1895 by Pope Leo XIII.

The costs of meeting military obligation could be high. The price of harness from specialist armourers in distant cities was increased by the delivery costs. Prices rose steeply, tripling in the first half of the sixteenth century. The cost of the white kersey cloth used for uniforms rose from the 7*d* per yard paid by citizens of Oxford in 1523 to the 2*s* (24*d* or 10p) paid by the parishioners of Marston thirty-five years later. Military obligation, however, was just one among many burdens borne by the county's inhabitants. The depopulation of whole villages following the Black Death had accelerated the clearance of land for sheep rearing, mainly on the great monastic estates. The subsequent dissolution of those monasteries had enabled a new class of entrepreneurial landowner to come to prominence and one way of increasing their profit was to enclose the common land, thereby depriving the peasantry of their living. One of those seen to have gained was Sir John Williams of Rycote. In 1549, several peasant risings took place across England, motivated by both religious and social discontent. Specific objections related both to Edward VI's extreme and autocratic Protestantism, and the enclosure of the common land. In Oxfordshire, a rising was led by a group which included the vicars of Barford St Michael and Chipping Norton, respectively James Webbe and Henry Joyes. Rycote was attacked by a mob which damaged the house and the recently enclosed deer-park. Lord Grey of Wilton was despatched with a force of 1,500 German and Swiss mercenaries which routed the rebels at their camp near Chipping Norton. In addition to many summary executions, ringleaders were ordered to be executed for treason. Webbe was hanged, drawn, and quartered, and Joyes was hanged in chains from his own church tower. Some, however, including the vicar of Bloxham, escaped punishment, but two citizens of Thame, held to be among the most seditious, went to the gallows. Blame for this and other risings which had broken out across the country contributed to the fall of the unpopular Protector Somerset, an event celebrated in Oxford. Somerset, Edward VI's uncle and regent, was accused of sympathy for, and even collusion with, the rebels, a standpoint unpopular with his fellow landowners and a convenient pretext for his downfall.

By the end of the century, some 40 per cent of Oxfordshire's land had been enclosed and a quarter of the rural population was impoverished. Rising food prices and loss of the land which had afforded them self-sufficiency now contributed to thoughts of another rising. The leader of this 1596 rising was a carpenter from Hampton Poyle near Kidlington, named Bartholomew Steer, who gathered a small group of likeminded men together. Sir Henry Norreys had been a guardian of the young Princess Elizabeth at Woodstock, and his son would become a distinguished soldier in the queen's service. By 1596, Sir Henry had become Lord Norris, the lord lieutenant of Oxfordshire, and lived at Rycote. He now became the first target of Steer's plot. The plan was to attack Rycote and seize the weapons stored there; to murder the seven local landowners most guilty of unrestrained enclosure; and to march on London, linking up with sympathisers from across the region. Although their summons to assemble on Enslow Hill went unanswered, they were nevertheless arrested; taken to London; tortured to reveal the extent of their plotting and, if possible, to implicate local gentry. In the end, those who survived this ordeal were returned to Oxfordshire to be tried and, inevitably, executed. This rising, however, did lead to legislation in 1597, restoring to arable use land which had been converted to pasture since Elizabeth's accession in 1558.

Oxfordshire in the Civil War

The county would play an important part during the course of the First Civil War: driven out of parliamentarian London, Charles I would remove his court to Oxford and closely surround the town with fortifications and an outer ring of fortified strongpoints; and the River Thames and the major routes which criss-crossed the county would facilitate the movement of armies across the country. As these armies jockeyed for position, they sought to establish garrisons to control territory and resources. Banbury and Wallingford both protected Oxford and acted as blocks to prevent the parliamentarians' westward expansion from their bases in London and East Anglia. The received wisdom of warfare held that battles were to be avoided as their outcomes were always unpredictable. The battles of Newbury and Edgehill, both fought just outside the county's boundaries, and Chalgrove Field and Cropredy Bridge, both inside, produced generally inconclusive results but affected morale, motivation, and reputations. Those villages in the contested areas around Banbury, such as Adderbury or Bodicote, which were alternately occupied by royalist or parliamentarian forces would suffer inordinate economic pain. As late as 1645 when the royalist cause was all but lost, Chipping Norton and Culham were plundered by the cavaliers and Banbury's royalist garrison raided villages in Northamptonshire carrying away goods, treasure, and livestock. Churches, including those at Banbury, Faringdon, and Enstone, where the village stocks were destroyed by soldiers in 1643, suffered extensive damage.

The unsatisfactory organisation of the militia levy system had been addressed by James I who repealed the old statutes in 1603. Henceforth, munitions would be kept in central armouries under the eyes of the lords lieutenant. In 1615, he ordered a reorganisation of the army, raising the Train(ed)-Bands as a national militia. Organisation, however, would continue at a local level and parliament nominated county leaders in 1641. In the coming Civil War, the Train(ed)-Bands would fight for whichever side they found themselves or their leaders supporting, and the armouries would be seized by whoever was quickest off the mark, possession being nine tenths of the law. Even before hostilities commenced, a dispute in mid-1642 had resulted in cannon being removed from Banbury Castle after a stand-off between the royalist earl of Northampton and Lord Brook, the parliamentarian. Those deemed to be persons 'fit to be entrusted' with organising the county militias included Viscount Saye and Sele of Broughton in Oxfordshire; Lord Paget and, later, Colonel Henry Bulstrode in Buckinghamshire; and Sir Jacob Astley in Berkshire. The militia of Buckinghamshire fought in the possibly spurious battle of Holman's Bridge outside Aylesbury, allegedly driving Prince Rupert's force back on Thame after inflicting heavy losses, and then at Edgehill. Astley was the royalist sergeant-major-general of foot; Saye and Seal and Bulstrode each raised a parliamentarian regiment of foot for the field army. Meanwhile, caught in the no-man's-land of the Thames Valley, it is likely that the militias carried out garrison, lines of communication, and outpost duties: Oxfordshire's for the royalists and Buckinghamshire's for parliament, while Berkshire's two militia regiments fought on opposing sides at Newbury in 1643.

Opposition to the king's policies had hardened, especially in solidly puritan Banbury before the war. Over forty Oxfordshire gentry, among them John Hampden, had refused to pay Charles I's arbitrary taxes such as ship money, and Sir Francis Wenman of Thame Park, the Hundred bailiff, refused to collect such taxes. William Fiennes, Viscount Saye and Sele, of Broughton Castle had continued the approach of Sir Anthony Cope of Hanwell in backing the citizens of Banbury in refusing to contribute to a forced loan being levied by the government in 1627. The next year, as also happened in Thame, objections were raised when troops were moved from Woodstock to Banbury to be billeted there at the cost to the town. A subsequent fire, albeit blamed without evidence, on the troops, heightened the townsfolk's resentment and levies of the controversial ship money remained unpaid in 1639. Moderate opposition to the king had previously been embraced by Viscount Falkland of Great Tew, but as it grew in strength, he shifted his ground and was killed fighting on the royalist side at the first battle of Newbury in 1643. Other local aristocrats, however, had never wavered from their loyalty to the king. Thomas Pope, 2nd earl of Downe, owner of large estates around Witney, raised a troop of horse and joined Charles I in Oxford as soon as war broke out. In 1648, those estates apart from Cogges and Wilcote were sequestrated by parliament. His uncle, who succeeded to the title, underwent a brief period of imprisonment by the king in Oxford, and was then, under the Commonwealth, arrested on suspicion of complicity in the 'cavalier' plot of 1656.

The Bishops' Wars constituted the first element in what would become the Wars of the Three Kingdoms when Charles I attempted to impose the organisation of the established Church of England onto Presbyterian Scotland. In 1639, he raised an army to enforce his wishes but in the absence of volunteers for this unpopular campaign, he was forced to resort to coercion. After an inconclusive campaign followed by a year-long hiatus, Charles attempted a second campaign in the summer of 1640, employing conscripts from the south of England this time. All over the southern counties, groups of pressed men were reluctantly gathering to be sent to Scotland. One such 600-strong contingent from Dorset found itself in Faringdon, billeted in inns and private houses. An unpopular officer became involved in a violent encounter with two of his company resulting in their deaths and the offending officer was then lynched by the outraged conscripts. Before the local trained bands could be mobilised to restore order, most of the conscripts had deserted, but several, including, conveniently, the supposed ringleaders, were caught, tried, and executed. Sir Simon Harcourt, of Stanton Harcourt, great-grandson of the earl of Oxford, was a professional soldier who fought mainly in the Low Countries against the Spanish forces but also in the Bishops' Wars. On the outbreak of the Irish Rebellion in 1641, he was commissioned as a colonel and posted as governor of Dublin. In an attempt, in March 1642, to destroy Kilgobbin Castle (Co. Dublin), one of the castles of the Dublin Pale, but at the time a base for families supporting the rebels, he was mortally wounded leading his force of government troops into an ambush and died the next day.

By the summer of 1642, the king's standard had been raised in Nottingham and civil war was declared. Members of Oxford University had already begun parading and learning military drill and, despite protestations by the city's two MPs that Oxford would become 'the seat of war', work would begin on fortifying the town in September 1642. However, those early attempts were neutralised during a brief occupation of the town by parliamentarian troops under Fiennes which lasted only until mid-October. The work on fortification resumed soon after, consolidating Oxford as the royalist capital, fervently loyal to the crown. Existing medieval defences were refurbished, especially in the south-western corner of the city. At the castle, what remained of the keep on the motte may have been adapted as a platform for cannon, ditches were recut around the motte, and a tunnel-like sally port, using ashlar blocks robbed from the original gatehouse, was inserted into the castle walls near the St George's Tower. The remains of Godstow Abbey had been converted into a house after the Dissolution and its perimeter wall was now adapted as part of the defences of the town. Rewley Abbey, too, was incorporated into the defences. Earthen ramparts and a massive redoubt guarding Magdalen Bridge were constructed, reportedly, but most unlikely, by a Richard Rallingson who had put his name to a plan. By early 1643, the existing fortifications were judged insufficient for the king's headquarters and William Legge, the royalist governor, may have been responsible for the improvements subsequently carried out by Sir Charles Lloyd or Sir Jacob Astley who both spent time in the city. A stronger tenaille trace, with outposts on the approach roads was built with bastioned redoubts connected by ramparts with palisades, ditches, and storm poles. A bastion on the city walls at Merton College was adapted for use as a gun platform to provide cover for the flooded water meadows. The Cherwell had been dammed in order to flood the meadows, and booms were stretched across the Thames. Ditches 24 feet (7.4 metres) wide and 12 feet (3.7 metres) deep have been excavated in building works around the city. These had been cut into gravel and revetted to avoid slide. While the Oxford fortifications constituted the most developed example of the time in Britain, the lack of resources available to the designers and builders still rendered them unsatisfactory and even 'amateurish' in Anthony Kemp's assessment. However, twice weekly when in residence, Charles I liked to promenade around the evolving fortifications to check on progress. Recent construction work on New College's Clore Music Studios in Mansfield Road has uncovered new evidence of the fortifications, and an interpretation panel and memorial plaque have been erected by the college, backed up by the surviving contemporary records in its archives.

Having previously been forced to sleep in his coach at Wolvercote, any move into civilised accommodation would be welcomed by Charles I, so it was into the buildings of Oxford University that he and his court repaired. Christ Church functioned as the centre of a diocese and its founding statutes specified that the college *cum* cathedral should provide a residence for monarchs and their households whenever they visited the city. Charles duly set up house there in the dean's lodgings. Queen Henrietta Maria moved into Merton College where she occupied an apartment in the Fitzjames Gatehouse, of the former warden, now absconded to the parliamentarians. Doorways were cut through the intervening garden walls of Corpus Christi and a path was laid to enable access between

Above: Godstow Abbey's precinct wall was incorporated into the Civil War defences of Oxford.

Right: Oxford city walls: this medieval bastion on the southern stretch may be the one, with a commanding view over the water meadows, converted to mount cannon in the Civil War.

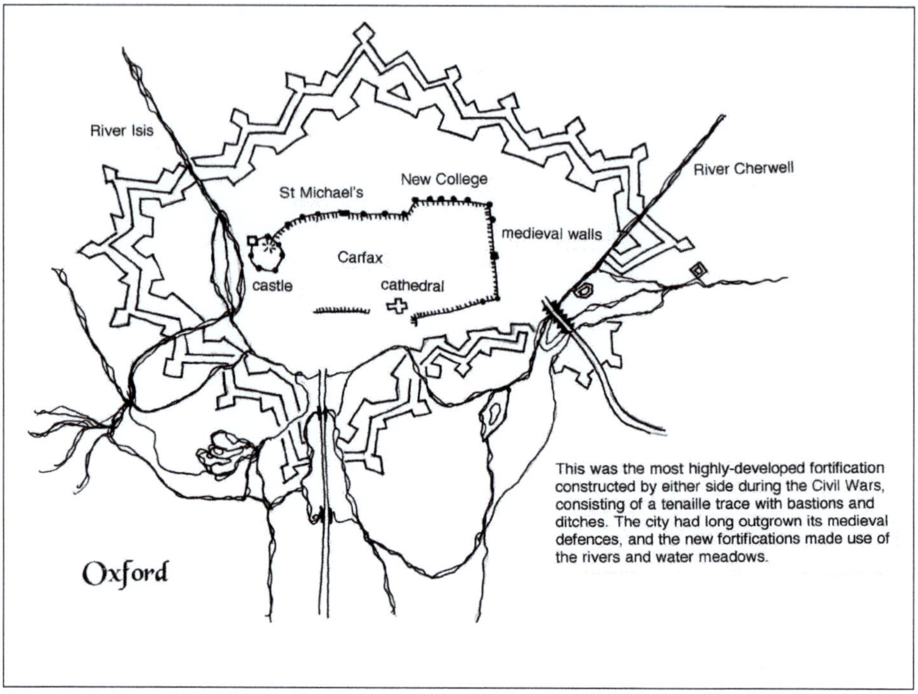

Plan of the Civil War defences of Oxford showing the extent, complexity, and sophistication of the works that were carried out by the citizens of Oxford under the oversight of Charles I.

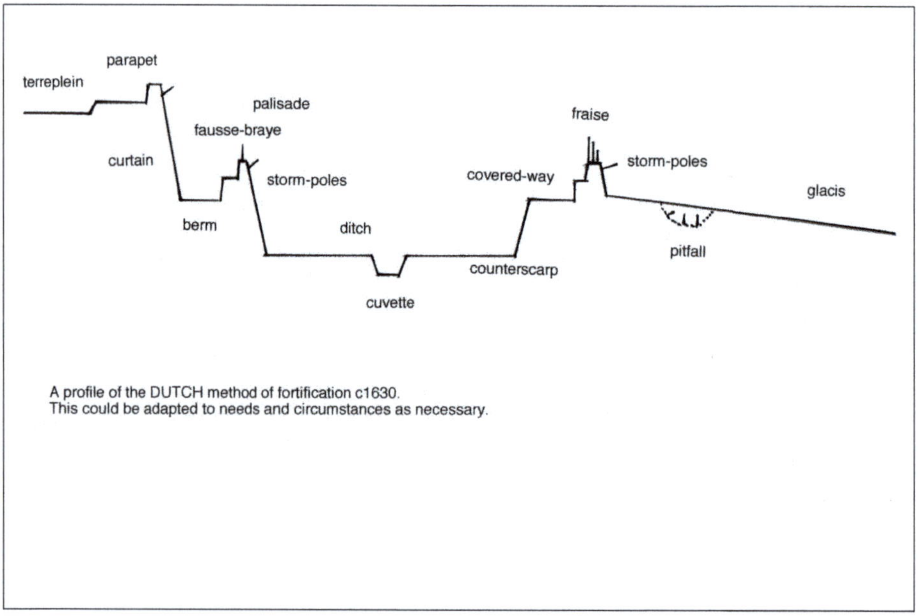

A cross-section of the Dutch system of fortification as practised at Oxford.

the two colleges. Finding suitable accommodation for the royal households was a military operation in itself and many a courtier exchanged luxury for discomfort or even squalor. Charles was accompanied by the offices of state with the council of war meeting in the cathedral's audit house. The Privy Council met in the cathedral chapterhouse and in Oriel College which housed not only the Treasury, but also members of the royal household and the editorial office of *Mercurius Aulicus*. This was the weekly royalist organ of public relations which was smuggled out for circulation in London in an attempt to counter parliamentarian comment. The Mint, run by Thomas Bushell of Enstone who had previously taken over the royal silver mines in Wales, moved into New Inn Hall; the chancery and law courts to Convocation House; and the Exchequer to Lincoln College. From January 1644, parliament was summoned to Oxford where the House of Commons sat in Convocation House with the lords in the upper schools. St Aldate's Church, standing between Pembroke and Christ Church, became a barracks for the eighty-strong royal foot guards, who paraded in Tom Quad, and the city's military governor. As a city either under siege or operating as a base for military operations, Oxford needed to establish the appropriate infrastructure. Brasenose, All Souls, and New Colleges became the arsenals and magazines, munitions being stored in such locations as the tower of New College; the law and logic schools became a granary; and Magdalen College Grove became a park for twenty pieces of artillery and the waggons which conveyed powder and shot. The town also housed foundries for manufacturing cannon and muskets in St Mary's College, now Frewin Hall in New Inn Hall Street, and in Christ Church. A factory producing swords was established in Wolvercote and uniforms were manufactured in the music and astronomy schools. The castle became a prison where those captured in battle, surrendering after sieges, or simply suspected of being parliamentarian sympathisers were incarcerated. With the majority of the nation's gunpowder production in parliamentarian hands, new facilities were urgently required. A gunpowder works at Oseney Mill was established and sources of the vital ingredient saltpetre were sought. It would mainly be found in tombs and dung heaps, and Chipping Norton church was among those whose floors would be dug up to extract it. Undergraduates who remained in the town were turned out of their colleges, and many were drafted into the garrison. Bored soldiery took to drink; their equally bored officers quarrelled and duelled; and insanitary conditions and food shortages caused general discontent and outbreaks of the plague and other diseases. Miseries were compounded for citizen and soldier alike by the psychopathic governor, Sir Arthur Aston, stories of whose gratuitous cruelty were detailed in a contemporary chronicle. Showing off in front of a group of ladies on Bullingdon Green, he was thrown by his horse, breaking his leg which then had to be amputated. His successor, one Legge, afforded ample opportunity for court wits to gloat. Few tears would subsequently be shed when

Aston was said to have been beaten to death with his own wooden leg at the siege of Drogheda in 1649.

Oxfordshire was initially assessed by parliament at £650 per week, a notional sum of which only a part could ever be collected. Taxes were, however, collected by Charles's alternative receivers from locations around Oxford and used to pay for the royalist army. The taxes of Banbury and Bloxham were assigned to Lord Byron to maintain six troops of Prince Rupert's cavalry. Some unfortunate communities occupying the no-man's-land of disputed areas found themselves paying twice. It was suggested that £30,000 should be levied from the citizens of Oxford to pay for the city's new fortifications but they offered their labour instead. As this onerous commitment of time and effort inevitably diminished, the entire population of Oxford—nobles, courtiers, women, and humble townsfolk—would eventually be compelled to provide one day's manual labour per week, working on these extensive fortifications, a requirement enforced by martial law with imprisonment as the governor's ultimate sanction. A further inevitability in a congested city full of troops living in unsanitary conditions was sickness, and throughout the occupation, some forty people died of plague, cholera, or dysentery every week. As if these privations were not enough, a devastating fire in 1644 destroyed many houses, shops, and workshops. It therefore comes as quite a surprise to hear that while the beleaguered citizens of Oxford received little comfort from their king, Charles, Rupert and the rest of the court were assured safe passage for traffic from London including physicians, wine, apparel, sporting guns, and dogs, while the royalist court continued to indulge in its anachronistic ceremonies, pointless protocols, and frivolous pastimes, such as hunting at Woodstock, as if nothing was happening in the outside world. When the king's falconer along with one of his favourite birds were captured by parliamentarian troops blockading Oxford, they were returned to the king unharmed as if by civilised neighbours.

In October 1642, the parliamentarian army under the earl of Essex and the royalist army led by the king were converging on the area where the three counties of Warwickshire, Northamptonshire, and Oxfordshire all meet. The royalists were encamped in villages including Cropredy and the parliamentarians around Kineton in Warwickshire. Battle was joined at Edgehill, and despite the best efforts of Prince Rupert to lose it, and of the parliamentarian infantry to win it, after a hard day's fighting and around 1,500 dead, the result remained inconclusive as the royalist army retired to Edgecote and Essex led his troops to Warwick. While the obvious course of action for the king would have been an advance on London, he chose to retreat to Oxford for the winter instead. After the battle, Prince Rupert went on to inflict extensive damage during the short siege of Broughton Castle, which was described as ruinous by Celia Fiennes in 1647. A further positive result for the royalists was Banbury Castle's surrender to the king, which ushered in a royalist occupation lasting over three years.

Despite numerous assaults, under the eighteen-year-old Sir William Compton, younger brother of the earl of Northampton, the town and castle, provided with its own gunpowder mill, together continued to serve as a vital outpost of Oxford throughout the war. This rather casts doubt on the claim that Ye Olde Reindeer Inn in Banbury's Parson Street had been Cromwell's HQ any time after October 1642, when he had arrived with his Cambridgeshire cavalry troopers, too late to influence the result of the battle of Edgehill.

While the religious wars of the sixteenth century and the Thirty Years' War (1618–48) imposed a continuous need for up-to-date fortifications on the towns of continental Europe, those in Britain had enjoyed longer periods of peace and had, for the most part, been naturally insulated against the violent meanderings of foreign armies. Thus, the comfort of manor houses had been substituted for the impregnability of castles, and residential suburbs had spread outside the walls of medieval towns. Much of the skirmishing of the Civil War period was carried out by lightly armed troops lacking the resources to transport along the terrible roads the heavy artillery necessary to conduct a siege, especially in winter. Therefore, any structure with stout walls might constitute a temporary fortress, repelling all but the most determined assault. The maximum penetration of a musket ball into an earth rampart was 30 inches (75 cm), which meant that far lesser thicknesses of masonry, especially if backed by earth, afforded an element of protection. Manor houses, especially those boasting a moat, could be made very secure with a bit of effort. It is said that woolpacks were strung along Broughton Castle's walls to absorb enemy shot, and many houses would have had their outer walls pierced by musket-loops. The house built in 1611 by Sir Thomas Spencer next to Yarnton church was reported in a nineteenth-century handbook for travellers as having four circular musket loops punched in its wall. Currently (2022), the house is swathed in plastic while asbestos is removed and extensive renovations are carried out, so this could not be verified. The house, originally of three ranges around a courtyard entered through a gatehouse, would be much reduced in size following losses incurred by the owners, the Spencer family, in the Civil War.

The continued security of Oxford depended on the ring of such fortified strongpoints, mainly composed of substantial manor houses, which surrounded the town, and strategic bridges such as at Islip or Wheatley, whose defence was aided in the winter months by the flooding of the surrounding fields. Gaunt House, at Standlake, controlling the Thames crossing at Newbridge, was a moated house besieged and bombarded in 1645, and only rebuilt *c.* 1660. Begbroke House, on the site of what is now St Philip's Priory, was occupied for the parliamentarians by Colonel Butler and appears to have suffered extensive damage as a new house, built with stone from the ruins of Woodstock Palace, was constructed in 1662. Other properties also suffered damage in the constant conflict. Hardwick Court, Whitchurch, had a wing added to replace parts of the

Sketch map to show royalist garrisons and houses held for the king around Oxford.

house built in 1526 and damaged in the Civil War. The royalist garrison of the bishop's palace at Cuddesdon quit the building in 1645, destroying it as they left in an act of scorched earth. Godstow Abbey, a Benedictine nunnery dating from 1133, near to the edge of Oxford, was another victim of such a policy. It had been fortified by its royalist garrison but, on its evacuation in May 1645, was burnt down, leaving the extant walled enclosure as the only survival. The already semi-derelict medieval Woodstock Palace was irreparably damaged during three weeks of siege and bombardment in 1646. The old house of Besselsleigh, complete with priest hole and belonging to the former speaker of the House of Commons whose son was an officer in the parliamentarian army, was captured from its royalist garrison late in 1644. Major-General Browne was unable to find enough spare troops to garrison it, so he ordered it to be slighted, by destroying the doors and walls, to prevent any future use as a defensive structure by potential 'ill neighbours', as he put it. The eastern portion of Culham Manor was demolished during the wars. Hinton Waldrist Manor survived intact after having parliamentarian troops billeted in it, but, for some, the impact of war was truly devastating. Bletchingdon House was held for the king by Colonel Sir Francis Windebank with a strong garrison of 200 men. In April 1645, his new wife was holding a soirée for her friends when a parliamentarian force appeared unexpectedly and summoned him to surrender. This he immediately agreed to do, chivalrously, it is said, to avoid endangering his wife and her guests. Instructions were quickly sent from London to install a parliamentarian garrison there to impede the king's return to Oxford following his latest foray into the field which would end in his defeat at Naseby. At this critical stage of the war, to those conducting his court martial in Oxford, Windebank's unforgivable surrender resulted in his being found guilty of cowardice and condemned to death, as Voltaire would later express it *pour encourager les autres*. He was shot by firing squad against the town wall abutting Merton College. For some it must have seemed that whatever stance they adopted, they could not avoid suffering. Thomas, Viscount Wenman of Thame Abbey, a kinsman of Hampden, was a moderate parliamentarian. His house was besieged, and his estate seized by the royalists and then, in 1648, as one of the negotiators, seeking an accommodation with the king, he was imprisoned by the parliamentarians for voting to accept Charles I's acquiescence to parliament's terms. The Crokes of Hampton Poyle were royalist supporters who were forced to pay a fine to avoid sequestration of their estates in 1646 but cut their losses and sold up two years later. John Milton, the poet, was another who appealed unsuccessfully against the sequestration of his royalist wife's family estate.

Further out from Oxford were further garrisons, such as Burford and Chipping Norton, most of which remained in place into the final stages of the war, with Deddington holding a royalist garrison until it was pulled back in 1645. Cornbury Park originated in a hunting lodge of Henry I in the Forest of Wychwood and developed as a grand house from 1630. It was held for the

A stretch of Oxford city wall adjoining Merton College, up against which Colonel Windebank of Bletchingdon House was shot by firing squad as a consequence of his misplaced chivalry.

king by Henry Danvers, earl of Danby, who had obtained the property in 1617. Overlooking the valley of the River Evenlode, it commanded routes used by the royalist forces based in Oxford and acted as part of that city's outer defences, combining with Bletchingdon and Woodstock Manors. Earthwork fortifications were dug, centred on Iron Age barrows, to straddle the main road and consisted of an artillery battery and ramparts and ditches to prevent the position being overrun. Radcot House was fortified to protect the bridge over the Thames and an earthwork battery, represented by some of the remaining earthworks, was built on top of the ruinous Radcot Castle to bombard the royalist defenders who surrendered in May 1646. A similar situation obtained in Faringdon where a royalist garrison was installed by Sir George Lisle, making Faringdon House his HQ, and fortifying it. Although the parliamentarians retook the town to open the supply route from the west, the house held out. Folly Hill, regarded as the likely site of a medieval castle, has traditionally been accepted as Cromwell's chosen location for a siege battery, during the spring of 1645. The garrison survived the ensuing bombardment, only surrendering to Fairfax after the fall of Oxford, but the spire of All Saints' church, which may have been acting as an observation post for the garrison, became collateral damage and was rebuilt in 1646 after the surrender. Cannon balls have recently been discovered in the house. Faringdon's successful resistance to successive assaults, only finally falling in June 1646 as one of the last royalist strongholds to hold out, meant that it attracted fugitives from those royalist garrisons which, by then, were falling like dominoes. Shirburn Castle remained a royalist garrison throughout the war, held by Richard Chamberlain, and only surrendering in May 1646. Stratton Audley manor, intermittently occupied by royalist troops as part of the outer defences of Oxford, had passed to the Borlase family, and the young Sir John was one of those MPs who joined the king in Oxford in 1642 and paid the penalty by having his estates sequestrated by parliament. A small circular earthwork there, 'Stuttles Bank', is said to represent a contemporary defensive work.

In the spring of 1643, the earl of Essex led a parliamentarian army into Oxfordshire with the intention of restricting royalist progress by besieging their capital of Oxford. He made his HQ at Thame and billeted his troops in the neighbouring villages, but his subsequent inaction provoked impatience amongst the parliamentarian leadership. The arrival of reinforcements spurred him to cross the river to Wheatley and to approach the royalist outpost at Shotover Hill, but an attack on the royalist garrison at Islip bridge was aborted when unanticipated superior numbers were encountered. At the time, the royalists in Oxford had received one shipment of ammunition from York and were further expecting a delivery of artillery. The queen had pawned her jewellery to purchase cannon in the Low Countries, shipped them into Bridlington, and was convoying them across hostile territory to Oxford, so it was vital that the parliamentarian forces be distracted. Acting on intelligence from a parliamentarian officer who felt unappreciated by his superiors, Rupert was able to second guess Essex and had three regiments of cavalry at hand, 2,500 troopers, when parliamentarian troops attacked Islip expecting little resistance. The turncoat, Colonel Hurry, had also informed Rupert of how thinly Essex had spread his troops. Rupert therefore felt justified in leading a force of 1,200 cavalry with 350 dragoons and 500 infantry, across the Thame at Chiselhampton, overrunning a picket at Tetsworth and completely surprising Sir Samuel Luke's Bedfordshire Dragoons, exhausted following their retreat from Islip, and camping without pickets at Postcombe and Chinnor with the rest of their force dispersed to Watlington and Thame. At Chinnor, fifty of the dragoons were killed and 120 more were taken prisoner. Unable to locate his intended prize, a convoy carrying the pay for Essex's army, Rupert judged it advisable to head back to Oxford before the parliamentarian response, led by Sir John Hampden with the troops from Watlington and Thame, could impede his dash for safety. Arriving at Chalgrove, Rupert despatched his infantry to secure the bridge and then turned to await his pursuers, using his retreating cavalry as the lure, and setting his dragoons in ambush, surprising Hampden's cavalry before sufficient reinforcements could arrive to support them. The dragoons had, in fact, jumped the gun by firing prematurely, so Rupert was forced to make a hurried cavalry charge. The result was almost inevitable: a rout of the parliamentarians; Hampden receiving a mortal wound; and around forty or so on each side being killed. Essex, who had set up his HQ in Thame, controlling the Oxford–Aylesbury road, was forced to withdraw, while Rupert made it back to Oxford in time to escort the queen on the final leg of her gruelling journey. She had successfully evaded the enemy and added further cannon and mortars to the defences of Oxford. This defeat of Essex at the battle of Chalgrove Field was just one contributor to the parliamentarian low point and further dented his reputation while raising the morale of the royalists. Colonel Hurry survived this battle, but having fought for every possible cause, he was eventually executed in Edinburgh in 1650.

Bicester was occupied intermittently by royalist troops from Oxford on foraging expeditions and was the scene of a skirmish in May 1643. That summer it was garrisoned by a force of royalist troops (reportedly, an unlikely 4,000) and Prince Rupert based a force of 1,000 cavalry there temporarily to supervise the delivery of provisions to Oxford. Royalist troops, camped on Culham Heath, were withdrawn into Oxford in June 1643. In August, Essex led an army composed of regiments drawn from the London Trained Bands to raise the siege of Gloucester. This force included five regiments under Sergeant-Major-General Mainwaring plus his own regiment of Redcoats who spent one night in Stratton Audley along the route chosen by Essex taking him through Bicester, skirting the Oxford outposts and aiming to exit Oxfordshire at Stow-on-the-Wold. Leading his seventy-strong company of dragoons, or mounted musketeers, attached to the parliamentarian cavalry, Captain Jeremiah Abercromby was killed in a skirmish nearby. On its last night in Oxfordshire, the army bivouacked with one unit out on a limb at Oddington near Stow. Although surrounded by royalist cavalry, it contrived to survive the threat of imminent attack until the rest of the army caught up and they all moved on into Gloucestershire to achieve their intended goal.

In the spring of 1644, Charles had been staying at Barton Court where he said 'goodbye' to the queen, never to see her again. The various contingents of the parliamentarian army rendezvoused at Abingdon which had been abandoned by the royalists. Barton Court held out but was burnt over the heads of its defenders. Timbers, showing evidence of parliamentarian musket balls were later reused in Barton Court Farm. In June 1644, Oxford's town and university regiments were mustered on Bullingdon Green for the defence of Oxford which was threatened with imminent siege. Sir William Waller had attempted a crossing of the Isis at Newbridge but was repulsed. Essex, however, was more successful, having attempted crossings of the Cherwell at Gosford and Enslow, he forded the river at Sandford. As the noose tightened around the city which had barely a fortnight's supplies and no realistic hope of relief, the king decided to decamp. By various tricks and deceptions; poor scouting by the parliamentarians; and a lack of co-operation between Waller and Essex, the king managed to slip between the two armies and to reach Burford, travelling on to Worcester from there. Essex then took half the parliamentarian force into the West Country while Waller was left to shadow the royalist field army. The royalist manoeuvres around the West Midlands continued until, pausing at Witney to receive reinforcements from the Oxford garrison, they were ready to challenge Waller who led a roughly equal force. With the royalist army on the east bank of the Cherwell and the parliamentarians on the west, the two forces moved north towards Banbury, in parallel, never more than 2 miles (3.2 km) apart. Waller then sought to exploit a gap in the royalist column by sending his cavalry across the river by the ford at Slat Mill and the bridge at Cropredy. Despite an initial element of success, these troops were quickly thrown back across the river by the royalist horse and only a stout defence by two regiments of the London Trained Bands prevented a rout. Once the royalists realised that strong parliamentarian reinforcements were on the way, Charles led his victorious troops to safety behind the defences of Oxford. The battle of Cropredy Bridge saw the parliamentarian army suffering significant losses of men, materiel, and face. Banbury town was overrun by Colonel John Fiennes, William's third son, in August 1644, and the castle was besieged, being bombarded from the churchyard of St Mary's by two mortars. Attempts were made to tunnel under the castle walls, but the workings soon became flooded by underground streams. For three months, the 400-strong royalist garrison successfully repulsed assaults by Fiennes and his 3,500 parliamentarian troops, until they were relieved by the timely arrival of a force under the earl of Northampton, come to rescue his little brother.

Abingdon started the war as a royalist town in 1642, and not until May 1644 did royalist forces withdraw. The bridge was then seized by parliamentarian troops who raided convoys taking supplies from Dorchester into Oxford. In January 1645, the battle of Culham Bridge was an unsuccessful attempt by the royalists to recapture and demolish the bridge. Repulsing this attack, Colonel Richard Browne took his troops across a ford to strike the royalists in the flank, an action in which Sir Henry Gage, the royalist commander, received mortal injuries. In late 1644, Browne had taken on responsibility for parliamentarian troops in Oxfordshire, Berkshire, and Buckinghamshire, as major-general of Oxfordshire, with his main force based in Abingdon. From early 1645 until well into the next year, he was attacked there on numerous occasions, on one of which a surprise attack penetrated right up to the abbey gate. Excavations published in 2007 uncovered ditches from the Civil War period which may represent royalist defences or additions made subsequent to the parliamentarian occupation of May 1644. The medieval Phyllis Court in Henley was the home and HQ of Sir Bulstrode Whitelocke, the local parliamentarian commander, who held the town throughout the war. Although the town itself was deemed not to be easily defensible, Whitelocke installed a garrison and fortified the court with a moat linked to the river and crossed by a timber drawbridge; projecting platforms for artillery; and an earthwork bastion faced with iron spikes as storm poles. After the war, he demolished the fortifications, re-landscaped the gardens, and continued in residence.

Oxford was seriously threatened for the second time in May 1645 when it was invested by Fairfax. Sir William Waller made Bicester his HQ where the parliamentarian horse were quartered. However, the besieging force was so harassed by raids that the siege was raised in the June. Ironically, it was this apparent royalist success which would lead to the decisive battle of Naseby and the defeat of the royalist field army. It would be a further year, though, before the siege of Oxford was renewed. This forced the defenders to construct a new line of fortifications outside the original line. Sir Thomas Glemham the new governor after Legge's fall from grace may have commissioned Bernard de Gomme, the Dutch engineer, to develop the defences designed by Sir Charles Lloyd and to draw up contingency plans in 1644. De Gomme had acted as Prince Rupert's adviser and had served on his staff rather than being in the front line as either besieger or besieged. His contribution centred on the application of the Dutch principles of fortification which ensured the provision of bastions large enough to carry sufficient guns adequately to flank the curtains. This, of course, was only possible on greenfield sites where construction was unimpeded by existing buildings. Even though his designs attempted to adhere to the orthodox, he was still forced to fall back on practices more common in field fortifications such as the shape and diminutive size of the salients and the *trous de loup,* pits with stakes in, at Oxford; and the palisades found at both Wallingford and Oxford. Every attempt was made to exploit existing features and a half-built mound in the gardens of New College, behind the medieval city wall, originally designed as a garden feature, was heightened to become either a platform for artillery or a viewpoint for observing the fall of shot. It would appear that the city's artillery park was well supplied with ordnance as the king had brought twenty-seven cannon with him after Edgehill and the queen had added more after her trek from Bridlington. By the end of the siege, local manufacture using bells requisitioned from Oxford's churches, and captured parliamentarian pieces had, despite the losses incurred at Naseby, brought the total ordnance eventually surrendered to thirty-eight pieces, along with seventy barrels of Oseney Mill's gunpowder.

November 1645 saw three regiments of parliamentarian troops occupying Thame, partly to prevent its further use by Prince Rupert as a base from which to attack Aylesbury; partly to defend against further attacks on the town by Colonel Legge from Oxford; and partly as a way of tightening the noose around Oxford. Thus, by December 1645, Oxfordshire was a shrinking royalist island in a sea of parliamentarian territory, but not until April 1646 did parliamentarian forces converge on Oxford from Witney and Abingdon, when Fairfax effectively blockaded the town with his cavalry. Woodstock Palace was assaulted, initially unsuccessfully, by the besieging forces, and the queen already having fled to the Low Countries, the king, too, left Oxford, apparently in disguise. He was heading for the Scottish army, currently besieging his vital stronghold of Newark-upon-Trent in Nottinghamshire. The estate plan of the Blenheim estate of *c.* 1705

Thame Grammar School, built in 1569, was forced to close during the Civil War when Thame was occupied by parliamentarian troops. It was used as a hospital during the First World War.

mentioned earlier, shows what appear to be artillery bastions attached to the wall surrounding the palace. Woodstock surrendered on 16 April and the siege of Oxford officially commenced on May Day. Fairfax erected a fortified camp for 3,000 troops at Headington Hill and built a bridge across the Cherwell at Marston to facilitate movement between sectors. Other troops occupied Cowley; the stable yard of Elsfield Manor, later the home of the writer John Buchan, was used as a gun park; and more troops sealed off the town on the north. At the same time, Faringdon, Wallingford, and Radcot were all blockaded. The besieging troops began a circumvallation starting in Headington and proceeding to St Clements. Its purpose was to keep the defenders from sallying forth; to cover the approach trenches for an assault; and to provide positions from which the artillery might bombard the royalist defences. Munitions were needed urgently so, as well as the large amount of powder sent from Abingdon, the lead roof of St Bartholomew's Chapel, standing within a medieval precinct wall, was melted down for musket balls. On 11 May, Fairfax issued the summons to surrender, and Sir Thomas Glemham advised the Privy Council, representing the king, that the town could no longer be defended. Following two frustrating weeks of an exchange of shot and indeterminate negotiations, it was finally agreed that the city would surrender, but not until 25 June would the keys be handed over. Negotiations for the surrender took place at the manor house at 15–17 Mill Lane, Marston, also referred to as 'Cromwell's House' or the 'Treaty House', which was the HQ of Fairfax during the siege. The surrender document was signed in what had been the meeting place of the Privy Council, the audit house of Christ Church. At the end, around 3,000 royalists marched out over Magdalen Bridge or through the North Port, protected by free passes. Princes Rupert and Maurice were allowed to leave on condition that they immediately quit the country.

Throughout the war, Wallingford was occupied by royalist troops as an outpost of Oxford. The castle's refortification included two gun platforms; its outer moat was filled in; a drawbridge was inserted into the town bridge; and the adjacent All Hallows Church was demolished to remove the threat of its use as a gun platform by an attacker. Following the fall of Oxford in 1646 the town was besieged and Colonel Blagge, commanding the garrison, threatened to fire the town if parliamentarian troops entered it. The garrison held out for twelve weeks but then, while surrender terms were being negotiated, they mutinied over pay. The surrender was brought forward, and the garrison was permitted to march 10 miles away before dispersing to their homes unhindered. A possible Civil War-era rampart was found in excavations in 2009.

As an *addendum* to the wars, the county saw the demise of one of several radical sects: the Levellers, led by John Lilburne and dedicated to the cause of egalitarianism. Seen as a threat to the new post-royalist order, parliament determined to clamp down on them. Lilburne had been arrested and confined in the Tower of London, and in May 1649, a large body of 12,000 of his followers, all deserters from the parliamentarian army, marched on London with the intention of freeing him. They were surprised at Burford by a strong government force led by Cromwell, and after a short resistance, the majority melted away, with around 400 taken prisoner. They were held in Burford church prior to the execution of a token three of their number by firing squad. Four months later, another Leveller rebellion occurred in Oxford. Here, the rebels, many of them soldiers, were arrested by their officers and confined in New College, but the external help they awaited failed to materialise and the rising collapsed. The inevitable repercussions included the execution by firing squad of seven of the civilians and two of the soldiers.

When hostilities broke out once more with Prince Charles leading a Scottish army into England, loyalties were again questioned. The citizens of Oxford had been the most loyal of Charles I's subjects up to his defeat in 1646, but by the time the conflict had been renewed in 1650, they sought a more peaceful existence. It was generally expected that Prince Charles would make Oxford his base for a move on London, so preparations for resistance were put in hand. Given the, probably only partial, slighting of the city's defences ordered by parliament in March 1647, the city's governor, Captain Draper, oversaw the construction of new fortifications, especially around New College, and prepared to receive reinforcements of regular troops to augment his hastily assembled volunteers under their newly commissioned officers, eagerly demonstrating their allegiance to the new regime. In the event, Charles got no further than the city of Worcester, where he suffered a resounding defeat. After the battle, his flight was directed by a local man, Francis Yates, who took the prince to a safe house, the first step in his successful escape to the continent. Subsequently, captured by parliamentarian troops but refusing to give anything away under interrogation, Yates was taken to Oxford and hanged. Charles was accompanied in his escape by Henry Wilmot of a Witney family who had fought alongside Charles throughout the wars and ended up commanding the royalist cavalry. After the death of his wife, in 1644 he married Anne Lee, herself a widow, who inherited Ditchley Park. Their son John was the notorious libertine, the 2nd earl of Rochester. After the war, Wilmot remained with Charles on the continent, his wife somehow managing to retain her estates on the basis that they were hers, not her husband's.

The Restoration of Charles II in 1660 would, twenty years on, eventually lead to a succession crisis precipitated by his lack of legitimate issue; the popular support for his natural son, James, duke of Monmouth; and the unconstitutional Catholicism of his brother James, duke of York. A parliament, elected in 1679, had been prevented from sitting for a whole year as a bill to exclude York from the succession was high on its agenda. In the wake of the bill's defeat in the Lords, the king announced another general election, dissolving parliament and ordering its removal to Oxford, away from London's volatile crowds. Echoing his father's occupation of forty years previously, and his own unappreciated evacuation in the Plague Year, complex arrangements for accommodating the king, his parliament, and the offices of state were set in train across the colleges and university buildings. The new parliament, still heavily weighted against the king's interests, met in March 1681. Confident that while the Commons would repeat their attempts to pass the Exclusion Bill and safe in the knowledge that the Lords would once more reject it, the king prorogued parliament after just one week, never to recall it in his lifetime. Following Charles's death and James's accession, Monmouth would be inveigled by those who opposed a Catholic monarch, into proclaiming himself king. In 1685, let down by those who had encouraged his rebellion, he was decisively defeated at Sedgemoor at the hands of an army he had himself created and which contained Oxfordshire militiamen and a troop of undergraduates from Christ Church despatched by the ultra-royalist Dean Fell. Along with many of his unfortunate followers, Monmouth was brutally executed.

The Development of the Armed Forces

The Regular Army

After the Restoration of Charles II in 1660, the former parliamentarian General Monck, by now the earl of Albemarle, had been commissioned by the king to establish new regiments to form a regular army, an institution hitherto regarded as an existential threat to the nation's constitution. Local militias such as that led by Sir Thomas Spencer of Yarnton, which welcomed the king to the opening of parliament in Oxford in 1681, would continue to serve but only as back-up to this standing army which had been put on a more regular standing by Monmouth, serving as the king's captain-general. As well as household troops for the monarch's personal protection, there were regiments of the line, permanently available for the defence of the realm or for foreign adventures. These regiments were usually associated with those responsible for raising them rather than specific localities, but by the time of George III, the value in promoting regional and local affiliations had been recognised. The 54th Regiment of Foot had been raised in 1755 and renumbered as the 52nd two years later. In 1782, it became the 52nd (Oxfordshire) Regiment of Foot recruiting mainly, but not exclusively, from the Oxford region. The 52nd, intermittently expanded with a second battalion, saw service in India, America, Ceylon, Spain, and Portugal, and was prominent in the final defeat of Napoleon at Waterloo. Following the successful development of the tactic of skirmishing by riflemen, in 1803, the 52nd retrained as light infantry, constituting the army's elite corps. After Waterloo, the regiment, once more reduced to a single battalion, served in Ireland, followed by much longer postings in different areas of Canada.

The Oxfordshire Militia

At the same time that Monck was setting up a force of regular troops, the militia was being re-established and the Oxfordshire Militia was embodied for the defeat of Monmouth's rebellion of 1685. The militia returns of 1697 record the strength of the Oxfordshire Militia under the lord lieutenant, the earl of Abingdon, and Colonel Lord Norreys. Declaring that every estate in the county had contributed to the roll, eight companies of infantry totalling 742 men, and one troop of 130 cavalry were available for service if required with comparable figures being recorded for both Berkshire and Buckinghamshire. Legislation was passed to regularise pay and to improve the discipline of the militiamen, but further reform would be needed. The county militias were notionally revived by Act of Parliament in 1757 but the Oxfordshire Militia Regiment was not actually embodied for a further twenty-one years at the time of the American War, by command of the lord lieutenant, the duke of Marlborough. Nearly 13,000 men in the county were eligible for militia service but only 560, fewer than 5 per cent, selected by ballot, were actually required to turn out for annual training, available for full-time service when summoned. The regiment was commanded by Lord Charles Spencer and officered by gentry including Jane Austen's brother. The Royal Oxfordshire Militia was one of a dozen militia regiments deployed to the south coast in 1795 as a precaution against invasion. Accommodated in tents at Seaford, outside Brighton, poorly paid and victims of the wartime inflation in food prices, 500 men of the regiment mutinied and looted foodstuffs from mills and shops. When order was eventually restored, two, some accounts say five, men were executed by firing squad; six more were flogged to within the proverbial inch of their lives; and the disgraced regiment lost its 'royal' honorific. The regiment served at different stations in Britain and Ireland throughout the French Wars with a brief hiatus around the 1802 Peace of Amiens at which time it fielded 966 men out of an increased establishment of 1,130. It remained embodied until 1816, carrying out guard duties at the Tower of London in 1811 with an establishment of 603 men. After Waterloo, the Militia, now with a strength of 622 men, slightly over its reduced establishment, entered a period of suspended animation with only intermittent periods of activity and, in 1832, along with every county militia, was suspended. The Buckinghamshire Militia, meanwhile, had been completed for service in 1760 with the same strength as that of its neighbour. It remained embodied throughout the French Wars serving in Ireland from 1798 as one of thirteen militia regiments deployed there to counter the threat of French invasion and, in 1814, it volunteered to serve briefly in France.

Volunteers in the French Wars

The French Revolution of 1789 came hot on the heels of the decisive French support for America during its War of Independence against British rule. This support, perceived as revenge for Britain's victories over France in the Seven Years' War, aroused fears of the import of dangerously subversive ideas from across the Channel. The excesses of the Gordon Riots of 1780, when it was necessary to mobilise the country's militias, were fresh in the minds of, especially, London's governing and mercantile classes. Volunteer units raised, generally by members of the propertied classes to defend their homes and livelihoods, were seen as the most effective defence against the anticipated depredations of the mob. Little attention to repelling the feared enemy invasion was evident and, across the country, armed volunteers expressed their motivation succinctly, as in this example recorded by Gee:

> Most, like the Bloxham & Banbury Volunteer Light Horse declared their intention of acting under the direction of the civil power in defence of the constitution, for the protection of person and property, the maintenance of quiet and good order, and for the support of justice.

These noble aspirations clearly chimed with the academic elite. Oxford University formed an armed association, and in 1798, Pembroke College subscribed £100 to a voluntary fund for continuing the war against France.

While the government had sought to bolster the inadequate militia by raising complementary volunteer companies for the augmentation of national defence, the volunteer movement had set off in a different, only vaguely parallel, direction under its own steam and, not always, with unqualified official approval. Volunteers for infantry companies were found mainly in the more densely populated areas, and Oxfordshire was one of seven rural counties where over half of its workers were employed in agriculture and was, incidentally, one of only two of those counties which failed to provide complete statistics for recording volunteer numbers. In general terms, rural counties generated fewer than half the number of volunteers as their more connected urban neighbours.

The volunteer cavalry units raised during the French Wars would be counted among the antecedents of the Queen's Own Oxfordshire Hussars yeomanry cavalry regiment. As early as 1788, a troop of yeomanry cavalry had been formed in Thame, but a more concerted effort to raise further such forces in Oxfordshire was initiated in 1794 at a meeting at Oxford's Star Inn at 34 Cornmarket Street, now demolished and replaced by the Clarendon Centre. The record of those attending gives us a helpful indication of the make-up of the new unit as they included the 'Nobility, Gentry, Freeholders and Yeomanry' of the county. At least seven further troops of cavalry of similar social composition were formed. These included the Loyal Oxfordshire Cavalry, the Charlbury Sharpshooters, the Bloxham & Banbury Light Horse and the Watlington County Fencible Cavalry, 'fencible' usually denoting veterans over the normal age for military service. Similar units in areas of former Berkshire included the Abingdon Cavalry with two further troops in Wantage and in Faringdon and Shrivenham. More than a dozen companies of infantry were also raised in the county. In 1803, three companies of volunteer infantry were raised in Thame with further such units forming in Oxford, Burford, and Langtree, among other localities.

Oxford was HQ for the Army's No. 12 South Inland District, which included the counties of Oxfordshire, Bedfordshire, Northamptonshire, and Buckinghamshire under Lieutenant-General Gwyn. In 1806, Oxfordshire's contingent comprised seven yeomanry cavalry units each with one troop ranging in strength from the thirty-nine troopers of the Ploughly troop to the ninety of the Bloxham & Banbury Light Horse. There were also fifteen regiments of volunteer infantry, the largest being the Oxford Regiment, fielding ten companies but some 114 short of its establishment of 800. Eight of those regiments had an establishment of 180 men in three companies and the rest, ninety men in a single company, with most of these units getting close to achieving those targets. Oxfordshire, thus, recorded combined strengths of 395 cavalry and 1,949 infantry. In Gwyn's opinion, all the yeomanry units' horses were in good condition; the Oxford Loyal Yeomanry, the North Wooton Yeomanry, and the Oxford Regiment of Volunteer Infantry were all deemed 'fit to act with troops of the Line'; but, while most of the other units were, in his estimation, still working towards 'Improving in Discipline', there were others which, unfortunately, remained 'Deficient in Discipline'.

In areas formerly in Berkshire, along with an infantry unit formed at Wantage, the Abingdon Independent Cavalry had been raised in 1794, and in 1804, joined with three similar troops to form the 1st Regiment of Berkshire Gentlemen and Yeomanry Cavalry. A separate unit, the Berkshire Provisional Cavalry, had been raised in 1797–8 with six troops: 'A' Troop being based at Abingdon and 'F' Troop at Faringdon. It served in Bristol and elsewhere in the South West prior to being disbanded in 1800, its senior officers being commissioned into the 1st Berkshire Cavalry whose occasional musters took place at the Red House on Wantage Down. In 1806, as part of the Home District with its London HQ at Horse Guards, the Vale of the White Horse Yeomanry Cavalry mustered six troops with an establishment of nearly 400 men, and a Faringdon and Shrivenham troop numbering 120. No specific mention is made of Abingdon in the Berkshire return as the town's yeomanry had become founder members of the 1st Berkshire Cavalry with an establishment of 221, in four troops. All these volunteers gathered for regular parades and training, but it is doubtful that they were allocated many real or meaningful duties.

Civil Unrest

After the battle of Trafalgar in 1805, around 100 French POWs were billeted in Thame on parole. However, it was not against the French that the Volunteers would be mobilised, but their own neighbours and colleagues. There were food riots in Banbury in 1800, and the cavalry charged into a crowd of protestors causing a child's death. Ringleaders, mainly from outside the town itself, were arrested and taken to Oxford where their arrival sparked a further riot. Members of the volunteer corps, purportedly the agents of order, were not above joining in, confirming the low esteem in which they were held by many. These volunteers, mainly craftsmen and tradesmen, represented the town dwellers most affected by the rising cost of living, particularly for foodstuffs. Their uniformed presence in disturbances was seen as deliberate intimidation by the farmers, who saw themselves as socially superior, but whose prices were the focus of protest. Disturbances also occurred in Oxford when protesters forced farmers to bring food to market at a fixed price. A request by the vice-chancellor of the university for regular cavalry to restore order was seen as a slight by the mayor and town clerk. They felt that the local Armed Association could perfectly well be entrusted with the task, and that to bring in regular troops showed a lack of confidence in the volunteer corps. The general consensus was, however, that volunteers would protect life and property but that their sympathies lay with the protesters' attempts to regulate prices.

As well as rising prices, the rural population was disturbed by enclosure. A new cut to divert the River Ray to improve Otmoor caused flooding of farmers' lands upstream. Those affected then broke down the embankments and were indicted for felony. However, the jury was ordered to acquit because the farmers' actions in seeking to avoid the flooding of their lands was regarded as legitimate. Unfortunately, this judgement was interpreted as an award of tacit official approval, exonerating the anti-enclosure parties, who then escalated their assault on the fences. Owing to conflicting loyalties, it became impossible to recruit special constables, and magistrates began calling in troops. The 1st Regiment of Oxfordshire Yeomanry Cavalry, comprising the former Wooton and Woodstock troops, set up its HQ in Islip alongside a force of regular foot guards. The protesters' campaign then culminated in a crowd of up to 1,000 people destroying fences on Otmoor in September 1830. Forty-two activists were arrested and conveyed from Islip to Oxford under armed guard, to be met by a mob, hundreds strong, which ensured the escape of the prisoners. Better organised by now, the protesters, armed with pitchforks and sometimes guns, mounted regular nightly raids on the enclosure fences. The yeomanry was called in and regular troops mounted guard and patrolled the Moor. It would take five further interventions by the yeomanry over the next few years before the problem was fully resolved in 1835. One factor was a drift toward more efficient policing by the civil authority. However, this would go wrong in Chipping Norton in 1845 when a man was killed by the town's overzealous new police-sergeant and the yeomanry proved reluctant to get involved in the ensuing riot, the last occasion on which their services would be requested.

A third matter exercising minds in the countryside was mechanisation in a situation where labour was plentiful, but employment opportunities were scarce, and the rural poor were losing their livelihoods to enclosure. In

1830, a crowd of several hundred people from the Banbury area, set fire to agricultural machinery in the so-called, country-wide, 'Swing Riots'. A troop of the Bloxham and Banbury yeomanry cavalry failed to make much impression on the rioters, being routed by them; specially sworn in constables had a little more luck; but it took a detachment of regular dragoons from Coventry finally to restore order. That same year, villagers in Benson, Crowmarsh, and Ewelme fired hay ricks and farm buildings, and smashed machinery with similar outrages reported from Chipping Norton. While many of the rioters were either imprisoned or transported, only a few were hanged. It can be argued that all this political activity and the authorities' response would eventually contribute to improvements in rural life and employment as well as precipitating the political reforms of 1832.

Military Infrastructure

Inland waterways had long provided convenient ways of transporting troops, their families, and munitions, reducing road travel times by two-thirds. The anti-invasion measures of the Napoleonic War had established a system for the rapid movement of troops in which the key routes were those from London to Liverpool and London to the Severn at Gloucester. The Thames was divided into sectors which would maintain day and night working and provide changeover points for horses. In Oxfordshire, two such sections—Henley to Oxford and Oxford to Lechlade—were established. The Oxford Canal, running from Oxford to Banbury and onward to the important junction at Braunston, formed part of the route to Liverpool used by troops being transported northwards for shipment to Ireland. Personnel, including the resident engineer of the Oxford Canal Company, were recruited by the commissary general to liaise with the boatmen and ensure a smooth passage. Each canal company billed the military for their transit based on tonnage and a toll for each lock passed. With the advent of the railways, however, use of the canals for troop movements was declining throughout the 1830s, and by 1850 would be completely phased out.

Although barracks had begun to be built on the invasion-prone south coast and in cities seen as likely to erupt in violent industrial action, troops elsewhere continued to be billeted in inns and private houses. This widespread and unpopular practice would continue in places such as Oxfordshire for a further couple of generations.

4

Victorian and Edwardian Oxfordshire, 1840–1914

After the turmoil of the years leading to the Reform Acts, attention turned to relationships with other countries and the expansion and maintenance of the British Empire. During the second half of the nineteenth century, both the regulars and the militia would undertake overseas service and the volunteer sector would be radically reorganised. Although the history of the regulars, the militias, and the volunteers are all intertwined, their separate and collective development will be outlined below under their own headings. The Cardwell reforms which established localisation depots brought, over the objections of the university authorities, a permanent barracks to Oxford, a city which had experienced little military involvement since the Civil War. With the consolidation of the yeomanry and the introduction of the Rifle Volunteer Corps, most of the county's small towns would also now host a military presence.

The Queen's Own Oxfordshire Hussars Yeomanry (QOOH)

We have seen how volunteer yeomanry cavalry units were raised across the country during the time of the French wars. The government had disbanded most of those units by 1828, but some, including two of Oxfordshire's units, continued on a self-funding basis for two more years until, in the face of worrying unrest, the government decided to restore them to the official list. Winning the 'Queen's Own' attribution from Queen Adelaide in 1835, the 1st Regiment of Oxfordshire Yeomanry Cavalry had its HQ in Oxford and numbered the county's aristocracy among its commandants and other officers, most notably the duke of Marlborough and Viscount Valentia. Annual manoeuvres lasting a fortnight took place at Blenheim and Oxford's Port Meadow, among other locations. Troopers were required to supply their own mounts, but uniforms and weaponry were subsidised by their wealthy patrons and the War Department at Horse Guards. The regiment's unwieldy title was changed to the Queen's Own

Oxfordshire Hussars soon after 1881. The Berkshire Yeomanry had followed a very similar trajectory but there had been a hiatus in the middle years of the century, which was only fully ended in 1871 when, as part of its 2nd Squadron, a fourth troop, 'D' Troop, was raised in Wantage. Annual camps were often held at Churn, on the Downs. With the establishment of an Oxford City police force in 1835; of a Berkshire Constabulary in 1856, subsuming police forces in Abingdon, Wantage, and Wallingford; and of an Oxfordshire county force in 1857; the requirement for the local yeomanry to turn out in aid of the civil power had been largely removed.

The terms of engagement for members of the yeomanry precluded service outside the British Isles, but when the army in South Africa was pinned down by the hit-and-run tactics of the Boer commandos, the call went out for volunteers to become mounted riflemen matching the tactics of the enemy, designated the Imperial Yeomanry. Volunteers from the QOOH formed the 40th Company of the 10th Battalion, and the 59th Company of the 15th Battalion, serving alongside companies from Buckinghamshire and Berkshire. The 39th and 58th Companies of the 10th and 15th Battalions were raised from the Royal Berkshire Yeomanry, whose use of that unofficial 'Royal' honorific ceased in 1902. Their successful experiences in South Africa led to the reorganisation of each of the yeomanry regiments into four squadrons with a machine-gun section.

The Oxfordshire Light Infantry

The regiment, with its single battalion, was involved in campaigns in India, in garrison duties in Gibraltar and Malta, and in home postings in England and Ireland, but far-reaching changes were imminent. The 85th King's Regiment of Light Infantry (Buckinghamshire Volunteers) had been assigned to Bullingdon, later Cowley Barracks with the 52nd, but as part of the reforms of the time, in 1881 it was detached to merge with the Shropshire Light Infantry. At the same time, the 52nd (Oxfordshire) Regiment of Foot was merged with the 43rd (Monmouthshire) Regiment of Foot, a fellow light infantry unit with whom it had enjoyed a shared history, and which would now form the Oxfordshire Light Infantry's extra battalion, numbered 1st and based at the regimental depot at Cowley, numbered on a contemporary plan as No. 42 Brigade Depot. Besides the two regular battalions forming the 43rd Regimental District, there were the 3rd (Buckinghamshire) Militia Battalion; the 4th (Oxfordshire) Militia Battalion; and four volunteer battalions comprising the two counties' former Rifle Volunteer Corps (RVC), combined and numbered: 1st (Oxford University), 2nd (Oxfordshire), 3rd (Buckinghamshire) and 4th (Eton College). In 1900, a company of volunteers drawn from the Buckinghamshire Militia battalion fought alongside their regular colleagues in South Africa. It was involved in mobile operations and then manned the blockhouses which would limit the Boers' ability to manoeuvre freely and would lead, by attrition, to their final defeat.

Haldane's reorganisations of 1908 (see below) which set up the Territorial Force (TF) had a direct impact on this structure. The two regular battalions, having either absorbed or affiliated with the Buckingham-based infantry units over the years, became the Oxfordshire and Buckinghamshire Light Infantry (OBLI); the 3rd Militia Battalion was disbanded; the 4th Militia Battalion became the 3rd (Special Reserve) Battalion; the 2nd Volunteer Battalion became the 4th Battalion (TF); the Buckinghamshire Battalion (TF) remained a discrete part of the regiment but based in Aylesbury; the Oxford University battalion joined the Senior OTC; and the Eton College battalion joined the Junior OTC. This left the OBLI with three regular and two TF battalions with four of them based for administrative purposes at Cowley Barracks. In 1912, motor transport vehicles of the Army Service Corps were reported as being quartered in St Giles, and by 1913, Morris Motors in Cowley were beginning to mass produce models such as the Morris Oxford as the military applications of motor vehicles were becoming more apparent.

The Oxfordshire Militia

Given the future amalgamation of the two units, both the Oxfordshire and Buckinghamshire militias will be dealt with here. The Oxfordshire Militia was revived in 1852 by the duke of Wellington and training, normally twenty-seven days each year, recommenced, initially at Woodstock and then in Oxford. Both militias were embodied for the Crimean War, the Oxfordshire serving on Corfu in the Ionian Islands guarding the lines of communication; and the Buckinghamshire engaged in guard duties at home to relieve regular troops. In 1881, the Buckinghamshire Militia became the 3rd Battalion, Oxfordshire Light Infantry, and the Oxfordshire Militia became its 4th Battalion. The 3rd Battalion spent most of 1900 in Ireland during the South African War and the 4th Battalion was based in Portsmouth and Gosport. Throughout all these years, the militia regiments had contributed hundreds of volunteers to the Regular Army. The next significant reorganisation was the creation of the Territorial Force (TF) out of the RVC but also to include a reorganisation of the militia regiments. After ultimately unsuccessful local opposition, the Royal Buckinghamshire Militia was disbanded, but many of its members elected to join their Oxfordshire comrades in 1908, in a new 3rd (Special Reserve) Battalion, OBLI (TF).

Rifle Volunteer Corps

In 1859, the nation was becoming alarmed by the manifest ambitions of Napoleon's nephew, Napoleon III of France, who appeared to be contemplating an invasion of England. Dissatisfaction with the performance of British troops in both the Indian Mutiny, as it was known in Britain, and the Crimean War, saw the National Rifle Association set up to raise standards of marksmanship and it was agreed that competition for prizes would get people interested in target shooting. A rifle range was opened at Hincksey in 1861, when there were

369 entries competing for ten prizes. It was also generally felt that the creation of a trained force of citizen volunteers would provide a much-needed backup to the Regular Army and militia. While the gentry and their rural tenants had the yeomanry cavalry, the urban middle classes felt that they, too, should have an opportunity to serve. The popular result was the Rifle Volunteer Corps (RVC), initially formed of individual groups, independent in terms of finance, uniforms and equipment, governance, and leadership. The earliest to be formed in Oxfordshire were the three companies formed in Oxford University in August 1859, but others soon followed from February 1860 in Oxford and Banbury. Oxford's 2nd Corps largely drew its recruits from the city's middle classes and most RVC would rely heavily on professionals, businessmen and civic authorities for patronage and leadership. Beckett has analysed the social composition of Oxfordshire's RVC using the original subscription lists submitted to the duke of Marlborough as lord lieutenant of the county. They show a preponderance of shopkeepers and tradesmen with smaller proportions of artisans and professional men. Only in Bicester and Deddington were there significant numbers of farmers, and only in Witney were a third of members drawn from the professions. By 1861, however, only 11 per cent of members were from the gentry and this had fallen to just 2 per cent by 1877, and this trend was mirrored in a general decline in upper-middle-class volunteering. Between 1861 and 1877, the largest number of volunteers was drawn from tradesmen, but craftsmen's membership, over that period, increased to one-third. One solution to the problem of enrolling adequate numbers to maintain unit viability was to woo employers, encouraging them to promote the RVC among their employees. While a workforce in an urban factory might enrol wholesale, only two instances of such commitment were to be found in Oxfordshire: in Banbury's Britannia Works and at the textile business of William Bliss in Chipping Norton. Finding the right leaders would be a recurrent problem for many corps. In Wallingford, the 3rd Berkshire RVC resorted to appointing a squire from across the (former) county border as their CO, as they could find no one more locally with the requisite military knowledge, time, experience, or motivation.

It soon became apparent that all these scattered and disparate units needed to be gathered into a larger organisation. Oxfordshire's nine RVC were grouped together in an administrative battalion, a measure receiving only grudging support from the 2nd Oxon RVC who accepted that some consistency was needed in the system but valued their autonomy. Within a short time, the War Department imposed more order by offering grants to units which met certain criteria. These included a fixed training regime; measurements for efficiency of drill, turnout, and marksmanship; regular attendance at drill nights by sufficient members to make training activities effective; and the provision of premises for the unit's administration, the secure storage of its arms and ammunition, and an indoor space for drill. The Wallingford corps would find ammunition storage a problem as they were refused permission to store it in the police station on the wholly understandable grounds that its security could not be guaranteed, and its presence there would invalidate the fire insurance. The Militia Armoury on New Road initially met all such needs for the Oxford University RVC.

Despite the increasing availability of funds from government, civic authorities, or wealthy patrons, finance remained a stumbling block to enrolment. Although support from persons of influence was often forthcoming—in 1861, the CO of Banbury RVC was Colonel North MP—many units were dependent on their members for finance: Wallingford's corps charged a joining fee of 10*s* 6*d* (half a guinea), with the same sum as the annual subscription and a higher sliding scale for officers, and Deddington's subscription was 5*s*. The cost of Oxford's uniform was £3 7*s*, and Banbury's was £4. These costs must be seen in a context in which the average agricultural labourer's wages were 9–12*s* per week. Magistrates in Watlington, along with community leaders in Banbury and Whitchurch, concluded that it was hard enough for the middle classes to afford to join, let alone labourers. The 5th Corps had formed at Woodstock in 1860, but soon split with a new 9th Corps remaining in Woodstock and the original 5th Corps migrating to Witney. Here, finance problems, combined with the difficulty of finding suitable officers, contributed to its disbandment three years later and Bicester went the same way in 1870, although the Banbury corps had managed to weather their early financial troubles in 1862. The average volunteer in 1861 was thirty years old and this may have been for financial rather than patriotic reasons. As official support relieved the pressure on their pockets, the average age of volunteers had reduced to nineteen by 1877, but the average length of service had decreased from five years to four by 1877. Turnover could be considerable. At Wallingford which enjoyed an initial membership of seventy-eight, the period 1870–3 saw around fifty leaving and the same number enrolling, raising all sorts of questions about the number of 'effectives' on roll, the loss of experienced volunteers, and the implications for training. Oxfordshire's original seven corps began with numbers ranging from 109 in Oxford city to just thirty in Thame so such fluctuations could make it difficult to create a cohesive unit with high morale. However, in October 1861, a shooting match for 7th Corps, Oxfordshire RVC, attracted over 300 entrants.

As well as constraints of personal finance and the scarcity of suitable officer material, there were other factors affecting recruitment. In 1888, the Oxford University RVC, recently redesignated as a volunteer battalion of the Oxfordshire Light Infantry, came close to folding as the distractions of sport and boating were curbing the undergraduates' enthusiasm for volunteering. The lack of interest in the RVC among all but a few farmers may reflect the greater appeal of the yeomanry cavalry and, for many farmers' sons who had reservations about joining the yeomanry, there were the light horse volunteers as an alternative. However, the Oxfordshire Light Horse Volunteers, raised in

Banbury in 1864, never fielded more than sixty sabres and disbanded in 1870 as so few felt able to attend drills, partly, again, owing to the cost of maintaining horses and kit. While in many of the remoter parts of the country, especially Scotland, the attractions of winning worthwhile prizes in shooting competitions and the opportunities for social mixing underpinned recruitment, areas such as Oxfordshire offered a whole range of competing activities. Shooting, however, which provided the original rationale for the RVC remained a key draw with many of the early RVC constructing their own rifle ranges. The Henley RVC had a miniature range off the Fair Mile and a full-size outdoor range at Nettlebed and a silver cup and a silver bugle were donated for the annual competition. The 5th Corps at Witney had a local builder erect a range for them in a cleared section of Cogges Wood, complete with markers and flagpole. However, a county such as Oxfordshire offered many alternative facilities and the RVC held no monopoly. In 1887, the first mention of a Deddington Rifle Association, independent of the Volunteers is seen. The Cherwell Miniature Rifle Club was mentioned in 1909 and again in 1910 when they were the winners of the City Miniature Rifle League which included a team from Oxford United Banks. Also in the county are the Bicester Town and District Rifle and Pistol Club, founded in 1906, a member of the Oxfordshire Rifle Association which itself dates back to 1862, with other constituent clubs in Abingdon (City of Oxford), Crowmarsh and Shrivenham. The Church Lads' Brigade (CLB) fielded a team in Chipping Norton, as did the Britannia Works in Banbury, many of the club competitions taking place at the Churn range. The first military installation on what would later become the vast Bicester Central Ordnance Depot was a 600-yard (550-metre) rifle range on Graven Hill, set up for the use of the local RVC. Another, less martial, activity that often originated with the volunteers and might attract members was the brass band. In 1903, Henley formed a town band with a nucleus of members from the former volunteers' band.

The demands and rewards of the volunteer may be seen in snapshots of the 6th Oxfordshire RVC at Deddington. This corps was formally established in 1860 in the town hall of 1806 with forty-one members and eleven honorary members. Corps activities, which appear to have been little changed over the years, centred around shooting, drill, parades, route marches, fund-raising, and social activities. The 1880 annual shooting match marked the twenty-first anniversary of this traditional Boxing Day event, held at the 900-yard (830-metre) Butts in 'Battlethorn Field'. Volunteers shot for prizes, which included a goose, a bottle of whisky, and a leg of mutton. In 1884, Deddington RVC beat Bicester at shooting by 630 to 517 points, and the corps even took part at a national event when four marksman brothers successfully represented Deddington at the national Wimbledon rifle competition. The 1887 fete in the Castle Grounds raised money for new targets at the Butts. In 1883, the annual Adjutant's Drill took place in the market place and, three years later, now 'C'

Company, 2nd Volunteer Battalion, Oxfordshire Light Infantry with ninety members, the Deddington corps paraded in the Castle Grounds. The corps provided a guard of honour for Prince Leopold's visit to Banbury in November 1882. In April 1883, twenty-six members marched to Aynho to join up with seventy-five members of the Banbury Company for drill and refreshments and, a month later, attended a full battalion drill in Oxford. A fete with the band of the Banbury corps in attendance in 1886 was followed by the annual dinner at the King's Head. Entertainments were held in the boys' schoolroom—a concert by the officers of the 2nd Oxford city RVC was put on in 1878. Although public grants did not extend to bands, both the Oxford and Banbury corps saw them as vital in promoting good relations with the wider community. In 1885, the deaths occurred of Sergeant-instructor Wallace after over twenty years with the corps, and of Colour-Sergeant Parish, aged only forty-one but with over twenty-five years membership of the corps behind him. In 1887, the problem of secure storage came up when a fire in a workshop adjacent to the churchyard necessitated the speedy removal of the ammunition stored there.

The Cardwell reforms brought the regulars, militiamen, and volunteers into the same regimental family in order to strengthen those local attachments which might engender pride in the unit; to aid the recruitment process; to foster a shared *esprit de corps*; and to promote co-operation between the different elements. This ambitious aspiration, however, was not always fulfilled. In May 1877, for instance, a brigade drill had been arranged by the district staff at Cowley Barracks to be held on Port Meadow in Oxford, but at least one volunteer battalion arrived from a distance and on a very wet day, to find it had been cancelled without them being so informed. As we have seen, the RVC initially became volunteer battalions and then went on to become integral to the new Territorial Force.

Military Infrastructure

Situated on the corner of Oxford Road and Hollow Way, Cowley, the Oxford Military Academy was set up in 1864 to prepare the sons of military officers for service in the Regular Army. The college bought the Cowley Middle Class School in 1876; the college hall was the former seventeenth-century manor house; the chapel was built in 1870; and an east wing added in 1877. The curriculum for boys from the age of thirteen included military riding; infantry drill; training with lance and sword; carbine drill; swimming and gymnastics. Although the dukes of Connaught and Cambridge, prominent military figures, were numbered among its patrons, the college could not compete in the same market as the new public schools and closed in 1896. The site was developed in 1912 by William Morris, later Lord Nuffield, as a car plant.

A new militia barracks, designed by J. C. Buckler in the style of a medieval castle with crenellations, and containing an armoury and drill hall, was opened on Oxford's New Road in 1854. When, in 1876, the militia was about to be absorbed into the Oxfordshire Light Infantry, the barracks was handed over as the HQ of the Oxfordshire Constabulary, formed in 1859. It was demolished in 1969. Up until then, the Buckinghamshire Militia had been based in their barracks in High Wycombe. Bullingdon, later renamed Cowley Barracks was built as the No. 42 Brigade Depot, the centre of the 43rd Regimental District in 1876, initially to house the Oxfordshire Light Infantry, Militia and Volunteers, and the Royal Buckinghamshire Militia. It was built to a universal War Office design in the style of a medieval fortress. The towered 'Keep', designed as a defensible armoury, contained specially strengthened concrete floors for the storage of large quantities of arms and ammunition for distribution to volunteers and recruits in a national emergency. Around a large parade ground were ranged barrack blocks, messes, stables, stores, married quarters, and a hospital, all enclosed by a high wall entered through an arched gateway.

The Marconi company was awarded a government contract to set up a chain of radio stations to link Britain with locations across the empire. The programme had only just got under way when the First World War broke out and Marconi's contract was cancelled. Only two of the proposed network of transmission stations had been built: Leafield, at Langley near Witney, and another near Cairo. The shortwave beam system then took over and the Leafield

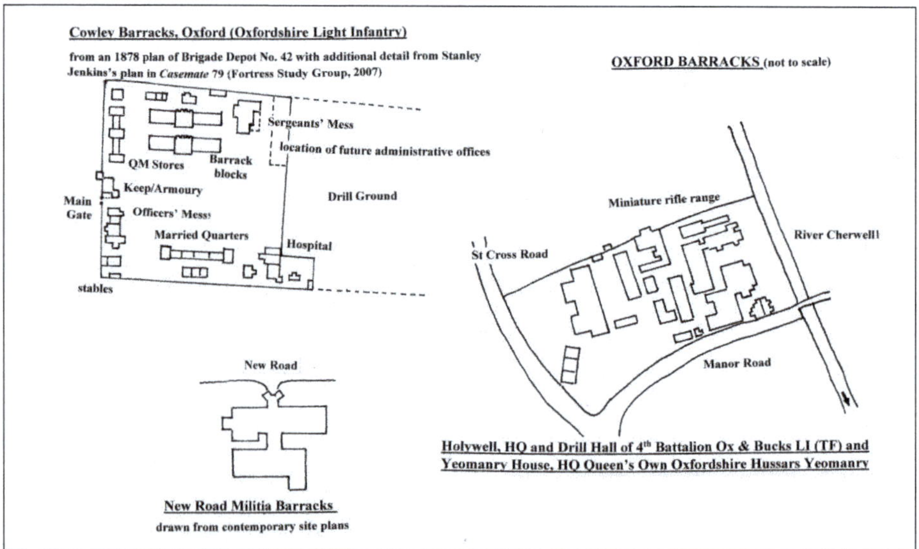

Oxford's barracks: sketch plans of Cowley Barracks, the New Road Militia Barracks, and the Holywell Territorial Force HQ, range, and drill hall. The 1872 plan shows a projecting corner tower at the north-east angle, which was not, in fact, built.

Cowley Barracks: the officers' mess, currently in use by Oxford Brookes University.

Cowley Barracks: 'Napier' barrack block, built to accommodate 112 other ranks and their NCOs. Along with its 'Moore' barrack-block twin, it was demolished for housing.

station had a long career under the GPO, only being decommissioned in 1986. The Clarendon Laboratory in Oxford opened in 1872 as the first purpose-built science laboratory in England and would be home to early research into the atom. The Townsend Building (Second Electrical Laboratory) opened in 1910 to the south of the Clarendon.

Drill Halls (see also Appendix V)

One of the War Office's stipulations in recognising RVC in their early days was access to a space providing for the secure storage of arms and ammunition; the efficient administration of the corps; appropriate spaces for indoor drill on winter evenings and for outdoor parades; and rifle ranges both indoor and outdoor. All sorts of premises were utilised: town halls in Banbury and Deddington; the seventeenth-century former Methodist Meeting House where John Wesley preached in Oxford and a former Friends' Meeting House in Witney, built in 1712 but superseded in 1828; a school room in Abingdon and a former girls' school in Faringdon; the Corn Exchanges in Witney and Faringdon; private houses in Oxford and in Wantage where there was accommodation for the yeomanry instructor and a barn next door for stabling; a converted skating rink and racquets court in Oxford; and converted domestic or commercial buildings in Wantage; the Spreadeagle in Thame; and the Red Lion and the Plough in Banbury. In Banbury, two rival Corn Exchanges had opened on the same day in 1857 but, following use of the (new) town hall, a drill hall was opened in Calthorpe Street. This proved inadequate and a move had been made to the former British School in Crouch Street prior to the outbreak of war. Purpose-built drill halls dating from the Victorian or Edwardian periods are scarce, with possible examples in Banbury, Henley, and Chipping Norton. The new town hall of 1901 in Henley, contained a basement drill hall, but would not be used as the opening of a new drill hall in Northfield End, for the yeomanry, rifle volunteers and CLB, paid for by Mr F. M. Drewett, a long-serving volunteer, was reported in *The Times* of 10 October 1900. The Kelly's Directory of 1911 records the yeomanry as being based in the White House, Market Street, with the OBLI in Badgeworth Lane, probably the hall reported in Northfield End. This would suggest that the current ARC in Queen's Hall in Friday Street, formerly reported as in operation in the 1890s, may not have been acquired, or built, until much later. Following the establishment of the Territorial Force (TF) and with the approach of war, the provision of new drill halls gathered pace with examples in Banbury (Crouch Street), Oxford (Holywell), Wallingford, Wantage, and Woodstock.

Reflecting the importance of marksmanship to the volunteers, ample facilities were provided both indoor and out. These included butts on Crouch Hill, Banbury; the full-length outdoor range of 1861 at Hinksey; The Bull, in Henley's Bell Street, housing a Morris Tube range where muskets and rifles could be fitted with a sleeve to fire small-bore ammunition in an indoor setting; the miniature range standing opposite the White Hart on Shirburn Street in Watlington; a similar range standing at the south end of Park Street, in Thame; the Watlington range opened in 1908 by Ian Fleming's father and now the Otmoor range of the Chiltern Rifle Club, formed in 1962; the range which opened in 1910 behind the new council school in St John's Road, Wallingford; and the miniature range at the depot of the 4th Battalion, OBLI, in Holywell, Oxford. Meanwhile, much of the outdoor military shooting by the regulars took place at Churn on the Downs.

Banbury: the new town hall, opened in 1854, which served for a while as a drill hall and armoury for the Rifle Volunteers.

Oxford: the former Methodist Meeting House in New Inn Hall Road, where John Wesley once preached, served as the HQ of the Queen's Own Oxfordshire Hussars in 1895.

Abingdon, Roysse's Room was the base for units of the Berkshire Yeomanry and the Volunteers of the Royal Berkshire Regiment.

Faringdon Corn Exchange was used as a drill hall for the Berkshire Rifle Volunteers.

Wallingford drill hall on Thames Street is still used by the local cadets.

Henley Town Hall was built in 1901 to incorporate a basement drill hall but was never used as such since alternative accommodation had been provided for the local Volunteers by a benefactor.

Wantage: the Alma drill hall opened on the eve of war in 1914 for the Berkshire TF.

The Woodstock drill hall dates from shortly after the establishment of the Territorial Force in 1908.

The Territorial Force, 1908–1914

Many different factors contributed to the establishment of the Territorial Force (TF) in 1908, but the main driver was the need for a home defence force, given the demands of empire on the Regular Army and its diminutive size when compared with the massive conscript armies of the European powers. The TF was set up at local level by County Territorial Associations (CTA) to be a mirror image of the Regular Army. There were fourteen regional TF divisions each consisting of a brigade of yeomanry cavalry with attached Royal Horse Artillery (RHA); three brigades of infantry, each of four battalions; field (RFA) and garrison or siege (RGA) artillery; Royal Engineers (RE) construction, electrical, and signals companies; Royal Army Medical Corps (RAMC) general hospitals, field ambulances, and casualty clearing stations; and Army Service Corps transport and supply columns. Oxfordshire's units belonged to the South Midland Division with its HQ in Warwick. The QOOH was part of the 2nd South Midland Mounted Brigade together with the Berkshire and Buckinghamshire Yeomanries and the Berkshire RHA. In line with similar units, the Berkshire Yeomanry was expanded to four, full squadrons, with 'D' Squadron based in Wantage. Annual training continued to take place at Churn. The recently renamed OBLI contributed its two battalions to the South Midland Infantry Brigade along with two battalions from Gloucestershire and Berkshire. Both cavalry and infantry brigades had their HQs in Oxford. The only other units of the TF resident in the county were the 3rd Southern General Hospital in Oxford and the third line depot of the 2nd Mounted Brigade's field ambulance at 1 Iffley Road, Oxford. The Oxford Journal of the 13 April 1910 has a photograph of 'nurses enlisted for service in the 3rd Army Field Hospital', presumably meaning the 3rd Southern General.

Elements of both the Berkshire Yeomanry and the 4th Battalion, Royal Berkshire Regiment (TF), were based in towns lying, since 1974, within Oxfordshire. TF units were scattered across the counties with squadrons of yeomanry and companies of infantry based in drill halls, and their constituent units meeting for regular drills in their designated drill stations located in halls, institutes, and public houses. Colonel, the Right Honourable the Duke of Marlborough, lord lieutenant of Oxfordshire, was *ex-officio* president of the Oxfordshire CTA with a dozen military members; six members representing the county, borough, and university; co-opted members as appropriate; and its secretariat based at 30 Magdalen Street, Oxford.

Throughout the early days of the TF in the years leading up to the outbreak of the First World War, newspapers are littered with references to parades: Blenheim Palace in 1911 when the entire Mounted Brigade gathered; manoeuvres and exercises on Salisbury Plain and Lulworth Cove; field days and annual camps in Nuneham Park and Headington Park; church parades; shooting competitions; point-to-point races;

annual inspections and sports days. Faringdon found itself at the centre of the Army Manoeuvres of 1911, establishing a feeding station at Church Path Farm and taking the opportunity to recruit to the volunteers at the Bull Inn in London Street. The town was flooded with politicians, military top brass, and foreign attaches, all come to observe the manoeuvres and to enjoy the hospitality of the Bell Inn.

Cadets

The earliest cadet corps in the county was initiated at the Linden House School in Headington which recruited forty-five of its seventy pupils aged from nine to seventeen, into the Oxford City Rifle Cadet Corps. The initial parade took place in March 1861 and with schools such as Magdalen College School joining, the corps quickly grew into a county-wide organisation, parallel to the RVC. Throughout this period, and until the years after the First World War, both the Boys Brigade (BB), founded in 1893, and the Church Lads' Brigade (CLB), founded in 1891, were organised as uniformed, paramilitary organisations and trained their members to drill and to shoot, while ensuring that the attitudes being inculcated were not exclusively warlike. In Abingdon, the BB had a drill hall in Ock Street, and Oxford, with its first company forming in 1888, was one of four English cities cited as being among the organisation's principal strongholds. Trinity Hall in Harpsden Road, Henley-upon-Thames, later home to a rifle club, hosted a company of the CLB. After the TF's formation, regiments promoted the formation of their affiliated Territorial Cadet Force (TCF), encouraging school based TCF units, along with both senior and junior OTC. In 1910, King Alfred's School, Wantage, purchased, for £96, a former fire engine house, built in 1878–80, as its OTC armoury. Incorporated into the Senior OTC, the OUOTC sought to provide a width of experience for those intending to make the army a career. It therefore comprised a cavalry squadron; an artillery battery; a signals section; a field ambulance section; and an entire infantry battalion. Drill, including that devised for the cyclist detachment, was carried out on Christ Church Meadow. Garsington was the scene of exercises against an imported enemy in 1913. The OUOTC's field days at Tackley involved Radley's Junior OTC contingent as well as those from further afield such as Eton and Harrow. In 1910, Burford GS Cadet Corps was affiliated to the OBLI which also raised the Cowley Cadet Corps, military consciousness being a common element for boys growing up in those years before the First World War. In 1901, after the Boer War, the Oxford Preparatory (later Dragon) School, launched a subscription for a memorial building consisting of a carpentry shop with a museum/library above, as a tribute to a former pupil. The St Clement's Company of the CLB were winners of the Regimental Inter-Battalion Dyson Cup for physical drill, arms, and shooting in August 1912. In September 1913, cadets of the 1st Witney BB camped at Lulworth and went onboard the battleship HMS *Orion* in Portland Harbour in Dorset.

Wantage, King Alfred's School OTC armoury was built as a fire-engine house but was bought by the school for the use by its cadet unit.

Change was in the Air

Although the railways had long been in operation, reliance on the horse was still widespread, with a new indoor riding school being opened in 1909 by Mr Rhodes to the rear of 171 Walton Street in Oxford. However, things were slowly changing. One of the earliest balloon flights had been made by James Sadler who took off from Christ Church Meadow in Oxford in October 1784. Ascending to a height of 3,600 feet (1,100 metres), he then travelled the 6 miles (9.6 km) to Woodeaton. Despite his scientific achievements, he received little recognition, a plaque memorialising this ground-breaking feat only appearing on the wall of Merton College in 1984. Special occasions—such as the installation of the politician William Grenville as chancellor of Oxford University in 1810—might be marked by the spectacle of a balloon flight; ascents in tethered balloons would soon become commonplace at fairs; and aeroplanes would begin to appear in the skies in the early years of the twentieth century. On Easter Monday 1910, crowds gathered in Banbury in the expectation of observing a flight by the pioneer aviator Claude Grahame-White, but they were to be disappointed as he failed to arrive. Meanwhile, Oxford's Port Meadow had been set up to operate as a civilian flying school, only for the timber hangars and fifteen aircraft to be destroyed in a gale in 1911. Unfortunately, the military were slow to capitalise on these trends, but an aircraft of the Air Battalion RE did appear at Port Meadow in August 1911. Sadly, on 11 September 1912, a Bristol monoplane, flown by two members of the Royal Flying Corps (RFC), crashed there, a military funeral taking place at Wolvercote church. That same month, more military aircraft appeared at Wolvercote Common or Port Meadow which by 1913 was in regular use by the RFC as an airfield, and Grahame-White himself finally made it there in the October.

The Vale of the White Horse, centred on Shrivenham and Faringdon, had provided the setting for the annual army manoeuvres of 1909 with 70,000 regulars involved, and culminating in an assault by the Red Army on the Blue Army defending Faringdon Folly, where both sides resorted to hurling turnips at each other. In 1913, however, the annual autumn manoeuvres were again held in the south Midlands, around Daventry in Northamptonshire, with 10,000 regulars, mainly cavalry regiments, billeted in Oxford, in South Park, Headington, and in Colonel Miller's parkland at Shotover House near Wheatley. This time, airships would be employed in a reconnaissance role, supporting these Whiteland forces which constituted the 'target' to be attacked. In March, the army's airship *Beta* had appeared in the skies over Oxford, possibly engaged in rehearsals for those manoeuvres, and in June, *Gamma* was seen over Blenheim. During the manoeuvres themselves, one of *Delta*'s propellers was repaired on University Parks. The other two forces in the exercise, Greenland and Brownland, were provided with squadrons of RFC and RNAS aircraft reporting on the Whiteland force's scripted fighting retreat. Two Bleriot XI aircraft of the RFC deployed to France a year later, and, *en route* to the manoeuvres, received attention from mechanics in Wantage. At the other end of the county, forces attacking Whiteland's eastern flank were converging on villages around Stokenchurch. It may be argued that many of the timely lessons thus learned in the skies above Oxfordshire would be effectively carried over into the action about to unfold on the continent of Europe. In the early months of the war during the BEF's Retreat from Mons, the otherwise unseen and unpredictable movements of the invading German army would be observed and reported by the reconnaissance aircraft of the RFC, enabling an orderly, if pressured, withdrawal and a successful counterattack.

5

Oxfordshire in the First World War, 1914–1918

For those at the far western end of the county, the outbreak of war was announced at 7:49 p.m. on 4 August 1914 by the pre-arranged signal of ten blasts of the hooter at the Swindon railway works, and agricultural labourers within earshot in Shrivenham hurried straightway to enlist. In Banbury, the QOOH and the 4th Battalion, OBLI, gathered at their Crouch Street drill hall to mobilise. Unofficial discussions between the French and British general staffs had resulted in a commitment for the Regular Army to supply a British Expeditionary Force (BEF) to fight alongside the French army in Flanders. However, the speed of the German advance through Belgium precipitated the Retreat from Mons, which saw much of that BEF destroyed. This meant that within the first few months of the war, the Territorial divisions, ostensibly forming a home defence force, were required to be deployed around the empire, either to release regular units for service on the Western Front or to serve there themselves. Lord Kitchener, appointed as war minister, had initiated mass recruitment from the very start of the war and over 2,000 had turned up at Oxford Town Hall to enlist into local regiments in August 1914, some newly recruited territorials being transported to camp in charabancs loaned by the Oxford Tramway Company. Around the county, packed meetings in venues such as Witney's Corn Exchange were held to raise recruits, with those bound for the 2/4th Battalion assembling in Oxford, including a large contingent of trainee teachers from Culham College, with more overflowing into other units. Some of this mass of recruits were able to join the second-line units of the yeomanry and the TF infantry and artillery, but the majority were sucked into Kitchener's New Armies, formed from scratch around cadres of old soldiers, reservists, and territorials, who were charged with producing a force to win the war. By 1915, there were recruiting offices in Oxford at the Carfax and at 47 High Street with another, temporarily, in Logic Lane. Recruits in Banbury attended the recruiting office in Cow Fair. Many

Witney Corn Exchange was used as a drill hall for both the local territorials and the Volunteer Training Corps, and as a recruiting office in the First World War.

towns located their recruiting offices in drill halls, town halls, labour exchanges, or even in commercial premises. One-off recruiting fairs were held across the county with such an event recorded in Woodstock at which men enlisted on the spot and were carted off before they could change their minds. Public meetings were held to nudge young men into enlisting and preachers would often attempt to shame their congregations into flocking to the colours. On a smaller scale than the 'Pals' battalions, local associations enlisted together. In Henley-upon-Thames, the entire membership of the Trinity Hall Rifle Club, founded in 1910 and shooting on a small-bore range, joined up, with some of the members employing their skills as snipers.

The Deployment of Local Units

The Yeomanry

The 1/1st Queen's Own Oxfordshire Hussars, as part of the 2nd (South Midland) Mounted Brigade, mobilised with the 1st Cavalry Division in Reading but was transferred to the new 2nd Cavalry Division, assembling at Churn, with its HQ in Goring. It was soon detached from its new division and went to France in September 1914, the first yeomanry unit to be deployed in France and Flanders. This was at Churchill's specific behest and intended as support for his naval division attempting, unsuccessfully as it turned out, to hold the important port of Antwerp. Following this setback, it remained in France as mounted

GHQ troops, serving there for the entire war, involved in fighting small actions and taking casualties as the British cavalry spent four years waiting to exploit the promised breakthrough on the Western Front which never came. The 2/1st served in home defence cyclist brigades in East Anglia, Kent, and Ireland. The 3/1st, formed in 1915, was attached to a reserve cavalry regiment at Tidworth in Hampshire, and then at the Curragh in Dublin.

Both the first- and second-line Berkshire Yeomanry regiments spent the war in unsettled states. The 1/1st remained with the 2nd Mounted Division and went to Gallipoli as dismounted troops, then regained its horses in Egypt only to be later converted into a unit of the new Machine Gun Corps, serving in France and Italy. The 2/1st served as mounted troops at home until 1916 when it was redeployed to East Anglia on anti-invasion duties as a cyclist unit.

The Oxfordshire and Buckinghamshire Light Infantry (OBLI)

This summary includes the thirteen battalions: three regular, three TF, five New Armies, and two garrison, which originated as Oxfordshire-raised units. Given the integrated nature of the regiment, the three TF battalions raised mainly in Buckinghamshire and those TF units of the Royal Berkshire Regiment which were based in towns which, since 1974, have been rehomed into Oxfordshire, are also recorded.

The 1st Battalion, based in Ahmednagar in India, was sent to Mesopotamia and went into captivity after Kut al Amara fell to Ottoman forces in 1916 after a long siege. Only around seventy of the 400 taken prisoner survived their captivity. It was reformed in October 1917 from drafts and fought up to the final defeat of the Ottoman forces in Palestine and Syria. The 2nd Battalion left Aldershot for France in mid-August 1914 and spent the whole war on the Western Front, taking part in every major battle from Mons to the final campaigns of Autumn 1918, which saw the comprehensive defeat of the German army. The 3rd (Special Reserve) Battalion served in Portsmouth, in camp on Portsdown Hill, and then in Cambridge Barracks and Fort Widley. Later, as part of the Dover Garrison, it continued to train recruits for drafts to frontline battalions. The 1/4th Battalion (TF) along with the Buckinghamshire Battalion (TF) went to Boulogne in March 1915 staying on the Western Front until November 1917 when both were posted to Italy and Austria, taking part in the defeat of the Austro-Hungarian armies. The 2/4th Battalion (TF) and the 2/1st Buckinghamshire Battalion (TF) had arrived in France by May 1916 where they remained. The 3/4th Battalion became the 4th (Reserve) Battalion, remaining at home and serving in the Tyne Garrison, 1917–18, alongside the corresponding 3/1st Buckinghamshire Battalion (TF). Four new battalions were raised from scratch as part of Kitchener's New Armies: the 5th (Service) Battalion (K1), the 6th (Service) Battalion (K2), and the 7th (Service) Battalion (K3) all formed in Oxford and served in France and elsewhere. The 8th (Service) Battalion (Pioneers) served at Salonika, 1915–18, and fought against the Bulgarian invasion of Greece. The 9th (Reserve) Battalion and the 10th (TF Home Service) Battalion both served at home throughout, in a training and an anti-invasion capacity, respectively. The Regiment's 1st Garrison Battalion was formed at Portland in 1915 and was despatched to India whilst the 2nd Garrison Battalion became the 11th (Garrison) Battalion in France. Two members of the 2/4th Battalion won the Victoria Cross, and nearly 6,000 officers and men of the regiment lost their lives. The 1/4th Battalion, the Royal Berkshire Regiment whose 'C' Company was based in Wantage and Wallingford, and whose 'F' Company in Abingdon, served initially in France, taking part in many of the major actions, but was then sent to Italy in November 1917, finishing the war in Austria.

Artillery and Service Corps Units Raised in Oxfordshire

Four Royal Garrison Artillery (RGA) siege batteries were raised in Oxfordshire, contributing to the heavy artillery element of the New Armies, the first of which, 128 Oxfordshire Heavy Battery, had been raised by Lt-Col. Hamersley, MP for Mid-Oxfordshire. Both 128 and 132 Batteries were camped in Headington in July 1915 and were still there in February 1916, prior to 128 Battery going to France in July 1916 to man a pair of 12-inch rail-mounted howitzers, and 132 Siege Battery taking its four 6-inch howitzers to Salonika the next month. Two further siege batteries, Nos 135 and 156, were also designated as 'Oxfordshire' batteries and were deployed to France in the summer of 1916. Strangely, 135 Battery had originally been raised from coast defence units on Tyneside, but 156 Battery was raised at Exeter College and trained at Wolvercote and on Christ Church Meadows. All these four units contained local men, some of whom are recorded as having previously served with the QOOH or the OBLI, with some among those recorded as casualties. The 346 MT Company ASC was raised in June 1915 and initially assigned to the 34th Division (K5 but renumbered K4), which sailed for France in January 1916. Based at Witney from at least August 1915 until February 1916, however, the company sailed for Salonika in May 1916 to serve as the 28th Divisional Supply Column but was then repurposed as army troops, attached to GHQ for deployment as necessary. The 67th (2nd Home Counties) Division was a home service formation centred on the Windsor area in 1917 with the four MT companies of its ASC Supply Column, based in Thame.

The Home Front

While Oxfordshire was neither on the coast expecting to be shelled by German cruisers or invaded by German troops, nor among the targets under aerial attack by the Zeppelins and the heavy bombers, the changes in everyday life were apparent to all. Young men and women were recruited into the armed forces; young women worked in munitions factories or on the land; Oxford's first policewoman took up her duties in June 1917; country houses and colleges became military hospitals or centres for military training; five airfields for training RFC pilots appeared; troops came to the area on training exercises; those too old or too young to enlist, joined the VTC; POWs worked in the fields; factories, workshops and cottage industries turned their hand to making munitions for the war effort; and schoolchildren were taught to knit comforts for the soldiers at the front—balaclavas, socks, pullovers and gloves—and to forage for nuts and berries. By the war's end, the pupils of Benson Village School had collected a third of a ton of blackberries to be made into jam for the troops. Specific events such as Banbury's 'Aeroplane Week' or 'Tank Week' and Witney's War Bonds Week, were held to focus fundraising activities on particular items as a way of connecting those at home to the fighting abroad.

The Volunteer Training Corps (VTC)

As early as September 1914, Oxford's Civilian Reserve was drilling on New College cricket ground. A month later, it had become the Civilian Volunteer Corps, drilling on the Parks and marching across Port Meadow and, by the end of the month, as the Oxford Volunteer Training Corps, it was holding a field day at Shotover. Witney's VTC held its first parade in the Corn Exchange in the October. Members of the VTC would share duties such as guarding railway bridges and other vulnerable points (VP) alongside the National Reserve composed of veterans. A. D. Godley of Magdalen College, soon to be appointed as the county commandant, raised his own corps—Godley's Own—from older staff from the college and the school. It numbered Sir Walter Raleigh, former fellow and professor of English literature, and Robert Bridges, the Poet Laureate, among its more illustrious membership. In March 1915, the Oxford VTC was inspected by Lt-Col. Sir Charles Cuyler in the grounds of New College and carried out field days at Witney the next month, and at Wytham Park in June. The 2nd (Banbury) Battalion, initially based in a Banbury malthouse, was inspected at Chipping Norton in July 1915. In November 1916, Field-Marshal Sir John French, C-in-C Home Forces, inspected what was by now the Oxfordshire Volunteer Regiment (VR) in the University Parks, addressing the men and emphasizing the War Office's appreciation of their efforts. Previously the War Office had been accused of attempting to strangle the volunteer movement at birth so maybe Sir John protested too much. In January 1917, the 1st (Oxford) Battalion, Oxfordshire VR, was inspected by Colonel Calley, Southern Command's Volunteer Force (VF) staff officer, on New College cricket ground, and a year later, 'A' and 'B' Companies of the Oxfordshire VR were inspected on New College Ground, giving a demonstration of bayonet fighting and PT.

One of the tasks which VTC members performed in their free time was general labouring at the Central Ordnance Depot (COD) at Didcot. They unloaded and packed ammunition and stores from railway trucks; laid railway track; and unloaded wagons and prefabricated huts, stacking their component parts. In Banbury, assistance with the guarding of POWs was another duty. The widespread digging of practice trenches was carried out in East Oxford Recreation Ground in February 1917; in Wallingford at Kinecroft (SU604892) in 1917; as well as in Cumnor and Chipping Norton. Features on Port Meadow in Oxford indicate that elements of an entire practice camp were constructed including slots for the timber posts of huts, and latrine pits. Training for volunteers included bomb (grenade) throwing on New College Ground, shooting and signalling, with a seventeen-year-old member of the Banbury Company winning a shooting competition in September 1915. In August 1917, a combined camp and sports meeting (including tug-of-war, potato race, and bomb-throwing) took place at Eynsham Hall. In July 1918, a Special Service battalion left for three months on the coast, covering for troops frantically despatched to France to counter the German 'Michael' offensive. As well as the Oxford battalion with its HQ in New College, there was a second battalion with its HQ in Banbury's Market Place, and the 2nd Battalion, Berkshire VR, had its HQ in Wallingford Market Place. Alongside the volunteers practising their military skills was the Oxfordshire Motor Volunteer Corps consisting of private individuals, still required, even as civilians, to learn military drill and to shoot, who contributed their vehicles for conveying the wounded from railhead to hospital. The Light Squadron consisted of two- and four-seater cars and motorcycles. There were sections in Oxford, Bicester, Wheatley, and Witney, whose members received instruction in the workings of the internal combustion engine and its maintenance. They would also be available to ferry staff officers or troops in an emergency.

Banbury marketplace, the HQ of the 2nd Battalion, Oxfordshire Volunteer Regiment, 1916–18.

The National Reserve, men who had served their time in the Regular Army but remained on the army's books, were mobilised for internal security duties. The Chipping Norton Company guarded POWs, while other units in Oxford and Kidlington, operating alongside the volunteers, guarded railway bridges to ensure the safe passage of troop trains and Red Cross hospital trains, and the secure movement of munitions to the ports, notably Southampton.

Training and Labour Units in Oxfordshire

In addition to locally raised units and those passing through, other troops were also seen in the county. In July 1915, 300 troopers of the Royal Horse Guards, the Blues, with 100 horses were camped by Godstow Nunnery, practising river crossings. In January 1915, Banbury saw the arrival of the 1st Battalion, Essex Regiment, *en route* from Mauritius, and the 4th Battalion, Worcestershire Regiment, from Burma, with its HQ in the Wesleyan school in West Street, carrying out training in the area prior to despatch to the Western Front. In 1916, the 17th Battalion, King's Royal Rifle Corps (KRRC), spent time training in Banbury before going on to Wimbledon as the 112th Training Reserve Battalion. They were followed by the 23rd, 19th, and 22nd Reserve Battalions, KRRC, providing drafts for the frontline units and serving as training battalions. They were all billeted in private houses in the town and used the surrounding countryside for exercises and route marches. The 30th and 31st Battalions, Royal Fusiliers, were also both training reserve battalions. From January to September 1916, the 30th spent time in Oxford and the 31st in Abingdon, prior to joining the 24th Reserve Brigade in Edinburgh, training recruits and manning anti-invasion defences. Nationally, around 400 Labour Companies were formed for general manual duties and the county hosted six of these companies: Nos 396, 574, and 646 Companies were based in Oxford and deployed on agricultural work; No. 639 Company did general labouring in Oxford; and Nos 381 and 382 Companies were employed in the Central Ordnance Depot at Didcot handling munitions.

Cadets

Many of the nation's fourteen- to seventeen-year-olds first joined uniformed youth organisations and then the VTC in order to receive military training prior to being conscripted into the armed forces. They were also heavily involved in fund raising, with the Junior OTC at Radley raising the money for two motor ambulances which were presented to the army in December 1915. Both the TCF and the JOTC attracted large numbers of recruits, with St Edward's School in Oxford mustering 118 boys in early 1916.

Air Defence

A system of spotting the incursions of Zeppelins, hitherto confined to the London area, was extended to Oxfordshire in 1915. Police officers were tasked with reporting sightings by telephone or telegram to the Admiralty initially, and then to Horse Guards, in London. Most aerial attacks by Zeppelins originated on the east coast around the Wash area, their radio messages being intercepted by the naval 'Y' stations, and warnings would be issued. So that less time would be wasted in factories shutting down when no actual attack was imminent, the progress of the Zeppelins would be tracked by the integration of the railway companies' communications capabilities into the system, Oxford becoming the HQ of Area 44 of the Railway Warning Organisation. Bodicote was one of two AA batteries defending the munitions factory at Warkworth, just over the border in Northamptonshire but known as Banbury, along with a second battery at Overthorpe Lodge. Each battery was armed with a single 18-pounder gun, on a high angle mounting, and sleeved to fire a 13-pound shell with the larger charge allowing a greater ceiling to be reached.

Until 1916, the Admiralty was responsible for air defence with the Royal Naval Air Service manning AA guns and fighter aircraft. Despite claims by Churchill, the first lord of the Admiralty, that incoming Zeppelins would get short shrift, the aircraft available to the RNAS were incapable of reaching the necessary height and certainly not quickly enough to provide any effective defence. Despite the objections of the army's RFC, which saw only an offensive role for itself on the continent, responsibility was finally handed over to designated RFC Home Defence squadrons.

Military Aviation in the First World War

Oxford's Port Meadow was already established as a flying field by the beginning of the war and quickly became a military aerodrome in 1914, seeing a succession of training squadrons between 1916 and 1918. Although it covered an extensive area and was equipped with one large flight shed and seven canvas *Bessoneau* hangars, its further development was limited by regular flooding. An American unit arrived in July 1918, but the proposed training depot station (TDS) never materialised. The national network of TDSs was set up in 1918 for all-through pilot training and to train aircrew, especially Americans, on the new Handley Page O/400 twin-engined bombers. These would constitute Britain's response to the German Giant and Gotha bombers, which were attacking London and would underpin Trenchard's rationale for an independent air force. Each TDS was provided with six or seven 1917-pattern general service (GS) aircraft sheds with distinctive bowstring Belfast Truss roofs and a single aircraft repair shed. This configuration was actually built at Bicester, Weston-on-the-Green, and Upper Heyford. Witney, however, appears to have made do with eight canvas *Bessoneau* hangars, but the whole programme was overtaken by events and the sheds at Upper Heyford were never fully completed. All five airfields had been closed down and largely destroyed by 1920, although the dormant Bicester and Weston-on-the-Green would be reactivated by the newly reorganised RAF. A coupled pair of First World War huts, probably the station workshops (286/17), survive at Weston-on-the-Green. A national technical training school was set up by the RFC in the University Museum in Parks Road, Oxford, and in 1918, Oxford was HQ of RAF No. 2 Group (South-eastern Area). Witney survived as an industrial estate until this century but appears to have been cleared away for new development.

Although the RFC officially remained a unit of the Regular Army, its equipment needs were decidedly individual. It therefore set up its own store facilities and trained RFC officers to manage them. The Equipment Officers' School of Instruction was established in Henley-on-Thames in 1917 using hotels and public halls for billets and classrooms for its eight-week course. Staff and trainees were accommodated in the Royal Hotel, which was also the officers' mess, and the Imperial Hotel, both in Station Road. Phillis Court had opened in 1906 as a country club, remaining open throughout the war, but its garage was requisitioned by the RFC for training officers in the management of motor vehicle maintenance. Trinity Hall in Harpsden Road was used as a classroom and for the end of course examinations. From April 1918, the school became the RAF Technical Officers' School of Instruction and actual aircraft were introduced for teaching rigging and engine maintenance. The school removed to RAF Halton in Buckinghamshire in early 1919.

Weston-on-the-Green airfield: coupled huts forming the station workshops (286/17).

Witney: the guardroom of the Royal Flying Corps' airfield.

Witney: a linked pair of RFC squash courts (2078/18)—an essential element of any airfield, providing for officers' physical fitness and social recreation.

Henley-upon-Thames: the Royal Hotel was requisitioned in 1917 as the officers' mess of the Royal Flying Corps Equipment Officers' School of Instruction.

Anti-Invasion Measures

For the entire duration of the war, it was feared that a German army would invade across the North Sea and land on Britain's east coast, so each community was required to form an emergency committee that would formulate contingency plans for such an event. This involved the reception of evacuated inhabitants and livestock from threatened areas; the availability of tools and labour to assist the military; the handing over of river transport to the Thames Conservancy; the disablement of vehicles and the destruction of fuel stocks; and the requirement to keep key routes such as the main roads between Oxford, Bicester, Banbury, Henley, Wallingford, Thame, and Witney, clear for the movement of troops, supplies, and munitions. Special constables and the VTC would ensure that all those activities identified by emergency planning exercises were carried out efficiently and effectively. An evacuation route from the Essex coast leading through Hertfordshire and into Oxfordshire was physically marked along its course by arrows, painted onto buildings. It followed byways so avoiding the main roads along which troops would be travelling. Moulsford and Gatehampton bridges were amongst the six Thames crossings slated for demolition in advance of an invasion force. Some of the wives of lockkeepers who had volunteered for the forces, took over their duties. Those men who remained in post were enrolled as special constables and ordered to inspect passing river traffic, especially at night using searchlights, and working in conjunction with Conservancy inspectors in patrol launches, local police, and the military.

Oxford University in the First World War

From 1908, the HQ of the Oxford University OTC was at 8–9 Alfred Street (now Pusey Street). A Delegacy for Military Instruction had been established in 1904 to prepare students for commissions in the armed forces, and to ensure that military history figured in the university curriculum. Before the war, candidates would take their degrees, complete their military instruction, and carry out attachments to Regular Army units. By the start of the war, it was realised that this peacetime process was no longer appropriate, so the OUOTC set up a committee to process applications for commissions in the army and, by early 1915, a school of instruction for officers had been established. In 1916, this arrangement was formalised as two Officer Training Battalions (OTB), each of around 750 men: No. 4 OTB using various colleges as venues; and No. 6 OTB at Balliol and Worcester Colleges. Companies were billeted in selected colleges, so Keble College, for instance, was home to No. 4 OTB's 'F' Company and then to 'E' and 'C' Companies. The four-month-long period of training included PT, drill, turn-out, shooting, bomb throwing, and bayonet fighting, with instruction in military law and how to behave like an officer and a gentleman. Some of the graduates of the OTBs would be posted to Special Reserve units such as the 3rd Battalion, OBLI, at initially Portsmouth and then Dover, not quite the front line but exposed to enough enemy action to gain useful experience, prior to postings to front-line units. In 1916, sixty-three members of the RFC were billeted in Jesus College, and in 1917, a School of Military Aeronautics occupied Pembroke College with further RFC training in Exeter College. The 2/4th Battalion, OBLI (TF), was raised in September 1914 with an orderly room in Exeter College, officers' accommodation in New College, and billets in Brasenose College. Other lodgers in Brasenose College included the members of 135 (Oxfordshire) Battery, RGA, *en route* from Tyneside to mobilise in Bristol; 100 members of Manchester University OTC; and RFC cadets. A fourth Oxfordshire heavy battery, No. 156, was raised in Exeter College and trained in Wolvercote. In February 1917, Australian officer cadets were billeted in Magdalen College, and Lincoln College hosted more RFC cadets. Drafts for the QOOH assembled for training under canvas in Christ Church Meadows, leaving for France in February 1915, with further drafts following at regular intervals until 1916 when recruitment into the TF was curtailed. Premises of other colleges such as Wadham, Hertford, Magdalen, New, Trinity, and St John's were used for training and billeting of troops, and to provide accommodation for the proliferation of the 3rd Southern General Hospital and its numerous annexes across the university and city. The university authorities graciously allowed Wytham Woods, on the west side of the city, to be used for trench digging practice.

Munitions

Didcot, in its central location on a main railway line, as Vauxhall Barracks, became one of the Army Ordnance Corps' four principal army stores depots. It covered 600 acres (240 ha), opening in June 1915 as a reserve for Woolwich Arsenal, which, although relatively untouched, remained under constant threat of Zeppelin attack. By 1918, there were almost 2,000 soldiers handling stores in forty-five warehouses. Seven million rounds of ammunition went from Didcot to the Western Front via rail to Southampton Docks. Originally operated by the army's ordnance department, Milton and Steventon depots opened in 1916 as No. 3 Stores Depot to supply the local RFC stations with aircraft components and other stores, finishing the war as No. 3 RAF Stores Depot, south-eastern area.

Morris Cars in Cowley had developed a system of assembling cars from parts sourced externally and they were able to adapt this approach for the production of hand grenades and shell casings. In 1916, Morris was awarded a contract by the Admiralty to fabricate mechanised mine sinkers which laid mines at a specified depth, by reverse-engineering from a captured German example, producing 2,000 a week by the end of the war. The factory was connected to Cowley Station by a light railway.

Banbury National Filling Factory No. 9 at Warkworth, just over the Northamptonshire border, drew much of its labour from the local area. Soon after the commencement of production in 1916, the workforce consisted of nearly 1,000 men and 550 women. In the course of the war, a total of 4 million shells containing high explosive, shrapnel, and mustard gas was produced. The shell-filling houses and the melt houses, where the picric acid was processed, were served by tramways, and protected by earth traverses. Raw materials were delivered and finished shells were despatched by rail. A satellite site at Middleton Road, Grimsbury, was reactivated in the Second World War. Fortunately, there was only a single fatality at the factory, but many of the employees and even new-born infants displayed the yellowed skin which characterised munitions workers. Little can now be seen in terms of surviving structures, but lengths of steam heating pipe and railway sleepers have been put to good use as cattle-pens and a single timber hut may yet survive, reputedly reused as a coffin store for Humphris undertakers, in Banbury.

As well as the larger concerns, many local firms were able to do their bit: the Oxford Optical Company produced trench periscopes; in July 1915, Messrs Collins and Sons of Magdalen Street received an order for seventy wagons for the army; Witney's woollen manufacturers, fulfilling government contracts, supplied thousands of blankets to the forces. Attempts were made to maintain morale by continuing traditional and introducing new events. Messrs Minty, the furniture makers, managed to take their workforce of 250 on a works outing, and the women of Warkworth Filling Factory played a football match to raise money for Banbury's Red Cross Hospital.

Agriculture was to become as important to national survival as was industry. In March 1915, female recruits were being trained for farm labour at Reading College and a training farm near Dorchester prepared workers for agricultural work. In July 1915, a demonstration of new farming was mounted at a model farm at Kelmscott whose agricultural labourers were mainly female. The Women's National Land Service Corps, with 300 members, was formed in 1916 at Blenheim Palace, where 2,000 acres (800 ha) of parkland were ploughed up for crops. The 9th duke of Marlborough was president of this forerunner of the Women's Land Army (WLA), which began life in January 1917. In May 1918, as part of a nationwide recruitment campaign, uniformed land girls, accompanied by a steam tractor, processed through Oxford led by local worthies and the minister of agriculture, an enrolment hut being set up by the Martyrs' Memorial. The rally was attended by Princess Mary who distributed prizes, with another such event being held in Banbury the next month. The Britannia Works in Banbury continued to supply machinery to the agricultural industry, so vital to the country when food imports were being destroyed on the high seas by enemy submarines.

Military Hospitals

The 3rd Southern General Hospital RAMC, TF

This was one of a national network of hospitals which would be brought on line in the event of a war. There was a nominal establishment of RAMC (TF) personnel who would mobilise TF members from local medical facilities. It was centred on the new examination schools in Oxford's High Street, but it could spread out into as many other premises in the city as was necessary. Contemporary newspaper reports suggest that college servants, enrolled in the TF, constituted the original nucleus of the general hospital's nursing and ancillary staff. Some of the constituent medical facilities would be staffed by these TF personnel while others by Voluntary Aid Detachments (VAD) most of which were under the auspices of the Red Cross and the St John Ambulance. Initially, the official potential capacity of the 3rd Southern was 336 officers' beds and 1,210 for other ranks. The examination schools in the High Street, officially opened on 16 August 1914, provided its nucleus with 346 beds, including ninety-four for orthopaedic cases and twenty-five for 'nerve cases'—presumably shellshock, neurasthenia, or PTSD. The nearby Masonic buildings and University College's Durham Building provided a further 124 beds. On the Woodstock Road, the Radcliffe Infirmary and Somerville College together accommodated 326 beds, the majority being for officers after 1916. University College's Radcliffe Building provided 109 beds for recuperating servicemen and the Cowley Road Workhouse with 382 beds, including 110 for malaria cases, served as an extra annexe as the numbers of casualties increased. As well as meeting general needs, local hospitals

The Radcliffe Infirmary on Woodstock Road, Oxford, together with Somerville College next door, constituted core elements of the 3rd Southern General Hospital (RAMC) in the First World War.

addressed specific conditions: New College Shelter with 109 beds for TB, septic surgical cases, and cerebro-spinal fever carriers; in St Aldate's Street, the town hall held 205 beds for malaria cases; and the Walton Street Eye Hospital had twelve specialist beds. The first casualties evacuated from the front arrived on hospital trains in Oxford in October 1914 to be met by Red Cross staff. Casualties arriving on hospital trains at railway stations including Oxford and Banbury would be transported on to the appropriate medical facility by volunteers, often members of the Oxfordshire Motor Volunteer Corps, driving their own vehicles.

Other Military Hospitals

The VADs comprising female nurses and male porters/handymen staffed a wide range of small hospitals in mainly private houses, adding hundreds of beds to those of the larger hospitals and their annexes. The University of Oxford VAD hospital occupied the nurses' home on Banbury Road. The sixty-bed Red Cross Auxiliary Hospital at Tesdale House, Abingdon, opened in March 1915 and had treated over 1,000 servicemen when it closed four years later. Buildings were often improvised, and the mission hall was taken down from the rectory garden in Stanford-in-the-Vale and re-erected in Abingdon by the Red Cross. A few larger establishments were also brought into emergency use. Littlemore Lunatic Asylum became the Ashurst War Hospital with a 580-bed specialist neurological section from May 1918 for two years, reopening in 1922 as Littlemore Hospital. Some VAD hospitals such as Hill Lodge Auxiliary Hospital in Chipping Norton, would continue after the war as memorial hospitals.

Much of the medical provision was provided through individual private enterprise. In around 1916, Miss Feilden moved into a cottage in the grounds and opened her mansion, High Wall in Headington's Pullens Lane, as an officers' convalescent home staffed by VADs under her direction. The Wingfield Convalescent Home had been built in 1872 for eight patients. In 1915, Miss Feilden purchased extra land adjacent to the old house to provide two twenty-bed huts for orthopaedic cases. In 1918, she increased the land available and expanded the capacity to 100 beds, seventy-five of them in the wooden huts. The hospital was one of several in the city affiliated to the 3rd Southern General Hospital. This facility would ultimately become the Nuffield Hospital. The Pump House in Faringdon Market Place is typical of many of the private houses made available to the Red Cross as auxiliary hospitals. It had sixteen beds and had accepted its first dozen casualties, mainly local men, early in the war. It soon became obvious that its facilities were inadequate and Kitemore House, Shellingford, the home of the superintendent, was given over, caring for nearly 250 patients in the next year. The son of the founder of the Singer Sewing-machine Company donated his spacious home in Steventon as the 213-bed Milton Hill Sectional Hospital. Volunteers also organised such enterprises as the Banbury Station Troops' Refreshment Fund which allowed the Red Cross to provide a tea stall for troops on the move.

POW Camps

The popular conception of the POW camp with barbed-wire fences and high guard towers patrolled by fierce dogs is apposite for only a very few camps in the First World War. Large numbers of POWs were organised into work gangs attached to farms or to building projects. They were guarded by the veterans of the National Defence Corps or the part-timers of the VTC. Thus, many camps were temporary while a particular job was being done. German POWs, for example, were camped by the former quarry on the Wantage–Faringdon road and worked in the fields. Norman Nicol's list of First World War POW camps includes just four in Oxfordshire, but it would appear from documents held in the National Archives that there were a few more than that. These include Enstone, Hook Norton, Banbury, and Earls Lane, Deddington from Nichol's list, plus Cumnor Camp at Charlbury and Watlington POW Camp from the TNA record of reports of inspections. Neithrop Workhouse in Banbury was a sub-camp of the camp at Poundbury outside Dorchester (Dorset), the size of a small town, which acted as a clearing house for despatching POWs to upwards of 100 work camps across the country. Banbury accommodated 200 German POWs who were employed in construction. Early in 1918, there were three German escapees from Neithrop in two separate bids for freedom, but they were all soon caught. In January 1919, three months after the end of hostilities, three German POWs absconded from the Deddington camp but were swiftly recaptured by the local policeman.

6

Oxfordshire during the Interwar Years, 1919–1939

The 1919 Housing Act allowed local councils to build council houses for rental. Schemes ranged from Banbury's 361-dwelling Easington housing estate in its slum clearance programme to a few houses in Stallpits Road, Shrivenham, which complemented the eight semi-detached houses built by Lady Barrington for occupation by disabled ex-servicemen who would bring new trades to the village. A competition was run to design homes for heroes in Oxford. Plans for 109 houses on a 9-acre (3.5 ha) site off Cowley Road in Oxford, designed by a local architect, were accepted and work started in June 1920. Experimental houses built of concrete blocks were completed in Botley Road, Oxford, and at Shotover. A housing scheme was begun in Bloxham, but local newspapers were still publishing pictures of people living in old tramcars and huts and reporting an attempt to revive the building of residential barges. Dinners, church services, and receptions were held in Oxford and Wallingford, among other places, for demobilised soldiers, and most towns and villages started thinking about war memorials. The agricultural sub-committee arranged courses at farms in Headington and Eynsham to train discharged officers as farmers and training was arranged for disabled servicemen to do jobs such as repairing clocks and making jewellery. The St Aldates Workshop trained disabled men in furniture making and boot repairs and the Abingdon Road Improvement Scheme offered work opportunities to the unemployed. The YMCA opened a Red Triangle Club in Oxford, and the Church Army provided a social centre in Chipping Norton. Rotherfield Court, near Henley, was converted as a hospital for shell-shocked soldiers in 1921. During the general strike, Didcot COD was involved in providing supplies for the special constables maintaining order and the distribution of food and fuel to the populace.

Stagnation and Rearmament

The Great War had, of course, been the war to end all wars, so few had any thoughts of re-establishing, or even maintaining, military pre-eminence. In fact, the politicians decided that Germany had been so profoundly beaten that even were they to begin the process of rearmament, it would take them at least ten years to catch up. The Ten-Year Rule, therefore, became a policy which rendered defence spending unnecessary. The defence budget in 1932 stood at £102 million, one-eighth of what had been spent in 1919, but it was in that year that the threat of a resurgent Germany forced a reappraisal. The Ten-Year Rule was abolished resulting in enormously accelerated increases in defence spending.

Aviation

By 1920, the county's five RAF airfields had been closed, and that autumn, there were reports of canvas hangars rotting at Witney. Tens of thousands of aircraft had been scrapped and the necessity for an independent RAF was being questioned with its very survival hanging in the balance. Only Trenchard's successful argument for the development of an independent strategic bomber force would ensure its continued existence. Contemporaneous with this official neglect of aviation was a public enthusiasm for flight. Private flying was on the increase and the Automobile Association saw the need to set up a network of flying fields for members to land and refuel. Such landing grounds, usually no more than a flat field and a fuel tank, were established at Banbury, Wallingford, and Chilworth near Streatley.

Given Britain's recent history of its very recent French alliance, it seems strange that it was France which was perceived as a threat in the 1920s. The post-war plans for developing the RAF not only included notions of maintaining parity with France in terms of aircraft numbers, but also led to new airfields being orientated toward the south. Fighter stations would be clustered around London and bomber stations would be sited along the line of the Thames Valley. Three of these new bomber airfields would be in Oxfordshire: at Abingdon, Bicester, and Upper Heyford. All three would conform to a regular pattern with robust buildings on the technical, administrative, training, and domestic sites, all ranged around the grass flying field. Both Upper Heyford's and Bicester's wartime buildings had been swept away by 1920, so the planners started with clean slates. Upper Heyford's were built in the mid-1920s to a style which would fail to find favour with the architects of the expansion period ten years later. Bicester's replacement structures came in two phases, roughly ten years apart. The old GS 'Belfast Truss' hangars of the TDSs had been superseded by the new 'A'-type aeroplane sheds, built to a design of 1924 to accommodate the larger aircraft which were coming into service. Six of these hangars were built at Upper Heyford—four at Abingdon and two at Bicester—all of which have survived. Four more hangars were planned for Bicester, but Upper Heyford had swallowed up the budget. Upper Heyford had a small, single-storey, two-room building with a bay window, where visiting pilots would report to the officer of the watch. Besides the hangars, many other station buildings survive from the earlier period at both airfields: the guardroom, officers' mess, and HQ building, at Bicester and Upper Heyford; sergeants' mess and single-storey barrack blocks at Bicester; the powerhouse, workshops, and engine test house at Upper Heyford; and terraces of married-quarters at both. At Upper Heyford, the officers' mess, now a free school, is particularly imposing. These new airfields were designed for large numbers of aircraft: Upper Heyford had three squadrons, each of twelve aircraft, with spares making a total of fifty-four, all stored under cover and the first squadrons to operate from there in 1928 flew Handley Page Hyderabads; Bicester opened in 1928 with a complement of Hawker Horsleys and then Harts; and Abingdon opened in 1932 flying Fairey Gordons.

The RAF was subject to a number of expansion schemes through the early 1930s, with new stations being added after 1935, at Benson, Harwell, and Brize Norton. To accommodate even larger aircraft, the 'A'-type aeroplane shed was itself superseded by the 'C'-type hangar, expanded to 300 feet (92 metres) long with a clear span of 150 feet (46 metres). Four of these were built at Harwell and three at Brize Norton in brick; four at Benson in concrete; two were added at

Upper Heyford airfield: one of six 'A'-type hangars (19a/24) erected in the 1920s, all of which survive.

Upper Heyford airfield: the station guardroom (166/23).

Upper Heyford airfield: the station HQ building (1610-11/26).

Upper Heyford airfield: the officers' mess of *c.* 1925, now a free school.

Bicester airfield: one of several 'E'-type barrack-block (865/27).

Bicester airfield: the station sick quarters (106/23).

Bicester and one at Abingdon, all in brick. Brize Norton was also provided with a smaller version as an aircraft repair shed and its Aircraft Storage Unit (ASU) also received a brick version of the 'C'-type hangar. These Expansion Period airfields were all designed to plans approved by the Royal Fine Arts Commission and the Council for the Protection of Rural England under the watchful eye of Sir Edwin Lutyens. A suite of neo-Baroque building designs was drawn by an Air Ministry architect, A. Bulloch FRIBA. These elegant structures, set in rolling countryside were intended to imbue the RAF, still the new kid on the block, with instant heritage and gravitas. Bicester and Harwell were each given a 'Fort'-type watch office after 1934, but Abingdon would wait to get its 'Villa'-type watch office at the end of the decade. Bicester got a new officers' mess to a design of 1934, now (2023) in use as a care home. At Harwell, a complete suite of Bulloch's Expansion Period structures was built. Many of these buildings remain either added to those of an earlier period as at Bicester; repurposed for the needs of the army at Abingdon; still being used by the RAF at Benson and Brize Norton; sandwiched between the research facilities at Harwell; or adapted for commercial or educational uses at Upper Heyford.

These 1930s airfields were each intended to fulfil a specific function. Brize Norton opened in 1937 as a Flying Training School (FTS) flying mainly Hawker Harts and Airspeed Oxfords. The FTS shared the site with No. 6 MU which ran the ASU, holding aircraft, distant from the anticipated focus of enemy attack, prior to issue to operational squadrons. The Air Ministry experimented with several new hangar types specifically designed for aircraft storage. Brize Norton was one of four ASUs which were provided with Lamella hangars. These shared the same dimensions as the 'C'-types, but their low-profile, bow-shaped roofs, supported on a lattice of triangular cells, comprising 2 inches (5 cm) of concrete and 9 inches (23 cm) of soil and turf as camouflage. Brize Norton had six Lamellas, dispersed in pairs, of which five appear to remain. Just prior to the outbreak of war, Weston-on-the-Green was brought back into service as Brize Norton's satellite airfield. Benson was expected to provide a pool of aircraft for No. 4 Group, Bomber Command, but its grass field would prove unsuitable and other roles would ultimately be found for it. Harwell opened in 1937 with Fairey Battle bombers and Upper Heyford had worked its way up to fielding two squadrons of more modern Bristol Blenheims by 1938. In 1936, Abingdon was HQ for Nos 1 and 2 Groups, RAF Bomber Command.

Bicester airfield: one of the two 'C'-type hangars (4292/35), photographed *c.* 1990.

Bicester airfield: the 'Fort'-type watch office (1959/34), photographed *c.* 1990.

Bicester airfield: the institute and airmen's mess (8055-60/38).

Harwell airfield: the station HQ building (1723/36).

Harwell airfield: one of the 'H'-type barrack blocks (11595-7/38).

Harwell airfield: the sergeants' mess (*c.* 1939).

Harwell airfield: the station sick quarters (1963/34).

The Army in the Interwar Period

As the army was demobilised, by early 1919, the OBLI quickly reverted to its pre-war establishment of three regular and two territorial battalions. The 1st Battalion served in Russia against the Bolsheviks and both first-line battalions served in Ireland and in the army of occupation in Germany. On the outbreak of war in 1939, the 1st Battalion had been back in England for over ten years and the 2nd Battalion had spent ten years in Burma and on the North-West Frontier of India from whence it would only return in June 1940.

The static nature of trench warfare and the development of aircraft as a reconnaissance arm had signalled the end of cavalry's usefulness in warfare. Many yeomanry regiments had already fought as infantry, cyclists, or machine-gunners so the writing had been on the wall for some considerable time. Much of the regular cavalry was mechanised and the yeomanry regiments soon followed suit. Only a few of them were permitted to retain their horses as most were redesignated as either armoured troops or gunners. When the newly constituted Territorial Army (TA) reformed in 1921, an amalgamation of the QOOH and their Worcestershire neighbours resulted in the 100th (Worcestershire & Oxfordshire) Yeomanry Army Field Brigade, RA (TA) whose two Oxfordshire elements: 399 Battery and 400 (Howitzer) Battery were based respectively at Yeomanry House, Oxford, and at the QOOH Crouch Street drill hall in Banbury. Although they had lost their cavalry chargers, until mechanised transport became available, their guns would remain reliant on horsepower. Re-equipped with 2-pounder A/T guns, it became, in 1938, the 48th (South Midland) Division's anti-tank (A/T) regiment. The Munich Crisis highlighted the country's unpreparedness for war, forcing a decision to double the size of the TA, whose every unit was cloned by providing a cadre of officers and NCOs around which a duplicate unit might be raised. This expansion, fortuitously, provided the opportunity to recreate the two separate yeomanry regiments, the Oxfordshire half becoming the 63 (Oxfordshire Yeomanry) A/T Regiment RA (TA). Both the OBLI's TA battalions also created duplicate units: the 5th Battalion and the 2nd Buckinghamshire Battalion, built around cadres of reservists and serving territorials.

The aftermath of the Great War, understandably, saw a public reluctant to embrace overtly military activities. One acceptable exception was the spectacular and the OBLI took part in a Floral Festival and Searchlight/Torchlight Tattoo in August 1925. This was repeated the following August in Oxford's South Park. The territorials' annual camps would almost be phased out, but the Yeomanry's 399 Battery camped at Weymouth in 1925, and the OBLI ran camps at Bicester, Swanage, Chisledon, and Weymouth during the 1920s and early 1930s. The 100th Field Brigade, formerly the QOOH, practised shooting their 18-pounder field guns and 4.5-inch howitzers on the ranges on Salisbury Plain, performing well in inter-unit competitions, but only in the alternate years in which live ammunition was available, one must assume. The Oxford City Rifle Association was making use of the St Cross OBLI range in 1925. The government drastically cut the funds of the cadet organisations during the Depression, but the CLB had become affiliated to the KRRC in 1924. The Trinity Hall Rifle Club in Henley-upon-Thames had recommenced shooting at the end of the war and in 1938 an outdoor range was opened at Hernes Park. Use was made of whatever was available. The armoury of the former 'F' Company, No. 4 OTB, stored in a basement at Keble College, was handed over to the OUOTC with a miniature range in a bicycle shed.

Despite the curbs on spending, the CTAs managed to secure funds for some new drill halls. The Berkshire CTA acquired land in Abingdon on the north side of Abbey House grounds for a drill hall in the late 1920s, a site now occupied by a Waitrose supermarket. Bicester's drill hall had gone out of use by 1933, but a new drill hall for the QOOH was built at Easington Farm in Banbury, incorporating a Cotswold barn, in 1938. The OUOTC had moved into St Michael's Street in 1920, but by 1929 were installed in the new Yeomanry House in Oxford's Manor Road, alongside 399 Battery. In 1927, the men of Witney must have decided, at long last that their poky little 200-year-old chapel was too small, and the Corn Exchange, too inconvenient, opening a new drill hall, Langdale Hall. Ten years later, two brand-new drill halls appeared in Oxford. Slade TAC was included in the OBLI's new barracks complex for its 2nd Battalion, with an adjacent militia camp for the six-month-long training of conscripted twenty- to twenty-two-year-olds begun in early 1939. The TAC was demolished in 2008 and replaced by seventy-two houses and flats as well as nearly 400 units of student accommodation. The raising of 252 (City of Oxford) HAA Battery necessitated the construction of Elsfield Hall.

Witney: Langdale Hall was built in 1927 as a replacement drill hall for the Witney company of the Oxfordshire & Buckinghamshire Light Infantry's 4th TA Battalion.

Banbury: the new drill hall of 1938 for the Queen's Own Oxfordshire Hussars field artillery battery.

Henley-upon-Thames: the Queen Street/Friday Street drill hall still used by cadet units.

Oxford: Elsfield Hall was built in the late 1930s to house the Oxford battery of a newly raised TA anti-aircraft regiment.

Headington's Slade Park was opened around 1938 as a new barracks and TA Centre for the Oxfordshire & Buckinghamshire Light Infantry.

Air Defence

It had been decided in 1925 that the newly reformed TA should take on the responsibility for the nation's AA defences. However, given the lack of funds, little was done beyond gestures such as the OBLI 4th Battalion's training with AA Lewis guns at Cowley Barracks, mounted by the TA in October 1925. It would be a further ten years before any real effort went into equipping and training the TA for this role. In 1937, the War Office bought the Beckett Estate in Shrivenham as an AA training camp, citing the village's enjoyment of some of the clearest skies in the south of England. Barracks, now named Wellington and Marlborough Halls, were built in the park for the officer cadets of two resident AA batteries. The Berkshire RHA was converted into a HAA regiment as the 80th (Berkshire) AA Brigade, later Regiment, in October 1938 with one of its four batteries based at the newly built Elsfield Hall. This was a specialist drill hall, large enough to accommodate the 3.7-inch mobile HAA guns, sound locators, searchlights, predictive instruments, and mechanical transport of this new, and highly technical, unit. The hall is currently occupied by the Myers-Briggs Company.

The (Royal) Observer Corps

The system of employing spotters, usually special constables, in the Great War, had helped to inform a defensive response to bombing raids. What had become the London Air Defence Area (LADA) would be expanded as Air Defence Great Britain (ADGB) and the early warning element would be institutionalised as the

Observer Corps—'Royal' from 1941. This was based on volunteers co-ordinated by the RAF and generally operating in triangles of three local cells reporting to a central, regional centre that would pass information relating to the sighting of hostile aircraft to the RAF Fighter Command filter rooms. By 1935, the roll-out of aircraft spotting posts had reached Oxfordshire, where thirteen would be established by 1938. In 1935, Oxford was the HQ of No. 4 Group, within the western area, and until 1941, its centre was the GPO at 42 Pembroke Street, established as a telephone exchange in 1923, and now, with Rochester House, the Story Museum. The HQ moved into the New Bodleian Library in 1941, remaining there for the duration. ROC posts generally consisted of little more than a vantage point, either a tall building or a hilltop with extensive views. Volunteers were trained to distinguish between friendly and hostile aircraft. Enemy aircraft would be reported by telephone to HQ and some attempt would be made to indicate its height, speed, and direction. Sometimes a timber shelter would be provided with only minimal facilities, or the local volunteers might improvise their own post, some having achieved two-storey brick posts by the end of the war.

Preparations for Air-Raid Precautions (ARP)

With the New ARP Act coming into force in 1938, local authorities were forced to review or initiate their emergency planning. This included the provision of shelters; the recruitment of wardens; the evacuation of civilians or the reception of evacuees; the issue of gas masks; and basic training in firefighting and first aid. Local authorities were required to provide air-raid shelters (ARS) for 10 per cent of the local population on the assumption that at any time the vast majority would be at home, school, or work where shelter accommodation was mandatory. However, the implementation of these plans was often left until the war had actually commenced with much work on ARS beginning only in early September 1939.

Depots

One of only three RAF stores depots surviving from the Great War, RAF Milton, No. 3 MU, was designated as one of the service's seven Universal Equipment Depot (UED) depots, each staffed by sixty RAF officers and 800–900 men, and responsible for the receipt, storage, and distribution of equipment, a system established in the mid-1930s. Now Milton Park, it was opened in April 1938 at the end of the High Street necessitating the demolition of cottages. By 1940, the scale of equipment had increased so greatly that an alternative system became necessary. Within No. 3 Region, the Milton Depot would retain responsibility for aircraft parts, but ground equipment would be moved to a depot at Woodcote and clothing and barrack equipment to Wembley. Subsequently more concentrations of equipment were further dispersed and, where appropriate the canal system was used for transport. RAF Akeman Street served as a sub-site throughout Milton's existence.

The RAOC's original intention was for the Didcot COD to be only temporary, but it was made permanent in 1923, when over 160 houses were built to accommodate civilian workers, recruited from the locality, supporting military personnel housed in Vauxhall Barracks. The Didcot COD took on the functions of the Royal Army Clothing Department from its closing Pimlico depot for just three years until a new, less damp, dedicated facility was opened in 1936 outside Burton-on-Trent in Staffordshire. On the outbreak of war, it would be one of only five CODs, rapidly reorganised to cope with the expanding needs of an increasingly technology-based army. Stores, and civilian storemen, working alongside RAOC personnel, were divided into the four categories of: 'ammunition', 'MT', 'technical', or 'weapons'.

Munitions

Morris Motors produced a stopgap armoured car, the CS9, based on their 15-cwt truck, and mounting a Vickers machine gun in its turret. A total of ninety-nine were issued to cavalry regiments in 1938 and saw service in France in 1940 with the 12th Royal Lancers, and in North Africa with the 11th Hussars. The Nuffield Organisation also developed the Cruiser tank as a commercial venture having obtained examples of the Russian T3 via a US licence. The first prototype Cruiser Mk III was delivered in 1937. This model went into production in 1939 with sixty-five being built, and fought in France where most were lost, and in the Western Desert. By 1936, plans were being made for the Morris Works to become a shadow factory for the aircraft industry in the event of war breaking out.

The Air Ministry realised that unless a constant supply of fuel could reach the country's airfields, a credible defence against aerial bombing would be impossible. From 1936, Air Force Reserve Depots (AFRD) holding 4,000 tons of fuel were being planned. Additionally, intermediate Air Force Distribution Depots (AFDD), one of which was built at Islip, consisted of four or six 500-ton tanks built to supply fuel to those airfields in their localities.

7

Oxfordshire during the Second World War, 1939–1945

To avoid the situation that had existed in the Great War where territorials, to the intense annoyance and frustration of Kitchener, could opt for home service, on the outbreak of war in September 1939, the county's TA units were immediately subsumed into the Regular Army. In this war, all units—regular, territorial, or conscript—would serve wherever they were directed at home or abroad. The OBLI depot became an Infantry Training Centre (ITC) and was then joined by the Hampshire Regiment to form a Primary Training Centre. Local airfields were mainly used as flying training schools or Operational Training Units (OTU) for Bomber Command. Industry produced tanks, trucks, aircraft, and munitions. However terrifying bombing raids might have been for individuals, the county, nevertheless, was fortunate to escape their effects relatively lightly.

The Deployment of Local Units

The Yeomanry Regiments

The QOOH fought the Second World War as an A/T unit, the 63rd (Oxfordshire Yeomanry) A/T Regiment RA (TA) consisting of Nos 249–252 Batteries. The regiment spent most of the war attached to 61st Infantry Division serving in England and Ulster until November 1944 when an intervention by Churchill, the regiment's honorary colonel, achieved a deployment to the continent with 21st Army Group, lasting until May 1945. The regiment finished the war equipped with the self-propelled 17-pounder A/T gun mounted on the Crusader tank body. An earlier intervention by Churchill had proved less glorious when one battery had been detached to join the reinforcements sailing into captivity in Singapore and slave labour in Burma and Thailand. As 145 Field Regiment RA (TA), the Berkshire Yeomanry, whose 'D' Squadron had proudly demonstrated its antiquated 18-pounder field guns in Wantage marketplace, was attached to one of the brigades of the 61st Infantry Division alongside the QOOH, remaining with that formation until early 1945. The longed-for posting, to India as it happened, eventually came but too late for action as Japan surrendered, and the regiment's landing on Japanese soil was, fortunately, unopposed.

The Oxfordshire and Buckinghamshire Light Infantry (OBLI)

The 1st Battalion and both TA battalions were sent to France in September 1939 as part of the BEF. Whilst the 1st Battalion, following fighting on the River Scheldt, having suffered 300 casualties, managed to reach Dunkirk to be evacuated, the others were less fortunate. The 4th Battalion was unable to fight its way through the encircling German forces and was captured, its members spending the rest of the war in POW and labour camps, with only four men escaping this fate. The Buckinghamshire TA Battalion fared slightly better, fighting through to Dunkirk but still losing three quarters of its establishment in the process. Having been brought back to strength and, following time in Northern Ireland, the 1st Battalion joined the 53rd (Welsh) Infantry Division in 1943 and commenced its training for D-Day. Landing in Normandy on 24 June, the battalion fought through the campaign in Northwestern Europe, finishing the war in Hamburg. The 2nd Battalion was given a new role in 1941, training as airborne troops and taking part in the D-Day campaign, landing by glider, to capture and hold the vital Pegasus Bridge on the eastern edge of the landing beaches. The battalion then fought through Normandy as ground troops until evacuated in September having suffered 50 per cent casualties, only to be rushed back in response to the Ardennes offensive emergency, not returning to the UK until February 1945. The next month they were back in their gliders for the Rhine crossing operation, losing half their strength once more, but continuing the advance further into Germany. Midway into 1945, an advance party of the 2nd Battalion had been sent to India to prepare for airborne landings in Malaya but were fortunately overtaken by events with the Japanese surrender.

Following its escape from France, the reformed 4th Battalion remained in the UK training conscripts. The 6th Battalion with a nucleus of mainly regular soldiers was recruited in the summer of 1940. Following training, it was despatched to India in 1942 and fought with Slim's 14th Army in Burma. The 7th Battalion, formed in October 1940 from men awaiting assignment, went to the Middle East and fought through Tunisia, taking part in the landings in Italy at Salerno and Anzio. Reduced to sixty men from a strength of 1,000, the battalion regrouped in Egypt and then returned to the fray, fighting up through Italy until, once more greatly reduced, it supplied replacements to other units. Brigaded with the 5th Battalion, the 4th Battalion's duplicate, the 2nd Buckinghamshire Battalion (TA), following service in Portsmouth Garrison and Northern Ireland, was broken up to reinforce units involved in the D-Day landings, but which had fallen below establishment. The 50th (Holding) Battalion, OBLI, was stationed on a section of the GHQ Line in Hampshire (TNA: WO166/151) in June 1940.

As part of 80 HAA Regiment, 252 (City of Oxford) HAA Battery (not to be confused with the QOOH's 252 A/T Battery) spent the first part of the war on the south coast as part of AA Command. It then sailed for North Africa in the Torch landings; took part in the amphibious landings in Sicily and Italy with its waterproofed, mobile 3.7-inch HAA guns; and fought its way up through Italy until December 1944 when it was disbanded to reinforce other units.

The Army in Oxfordshire

In 1939, there were few regular units in the county and the OBLI battalions would soon go their different ways. The 1st Battalion, Royal Irish Fusiliers, was at Thame but would soon be deployed to France. The 4th Battalion, Cheshire Regiment, was based at Letcombe Regis in September 1939 prior to going to France as a machine-gun unit attached to GHQ. At the same time, the 53 (Worcestershire Yeomanry) A/T Regiment, RA (TA), was in Wantage with its RHQ in the town hall. Billets for NCOs and other ranks were in 'The Elms' and the Masonic Hall in Grove Street, the Alma Drill Hall, The Swan, and the King Alfred's Head public houses, while the officers were housed in the Bear Hotel. Eynsham Hall provided an initial base for the Royal Canadian Army Service Corps when it arrived in 1939–40. The RAF considered Thame Park as a possible photo-reconnaissance interpretation centre but were beaten to it by the War Office who requisitioned it as Southern Command HQ in 1941. The HQ of Southern Command is usually recorded as Wilton House near Salisbury, so references to Thame Park as such in 1941 may simply be for the HQ of Southern Command's South Midland District, which would have been moved from its 1940 premises at 6 South Parks Road, Oxford, to more expansive accommodation. Detachments of the Berkshire Yeomanry were detailed as aircraft sentries on the Ridgeway, based at Kingston Bagpuize and neighbouring villages. While the major effort to protect the country from invasion after Dunkirk lay in static defences along the coast and in the major stop lines constructed inland, the mobile forces necessary to counter enemy forces were being assembled as the GHQ Mobile Reserve. These were mainly centrally located in Northamptonshire, Hertfordshire, and Cambridgeshire, but provision was made to respond to other threats. Tanks would be carried by rail to Swindon if they were needed around Wantage and the Berkshire Downs, or to protect airfields such as Harwell. By early September 1940, a new division had been added to IV Corps' strength, and when the 31st Independent Infantry Brigade, one of whose four battalions was the 2nd OBLI, arrived in July 1940, it selected Shotover House, outside Oxford, for its HQ, with its support units accommodated in Port Meadow. The brigade's job was to man the GHQ Line and to defend airfields. Also deployed to the area was 127 Brigade from 42nd Division at Wheatley. By October, the 55th Infantry Division had joined IV Corps, deployed along the line Banbury–Charlbury–Faringdon and on into Gloucestershire through Lechlade. Northgate House in Faringdon was the HQ of the 1st Armoured Brigade's RASC Company which joined the brigade in November 1940 and then sailed for Egypt. During most of 1941, two battalions of the Royal Berkshire Regiment, the 5th and the 7th were based, respectively at Burford and Kingston Bagpuize, for training, while the 8th Battalion spent some time based in Vauxhall Barracks, Didcot. Middleton Park at Middleton Stoney became the HQ and Ordnance Service Training School of the RAOC for the duration. In 1944, an RE training unit was occupying Shotover Park, and another engineer unit stationed in the county was the Royal Marines Engineers who occupied a camp in Butts Road, Faringdon. One Nissen hut, the former camp cinema in Butts Close, survived as the 150-seat Little Theatre until 1972 when the whole camp area became the Marines Drive housing estate. During the construction of the anti-invasion defences, RE Command Centres operated in Shrivenham and Oxford.

The RAF and the USAAF in Oxfordshire, 1939–1945

Airfields and Operations

While any threat of aerial attack had appeared to come from the south, then centring the bomber bases on Abingdon (still in 1936 the HQ of two Bomber Command Groups) made some sense. Once the threat shifted to the east, however, then the RAF's primary bomber response would need to come from Yorkshire, Lincolnshire, and East Anglia. The projected Wessex bomber bases therefore shifted their focus to training. Abingdon became HQ No. 6 (Training) Group, RAF Bomber Command, and then, from May 1942, HQ No. 91 (OTU) Group. So much was happening on the training front that a satellite airfield at Stanton Harcourt was opened in 1940, initially for night flying and then for (Blind) Beam Approach Training, with a second satellite at Mount Farm added from 1941. Abingdon only gained concrete runways in 1944 but had flown its Whitleys and Ansons of No. 10 OTU throughout. Furthermore, it had established a 91 Group Air Gunners' Instructors' School; contributed to 1,000-bomber raids; flown leafletting sorties; and developed anti-submarine tactics. Bicester witnessed the unveiling of the Halifax heavy bomber in 1939, but as No. 13 OTU, it flew predominantly Blenheims, using its satellite at Weston-on-the-Green for night flying. From 1943, training activities switched to preparing the Tactical Air Forces' fighter-bombers to provide support for ground forces. The third of the pre-war putative bomber bases was Upper Heyford and training activities commenced here, too, in September 1939 as soon as its two resident squadrons had left for France. By 1941, No. 16 OTU was flying Wellingtons and Hampdens on 1,000-bomber raids; dropping leaflets; and carrying out assorted raids over France, while adding the piloting of Mosquitos to its training repertoire. On the outbreak of war, Harwell's Battles deployed to France, and soon No. 15 OTU's Wellingtons and Ansons would be focused on developing the navigational skills required for Bomber Command's night bombing campaigns. Activities included ferrying Wellingtons to West Africa via Gibraltar and participating in 1,000-bomber raids. In April 1944, Harwell's role, by now part of No. 38 (Airborne Forces) Group, changed to glider training in preparation for the Normandy landings. Crews trained on Albemarles and Stirlings: acting as Pathfinders; dropping small parties of troops to set up navigational beacons; carrying out supply drops for SOE; and towing loaded Horsa gliders on operations both on D-Day and for the ill-fated Arnhem adventure. Following other varied training activities, at the end of the war, Harwell's proximity to Oxford's science facilities prompted its transfer to the Ministry of Supply to become the centre of atomic research. Brize Norton's No. 2 SFTS carried out pilot training, including Beam Approach flying until 1942 when it became a Heavy Glider Conversion Unit for army glider pilots using Horsa gliders and Whitley tugs. Its runways were resurfaced in 1943 and flying transferred to Grove. In March 1944, Brize transferred as an operational station to No. 38 (Airborne Forces) Group and was involved in the invasion of Normandy, the Arnhem operation, and, having replaced the pilot losses over Arnhem, the Rhine crossing. Kidlington opened in 1939 as No. 6 SFTS, but soon took in No. 15 SFTS when Brize Norton was bombed. With over 100 Harvards on the site, use of the Relief Landing Ground (RLG) at Weston-on-the-Green was increased until Barford St John was opened in 1941 as a RLG for Kidlington's Airspeed Oxfords. It was upgraded as a bomber airfield in 1943 with three paved runways and reopened as a satellite of Upper Heyford, operating as No. 16 OTU flying Wellingtons until the end of 1944 when it switched to Mosquitos. Chipping Norton opened in July 1940 as a temporary home for No. 15 SFTS with its HQ in Oldner House, but soon passed to No. 6 SFTS which subsequently became No. 6 (P)AFU flying Oxfords. Grove had been intended as a spare bomber base but spent the first years of the war supporting flying training, particularly the gliders from Brize Norton. In 1943, the airfield passed to the IXth USAAF Support Command as a maintenance base for, mainly, Dakotas. Watchfield took in No. 3 ERFTS and both Nos 4 and 11 Air Observer and Navigator Schools, evacuated from the bombing of Southampton Water. It was first given over to Blind Approach Training, but then shifted its emphasis to investigating the enemy's use of intersecting navigational beams for directing bombers onto their targets, becoming the Wireless Intelligence Development Unit flying specially adapted Ansons. Further research work included calibrating blind approach beacons using Oxfords. Flying training could only be a dangerous distraction to all this highly secret and technically complex activity, so the flying schools moved out and the School of Flying Control took over. No. 3 FTS, a refugee from the Solent via Watchfield, took up residence in Shellingford from 1941, training British, Czech, and Dutch aircrew on Tiger Moths and army glider pilots from 1942. Broadwell opened at the beginning of 1944 under Transport Command charged with delivering airborne troops and supplies; carrying out shuttle services to the continent post D-Day; and retrieving wounded troops to hospital staging posts. Flying Dakotas, Broadwell's squadrons towed Horsa gliders to Normandy on 6 June; delivered an airborne battalion with all its jeeps, trailers, motorcycles, and heavy weapons to Arnhem; resupplied the isolated paratroops there; and took part in Operation Varsity, the Rhine crossing. Having served as a RLG for Shellingford during the first half of 1942, Kingston Bagpuize became a training ground for glider pilots from No. 1 GTS at Thame, over the Buckinghamshire border. Then, in January 1944, engineers of IXth USAAF laid an experimental wire mesh runway to enable fast refuelling and rearming of the fifty P-47s that would operate from there throughout the D-Day campaign, but, by the end of the year, the airfield was being operated by No. 3 MU as a depot. Akeman Street began as a SLG for Brize Norton, used by No. 2 SFTS but was later allocated to Little Rissington's No. 6 (P)AFU in Gloucestershire. Barford St John was used as a test site for Glosters' new Meteor jet fighter throughout 1943.

Although Benson began the war as a bomber OTU, its training activities were gradually replaced by photographic reconnaissance (PR) missions using sky-blue, unarmed Spitfires. This work took over completely from 1941, when the very first Mosquitos were flown. Mount Farm had been equipped with hard runways from 1940 and was therefore much in demand for heavy bomber training, but it was reclaimed for PR operations while Benson's concrete runways were being laid in 1942. In early 1943, it welcomed PR units of the VIIIth USAAF. A year later, an entire PR Group of the IXth USAAF, eventually consisting of four squadrons flying Spitfires and P-38 Lightnings, arrived at the newly opened Chalgrove to begin preparatory reconnaissance for the D-Day landings. All this PR product was processed at Nuneham Courtenay and at Medmenham House close to Henley where support was provided at Phyllis Court.

HQ No. 40 (Equipment) Group, RAF Maintenance Command, formed at Andover and moved into Caldecott House, Abingdon, at the end of 1939, where it remained for the duration. After the war, the building became a Barnardo's children's home until its demolition in 1972. The group was responsible for all equipment custody and distribution to RAF stations at home and abroad, including MT reserves and allotments. It would set up the UEDs such as RAF Milton, and after D-Day, it took over Bicester, servicing the needs of the TAFs. In 1940, the Morris Motor Works, Cowley, became the HQ of No. 43 (Repair)

Group, RAF Maintenance Command, later moving to Merton College. On the merger of the RAF Salvage and Repair Groups in 1941, their joint HQ was set up in Magdalen College.

Alongside the large Aircraft Storage Units (ASU) such as Brize Norton, there was a network of smaller Satellite Landing Grounds (SLG) for the dispersal and storage of aircraft prior to their delivery to airfields. Several of these SLGs operated in Oxfordshire: at Barton Abbey near the Heyfords (No. 28), Glympton (No. 23), Starveall Farm near Woodstock (No. 2), Slade Farm near Kirtlington (No. 1), Middle Farm near Mixbury (No. 3), and Bushy Barn near Pusey (No. 44). These were often little more than clearings in wooded areas allowing space for take-off and landing but affording cover for aircraft dispersed under the trees. Minimal buildings were provided, such as the surviving tractor shed at Barton Abbey and the Robins hangar at Starveall farm. A range of aircraft were stored, from Whitleys and Tiger Moths at Bushy Barn to Spitfires and Wellingtons at Barton Abbey. In 1944, the Royal Naval Air Station (RNAS) *Hornbill* at Culham was set up to operate as an Aircraft Receipt and Despatch Unit for the Fleet Air Arm (FAA). It comprised large numbers of FAA hangars: predominantly Pentads, Mainhills, and Fromson-Massillons, examples of which still (2022) survive on the industrial site next to the laboratories.

After 1941, the IXth USAAF took over several airfields and other properties mainly for use by its Service Command: Grove and Kingston Bagpuize were air depots; Ashdown Park and Cokethorpe were transport and aviation engineer bases; but Mount Farm and Chalgrove were both used for flying PR sorties and for processing the product.

Starveall Farm, No. 2 Satellite Landing Ground, used for the storage of aircraft prior to their issue to operational squadrons, was provided with this Robins Type 'B' hangar (2204/41).

Airfield Design in the Second World War

Contrasting with the polite elegance of the expansion period airfields, the wartime builds were utilitarian and ramshackle. Many of the new airfields had only grass runways—even the long-established Abingdon only received hard runways in 1944—but some, such as Broadwell, Barford St John, and Chalgrove, had acquired concrete or tarmac runways. Others, such as Chipping Norton and Weston-on-the-Green, made do with Sommerfield tracks laid on the grass. The US Air Force carried out trials with wire mesh at Kingston Bagpuize, used for a short while by US fighters in 1944, prior to rolling out the system in France after D-Day. All these new airfields relied for protection on the principle of dispersal. No longer would buildings be concentrated in dense groupings but would be spread out around the airfield with communal sites dispersed even further, outside the perimeter. Camouflage often consisted of simulated hedges across the flying field and at Chipping Norton, a fake road crossed one of its two runways. Accommodation at some places was initially tented but soon dozens of huts appeared: 'temporary brick' (tb) or 'half-brick'—that is single thickness walls with external buttresses; Nissen huts with curved corrugated-iron or asbestos sheeting on a brick dwarf wall; the similar but larger Romney and Iris huts; or the timber Ministry of Works hut. Agglomerations of these temporary structures nevertheless covered large areas of countryside, accommodating populations the size of small towns.

Air traffic control was provided from a watch office. Upper Heyford had one of the earliest wartime designs in brick with a timber superstructure (518/40). By contrast, the chief flying instructor's watch office at Shellingford (641/41) was a small bungalow with bay windows. A more substantial standard wartime design would appear in 1941 on two floors with a balcony facing the flying field. Edgehill (Shenington), recently spectacularly converted into a dwelling, is an example of the design allocated to bomber satellite airfields (7345/41 Type 'B') with a briefing room attached to the two-storey tower. Chipping Norton, Barford St John, and Enstone had a transitional design (13726/41) for bomber satellites and OTUs. The final version of the all-purpose watch office (12779/41, 13079/41, and 343/43) was built at Mount Farm, Stanton Harcourt, Broadwell, and Kingston Bagpuize. The watch office at Watchfield was very much a one-off design consisting of two floors, the upper one of which was semi-hexagonal fronted, with a three-level octagonal superstructure and a further lookout cabin. At Harwell, the upper part of the 1930s 'Fort'-type watch office was replaced by a new upper storey on the same footprint as the existing lower floor. This was demolished in 1990.

Hangars consisting of steel frameworks clad in corrugated-iron sheeting were designed to be put up quickly and just as equally speedily relocated. The most common was the T2, six of which were erected at Grove to be used for storing aircraft parts or as assembly shops, apart from housing aircraft. Smaller numbers

Shellingford airfield: the watch office and chief flying instructor's office (641/41) in temporary brick with two bay-windows, photographed in 1996 but since destroyed.

Edgehill airfield (now Shenington): the watch office designed for bomber satellite stations (7345/41 Type 'B'), photographed *c.* 1995.

Edgehill airfield (now Shenington): the watch office now converted into a family house by Joe Gibbs whose family has farmed the land since before the war, photographed in 2022.

Above left: Kingston Bagpuize airfield: the standard watch office (343/43) built at most airfields during the second half of the war. Another example remains at Broadwell.

Above right: Watchfield airfield: a reconstruction drawing by Mike Bardell of the one-off watch office, since destroyed.

were provided elsewhere, with two each at Broadwell and Chalgrove and singles at Barford St John, Edgehill, Enstone, Kingston Bagpuize, Stanton Harcourt, and Weston-on-the-Green. The Ministry of Aircraft Production (MAP) erected large, gabled B1 hangars for maintenance to be carried out by civilian workers, and single examples were supplied at Barford St John, Edgehill, Enstone, and Stanton Harcourt. Other hangar types included transportable Bellman hangars at Watchfield (five), Kidlington (two) Akeman Street (one), and Chipping Norton (two); a pair of American Butler hangars at Kingston Bagpuize; and pre-war, civilian flying school hangars at Kidlington. Mount Farm, as a satellite airfield, was never intended to have hangars, but intensity of use necessitated the provision of Blister hangars. These were also erected at Akeman Street, Watchfield, Enstone, Chipping Norton, Shellingford, and Weston-on-the-Green which was also provided with two canvas twelve-bay *Bessoneau* hangars. Grove also had two Robins hangars for storing aircraft parts, and Edgehill had one to conceal the experimental Meteor jet during development trials there. Of the naval hangars, the Pentad was the equivalent of the T2 but with sloping sides; the Fromson-Massillon was similar to the Blister but more substantial, and the Mainhill Type 'A' was somewhere in-between with a high curved roof. Culham, with its need to store large numbers of naval aircraft, was generously provided with eighteen Pentads, twenty-one Mainhills, and fourteen Fromsons.

Each airfield's instructional site was equipped with a collection of quite distinctive synthetic training structures. These included two-storey bombing

Enstone airfield: A T2 transportable hangar (3653/42) comprising steel sheets on a steel frame, designed to be speedily erected, dismantled, and re-erected as necessary.

Culham Royal Naval Air Station: a Pentad hangar (3304/43), designed to store Fleet Air Arm aircraft with wings folded, one of originally eighteen of this pattern on the site.

Culham Royal Naval Air Station: a Mainhill Type 'A' hangar, another FAA type.

teachers for bomb-aimers and turret trainers for air gunners; link trainers which were electro-mechanical flight simulators; and navigation trainers. Most of these structures were built of tb but some might be inserted into Nissen huts. One combined turret trainer and bomb teacher has been cleverly converted into a house at Stanton Harcourt. It has been implied that some of these training structures originated from Harwell, citing the 'Harwell Box'. This latter invention of 1940, described as a torture chamber for wireless operators, was designed to train W/T personnel in the worst possible conditions, some even reproducing the conditions which would induce airsickness. A typical W/T instruction centre would contain six Harwell Boxes.

Hangars would be dispersed around the airfield, but one would often provide a centrepiece for the technical site with its workshops; fabric, parachute, respirator, dinghy, and equipment stores; armoury and photographic shop; MT sheds; and crew locker rooms. Domestic or 'communal' sites dotted some way outside the airfield perimeter included huts for sleeping, for ablutions, and messes for eating. A separate site included the station HQ, administrative offices, and, usually, a robust operations block. The larger OTUs typically had a complement of between 2,500 and 3,000 personnel, making a significant impact on the local landscape, hostelries, and populace.

The Home Guard

There were six battalions of the Oxfordshire Home Guard, parented by the OBLI, proudly wearing its cap-badge, based on towns, with a seventh based on the university, all under the control of the South Midland District of Southern Command and mustering some 13,500 members. Additionally, there were LAA and MT units. Employers such as the GWR yards raised Home Guard units, and the de Havilland Works in Witney raised a full platoon. Until membership became compulsory, efforts were made to publicise the work of the local Home Guard and to recruit members. Banbury Fair in 1941 was given over to social events and demonstrations featuring its work. Battalions were centred on large towns but companies in rural areas would be composed of sections or platoons based in the surrounding villages. The 2nd Battalion had five companies centred on Bicester, Hethe, Deddington, Woodstock, and Kidlington. The company recruiting around Bicester itself had six platoons based in Fringford, Launton, the Heyfords, Steeple Aston, Blackthorn, and Stratton Audley.

Unit HQs were located in whatever premises were available, with those chosen in the early days often proving unsuitable as the force expanded. The 4th Battalion's initial HQ was in Church Road, Wheatley, but moved to The Swan in Tetsworth. In Bicester, the Home Guard joined the ARP control in Claremont House but moved to the Lodge at the Garth, also using the Bell Inn. In Culham,

Stanton Harcourt airfield: a turret instructional building Type 'A' and integral Air Ministry laboratory bombing teacher (937/43) now converted into a dwelling.

Shellingford airfield: fire tender shed (12563/40), together with a fuel tanker garage, the usual accompaniment to the watch office.

the hall of the Royal British Legion (RBL) was used; as were South Leigh railway station and Church Farm, West Hanney. Deddington Home Guard was recorded as requisitioning the town hall but was nevertheless charged a rent of £10 *per annum*. Home Guard lookouts were set up using such prominent viewpoints as church towers, only to be used as OPs rather than defence posts, and Faringdon Folly Tower. Training took place as locally as possible and rifle ranges were set up in such spots as Bloxham, Wheatley, Slade Camp, and Shotover Park. In Oxford, there was an assault course in Jackdaw Lane, and a grenade range in a former brickfield in Old Road. For times when larger formations could train together, more extensive areas such as the site of the former Banbury shell-filling factory served as a training ground. Three of the eleven battalions of the Berkshire Home Guard, all badged to the Royal Berkshire Regiment, were based in areas now in Oxfordshire: the 1st, 4th, and 5th Battalions in Abingdon, Pangbourne, and Wantage respectively.

Home Guard duties included carrying out patrols; guarding vulnerable points such as factories, bridges, telephone exchanges, and public utilities; manning roadblocks and monitoring traffic movements. After the disaster of Dunkirk, when invasion fever was at its height with a fear of saboteurs and the notorious but delusional Fifth Column, the Home Guard was put to ensuring internal

Bicester's Claremont House was the HQ of the local ARP and Home Guard units.

security. One way was to regulate movement and barricades were erected wherever it seemed to be a good idea. One of the local designs consisted of a tree trunk, one end of which was pivoted on a large tree stump or bollard or something similar, while a huge steel axle was fitted to the other end to which was affixed a large Oxfordshire wagon wheel. The trunk could thus be trundled across the road and jammed firmly against a wall or suchlike on the other side, closing the road. This description is taken from an article relating to the Finstock Home Guard and a photograph in Pevsner's *Oxfordshire* shows a similar contrivance operating across Burford High Street. As the expectation of invasion receded, the Home Guard took on the responsibility for manning both the hardened constructions of the Defence Lines, and much of the country's AA defences. Particularly important VPs such as the Leafield Wireless Station continued to be guarded by home guardsmen throughout the war.

With a regular army largely intact but having abandoned most of its weaponry and vehicles in France, arming the Home Guard would be a slow process. Although rifles soon began to appear, it would be necessary to improvise heavy weapons. The more cynical commentators have suggested, with benefit of hindsight, that these 'sub-artillery' pieces were intended to distract their crews from their lack of personal weapons. These new weapons included Smith Guns, designed to be towed by an Austin 7 car and firing ammunition so volatile the RAF depots segregated it from the bombs and SAA; Northover Projectors, which fired self-igniting phosphorous bombs from a drainpipe on legs; and spigot mortars, which, mounted on large concrete domed drums in brick-lined pits with ammunition lockers, fired HE or anti-personnel projectiles at an ideal range of 100 metres—very much whites of the eyes stuff. The top of a buried spigot mortar pedestal can be seen protruding through the grass in front of a loop-holed wall at Charney Bassett. Gradually, with intensive training, good leadership, and the enthusiasm and energy of youths awaiting call-up, the Home Guard grew to become a professional force, light years away from the early Dad's Army days. Just as the VTC of the Great War had attracted unlikely recruits to its ranks, the Oxford Home Guard recruited academics such as Kurt Mendelssohn of the Clarendon Laboratory.

Specialist Home Guard Units

The Upper Thames River Patrol (UTP), officially the 12th (UTP) Battalion, Berkshire Home Guard, with its HQ in Reading, patrolled the river from Lechlade to Teddington. Founded by the MP for Abingdon with the co-operation of the Thames Conservancy and the permission of the War Office, a force of up to 5,000 men, mainly watermen, and forty Wallingford women, received Home Guard training and either crewed patrol boats on the river, or provided riverbank or towpath patrols and support services. For the purposes of the UTP's patrols, the Thames was divided into five stretches: Section A from

Lechlade to Cleeve Lock at Goring was wholly in Oxfordshire, as was a large part of Section B from Goring to Sonning. Each boat was allocated a stretch of river within an area with the Abingdon area HQ at Abingdon Football Club and the Radley detachment in the college boathouse. In the event of an invasion, it would have been the UTP's responsibility to destroy locks and bridges over the Thames on the orders of the military authorities and to gather intelligence about enemy strengths and movements. Lock keepers were provided with ARS and kept a check on all river traffic from their vantage points at the river's choke points. The UTP liaised with land-based Home Guard, the field army, the ARP organisations, and the police. Their launches, generally privately owned and often crewed by their owners, as well as patrolling all day, every day, were to be available to ferry troops across the river as required. Crewmen, all with full-time day jobs, gave up a minimum of seven and a half hours per week on these duties.

The Home Guard was also responsible for manning AA defences including ZAA rocket batteries and the LAA guns protecting industrial sites (see below). The South Midland Home Guard Transport Column had its HQ in Oxford with two of its five MT Companies—Nos 2144 and 2147. Among the range of specialist appointments held by Home Guard officers—ammunition, gas, signals, and transport—was that of pigeon officer. Disappointment must have come to the reverend lieutenant who held this post in Bicester, when the post was abolished in 1944.

The Auxiliary Units

Remaining a secret for several decades after the war had finished, the auxiliary units were cells or 'patrols' of up to ten men who, in the event of an invasion, would go underground to harass the enemy by taking out couriers and sentries, disrupting transport, blowing up railway lines, and generally causing murder and mayhem. Unnoticed by the locals, they would repair to standard 'operational bases' (OB), equipped with food, arms, and explosives and generally hidden in woodland or under isolated buildings. Their life expectancy was thought to be around a fortnight and little if any consideration was ever given to the reprisals which would inevitably result from their activities. These patrols, composed of dependable types with the right skill set, ranging from Boy Scouts to septuagenarian poachers, were confined to coastal areas; those areas to which royalty, parliament, and government would be evacuated such as Worcestershire; with the odd patrol located near vital intelligence gathering sites. Oxfordshire therefore had no working patrols, but its central location in the country saw Faringdon selected as a national administrative and training centre, with Northgate House in London Street, becoming the first auxiliary units' HQ. This soon proved both too small and too public, so Coleshill House became the auxiliary units' new HQ and training base. Reporting to the post office at Highworth, the auxiliers themselves came from all over the country

Above: Faringdon: Northgate House in London Street was the first national HQ of the secret, stay-behind auxiliary units.

Left: Coleshill House: the interior of the original demonstration operational base for Auxiliers from all over the country while attending residential training courses. Pictured are some of the stalwarts of the CBA and English Heritage Defence of Britain Project which recorded twentieth-century military sites.

for training in explosives, weapons handling, unarmed combat, assassination, intelligence gathering, living off the land, and personal survival. Its outbuildings housed a small unit building radio sets for the operatives of the highly secret Special Duties Section, often those such as GPs and others with legitimate reasons for travelling the countryside, who would clandestinely report on the enemy's movements, garrisons, dumps of fuel and munitions and future plans. There was a firing range for the use of Auxiliary Units with their sniper rifles and Thompson sub-machine guns at Badbury Hill. Coleshill House was destroyed by fire in 1952, but many of the outbuildings survive along with a guardhouse, a generator building, and a demonstration OB.

Anti-Invasion Defences

From May 1940, the country had to face up to the strong possibility that there would be a German invasion. This could come from across the English Channel or the North Sea; into the Bristol Channel from Brittany; into west Wales or Merseyside via Ireland; into Scotland or the north-east coast of England from Norway; or into East Anglia from Holland. All these coastal areas were defended by coast artillery batteries, minefields, pillboxes, and beach obstacles, together forming the Coastal Crust. Some way inland, an A/T barrier, known as the Forward Defence Line or GHQ Line, was constructed using waterways stretching from the Somerset coast to the North Downs and on to the Medway, across the Thames into Essex and up through Cambridgeshire to the Nene, through Lincolnshire to the Humber, and on through Yorkshire and as far into Scotland as the Tay. Other stop lines, generally aligned along waterways or railway embankments as A/T obstacles, were built to funnel an invading force into killing zones. The purpose of these defences was to delay the invaders until the Royal Navy could sail from its northern bases to interdict reinforcement and resupply, and for the mobile reserves held in readiness in the Aldershot keep and the south and East Midlands, to confront and defeat the enemy.

The GHQ Red Line

The main GHQ Green/Blue Line, in the south of the country, ran from the coast near Weston-Super-Mare, through the Somerset Levels and along the Kennet and Avon Canal to Reading. This was supported by the GHQ Red Line, which ran along the River Thames from Lechlade to Reading. Where necessary, the river was supplemented by A/T ditches, as noted in the REs' Reconnaissance Report on the Forward Defence Line (TNA: WO/199/55), initiated in June 1940, particularly where the line diverged from the river to avoid going through Oxford. Between Abingdon and Pangbourne, the Thames again provided a perfectly viable A/T obstacle. Defences, some of them hardened, were built to strengthen this continuous A/T obstacle. These consisted of concrete, shellproof A/T gun emplacements and pillboxes for automatic weapons; fieldworks protected by barbed wire and mines; and bridges either blocked by A/T obstacles or prepared for demolition. These defences stood ready to be occupied by regular troops stationed along the line and home guardsmen in their home localities. The pillboxes and A/T gun emplacements were constructed by building contractors under the direction of RE officers, to standard designs issued by the War Office's Directorate of Fortifications & Works' relevant department (DFW3). The A/T emplacements, designed to house the standard 2-pounder A/T gun which was an adequate match for the current German armour, were sited to enfilade the A/T ditch. The exception is Radcot Bridge where the emplacement was sited to fire directly down the A4095 road which is the only possible approach across the marshy ground. Pillboxes housing infantry manning Bren guns were supplemented by earthwork section posts and a few open hexagonal pits mounting 6-pounder Hotchkiss guns salvaged from Edwardian battleships for use in First World War tanks and subsequently retained in the ordnance stores. Along the river between Lechlade and Radcot were thirteen shellproof Type 22(s) pillboxes on the riverbank, some on raised, concrete plinths to withstand flooding. Tadpole Bridge and Newbridge were both protected by pillboxes and spigot mortars with a further spigot mortar installed at Swinford Bridge, still on the Thames but to the rear of the Red Line.

The next stretch from Appleton Lower Common to Abingdon constitutes a cut-off running south of Oxford and an artificial A/T ditch was required between Fyfield and Kingston Bagpuize, part of an 8-mile-long (13-km-long) stretch which would see the line re-joining the river beyond Abingdon at Culham, where two A/T emplacements were built on the old disused bridge itself. This stretch was heavily fortified with A/T emplacements in pairs, firing along lengths of ditch meeting at obtuse angles to produce defensible re-entrants. In 1991, members of the Ridgeway Aviation and Military Research Group, with the co-operation of the farmer and with information from wartime aerial photographs, carried out an excavation of a section of the ditch fronting an A/T gun emplacement. The ditch was found to be 15 feet (4.6 metres) across and 6 feet (1.8 metres) deep, with low banks on both lips. Roads were provided with roadblocks and A/T blocks covered by pillboxes and fieldworks. The defences follow the river from Culham as far as Clifton Lock where the line cuts off the loop in the river to defend land overlooked from Wittenham Clumps, re-joining the river at Dorchester where A/T emplacements are placed at each end of Dyke Hills. The meadows at Benson are similarly protected and the stretch from Wallingford to Goring is protected by up to twenty pillboxes and A/T emplacements with particular attention given to the bridges at Moulsford, Cholsey, Shillingford, and Gatehampton. The meadows at Pangbourne, south of the river, could be flooded by sluices protected by pillboxes and A/T emplacements. From here, the Red Line ran south through the Sulham Valley, to re-combine with the Blue Line at Theale.

The GHQ Red Line represents one of the most heavily defended constructions in the country. Colin Alexander has estimated that over 25,000 tons of concrete went into the building of over 150 hardened structures along the 50 or so miles (80 km) of the line. The two most common of these were the DFW3/28a A/T emplacement for a 2-pounder A/T gun in the main chamber, usually with a side chamber for one or more Bren guns. The other common element was the DFW3/22(s), a hexagonal pillbox with five 42-inch-thick (107-cm-thick) shellproof walls and a thinner rear wall just 15 inches (38 cm) thick, saving precious concrete but dependent on enemy troops refraining from unsportingly attacking from the rear. There were five loopholes for Bren guns, and pistol loops on one or both sides of the doorway in the rear face. All these structures were built early in the building campaign and the majority were built using reusable timber shuttering with prefabricated concrete loopholes slotted in as the pour reached the appropriate height. The exceptions were shuttered either in brick or in corrugated iron. Many were built in low-lying riverside locations making it necessary to raise them up on concrete plinths. At Carmel College, a boathouse was adapted as a defence position on the riverbank. Roadblocks composed of A/T blocks, cylinders, or pimples can be seen at Lower Appleton Common; Peat Moor Lane, Marcham; New Barn Farm, Long Wittenham; and Waterloo Bridge on the A329 road. In total, between Kelmscott and Pangbourne, there were forty-two DFW3/28a and two DFW3/28 A/T emplacements; nine 6-pounder A/T gun-pits; fifty-five DFW3/22(s) pillboxes; and two concrete infantry breastworks at Radcot Bridge.

Marcham (SU453973): a standard GHQ Line emplacement for a 2-pounder anti-tank gun with a chamber for additional Bren guns (DFW3/28a).

Kelmscot (SU267991): a standard GHQ Line (Red) shellproof pillbox (DFW3/22s) built on the bank of the Thames and raised on a concrete plinth to counter seasonal flooding. It has the characteristic thin rear wall which may have economised on cement but not on safety. (*Colin Alexander*)

Long Wittenham, New Barn Farm (SU554946): a group of large, pyramidal A/T blocks straddling a road and fronting an A/T gun emplacement.

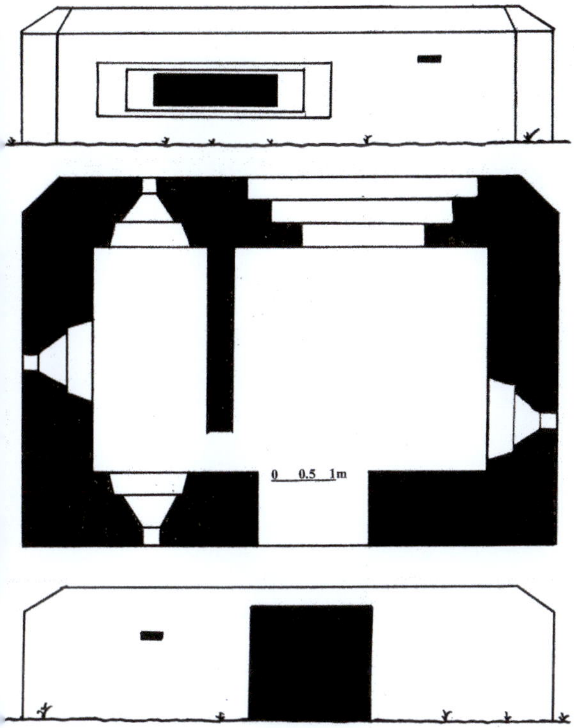

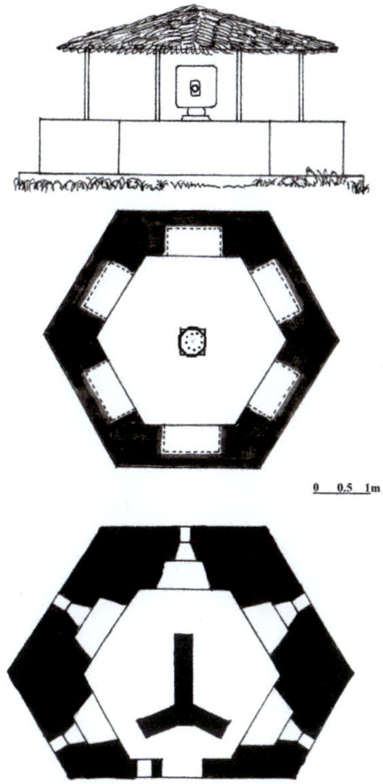

Above left: Plan and elevations of the Type DFW3/28a emplacement for a 2-pounder A/T gun (after *Alexander*).

Above right: Top: plan and elevation of an open pit for a 6-pounder Hotchkiss gun with overhead camouflage. *Bottom:* plan of a Type DFW3/22(s) pillbox for five Bren guns (after *Alexander*).

The Oxford Canal/River Cherwell Stop Line

An instruction issued by the commanding RE of Southern Command in July 1940, mentions an 'Oxford' stop line. This is almost certainly the defensive line based on the River Cherwell and the Oxford Canal, running from Gloucester Green near the centre of Oxford, north past Banbury to Hawkesbury where it joins the Coventry Canal and becomes part of the ring of defended water obstacles surrounding Birmingham's vital industrial centres. In the southern sector of this line, there appear to have been hardened defences only on crossing points. At least three pillboxes were grouped around what is now the A34/A40 crossing, and pairs of pillboxes were constructed to defend the bridges at Kidlington, Somerton, and Thrupp with singles at Enslow and Heyford, and tall A/T cylinders near Lower Heyford Station. Three of those which survive were DFW3/24 hexagonal splinter-proof pillboxes with walls 15 inches (38 cm) thick, with five loopholes for Bren guns and pistol loops flanking the doorway in the longer rear wall. At Thrupp, there was also a DFW3/26 square pillbox with four loopholes and a low doorway. Commanding the rail crossing over the River Cherwell between Kidlington and Islip (SP513133), is a DFW3/24 pillbox. It is interesting to note local differences as the Oxfordshire section, in Southern Command, employs standard War Office designs, whereas the Warwickshire section to the north of Banbury in Western Command, with one exception, used STENT prefabricated pillboxes and more robust A/T blocks.

Above: Somerton (SP495290): a standard, hexagonal, splinter-proof Type DFW3/24 pillbox, one of a pair on a road crossing of the River Cherwell/Oxford Canal stop line.

Below: Thrupp (SP482157): a standard, square, splinter-proof Type DFW3/26 pillbox covering a rail crossing of the River Cherwell/Oxford Canal stop line.

A/T Islands/Nodal Points/Centres of Resistance and Vulnerable Points (VP)

The first plans for countering invading forces between the coast and the linear defence lines, identified transport hubs. Initially named A/T Islands, next as nodal points and then as centres of resistance, their all-round defences circled the centres of the selected towns and villages and consisted of blocks on road and rail approaches, junctions, and river crossings, sometimes backed up by pillboxes or fieldworks. Such designated strongpoints in the South Midland area in August 1941, were Shellingford, Oxford, Radcot, Abingdon, Banbury, Faringdon, Bicester, Burford, and Witney. From the early days, Faringdon had been an A/T Island, defended by a company of Royal Marines in the summer of 1940. Local pillboxes were built by AE Baker & Sons: one at the foot of Folly Hill, with an accompanying roadblock; and another, now crowned with a statue, at the bottom of the hill on the A4095 Radcot road out of Faringdon; and in Coach Lane, a loophole was inserted in the wall of the former police station. Witney was defended by small 'Norcon' pillboxes—upended sewer-pipes with loopholes cut in them, and loopholed walls. Burford's bridge over the River Windrush was defended by a DFW3/22 pillbox and a moveable barrier was installed across the High Street. Bicester's redesignation as a 'Centre of Resistance' rather than an A/T Island in 1942, brought a pioneer company to help beef up the town's defences. Once the danger of invasion receded, later defence schemes redefined Didcot, Banbury, and Oxford as 'defiles' to be defended, but not permanently fortified like the former nodal points. Although the regular troops had moved on, home guardsmen were permitted to include existing fixed defences in their plans, manning pillboxes in an emergency as appropriate.

As well as these nodal points, there were dozens of Vulnerable Points (VP) which ranged from public utilities such as telephone exchanges or reservoirs to key bridges, munitions plants, or storehouses. One alternative to the pillbox was the insertion of loopholes into existing walls or buildings and many examples may be seen in the county ranging from the gable end of a stone house in Charlbury; to the parapet of a railway bridge in Bicester; to garden walls in Islip and Witney; and a police station in Faringdon. A Norcon pillbox stands at the end of the Ridings, guarding the OBLI's Slade Camp in Brasenose Wood. Steventon Depot had guard posts similar to those built to defend Royal Ordnance Factories.

Airfield Defences

The fear of invasion prompted measures to defend airfields against saboteurs and the threat of airborne landings, and this latter threat survived well into the war. To prioritise the provision of fixed defences, the Air Ministry invited Maj.-Gen. Taylor, inspector general of fortifications at the War Office, to formulate

Witney (SP362097): a Norcon pillbox, constructed from sewer pipe, one of a pair on the Cogges side of the river.

Steventon Depot (SU451921): a guard-post used for both security and fire watching.

a policy. Taylor allocated airfields to categories reflecting their vulnerability to attack and their potential contribution to defence. Inland Oxfordshire and Berkshire remained outside the high priorities of Class I, but, recognising the importance of the bomber force in countering an invasion, Abingdon, Benson, Bicester, Harwell, and Upper Heyford were all included in the next level of Class IIa, along with Mount Farm, as yet still under construction. Brize Norton, as an ASU, fell into Class IIc, while Kidlington, Akeman Street, Barford St John, Chipping Norton, Weston-on-the-Green, Watchfield, and Witney all came into Class III, the lowest category. Airfields in Class IIa would have up to twenty-four pillboxes, some facing onto the flying field and some facing away; rifle pits with overhead cover and barbed wire; three improvised armoured vehicles; and eight AA posts. Bicester, inspected in April 1941, showed an almost completed scheme of seven inward facing and thirteen outward facing pillboxes and eight rifle pits. Its garrison would have been 225 men armed with light machine guns, rifles, and initially First World War-vintage Lewis guns. RAF ground staff supplemented troops, drawn from 'Young Soldier' battalions. In 1942, the RAF regiment was formed for airfield defence and the tactic of perimeter defence was changed to one of defended localities (DL) or strongpoints at strategic points around the airfield. Another innovation was the specialist Battle HQ (BHQ) which was designed in 1941. This consisted of a square concrete cupola affording 360-degree visibility over the flying field, atop a sunken PBX, messengers' room, and office, from which the garrison commander might direct the defence of the airfield in some degree of security. Most BHQs were built to a standard design (11008/41), but at Kidlington, a different design of unknown appearance (TP3689/40), has been recorded, and the cupola of the destroyed BHQ at Benson appears in photographs to have been ten-sided. At Bicester, one of the DLs survives with two FC Construction 'mushroom' pillboxes and two covered trenches, of shallow V or W shape, and hence known as 'Seagull Trenches'. Another DL formerly consisted of a BHQ and five pillboxes. The FC construction pillbox has a domed roof carried on a central cruciform anti-ricochet wall. This cantilevered design gave a 360-degree field of fire with movable machine guns mounted on a tubular steel rail fixed to the lip of the circular wall under its overhanging canopy. One example at Bicester had an attached Stanton shelter. Other surviving defence structures include some of the eight, long, ARS, each with ten rifle loops facing the field and one in each end, which stand in front of the four hangars; one isolated pillbox; and a hexagonal loopholed shelter in front of the watch office. An apparently locally designed pillbox was employed at Harwell and Akeman Street. This is made up as a cylinder of three prefabricated curved concrete panels, six, evenly spaced, loopholes and steel doors, with a removable cupola with LMG mounting, installed by crane using its built-in lifting eyes. At Kidlington, a more conventional hexagonal, splinter-proof DFW3/24 pillbox stood until recently.

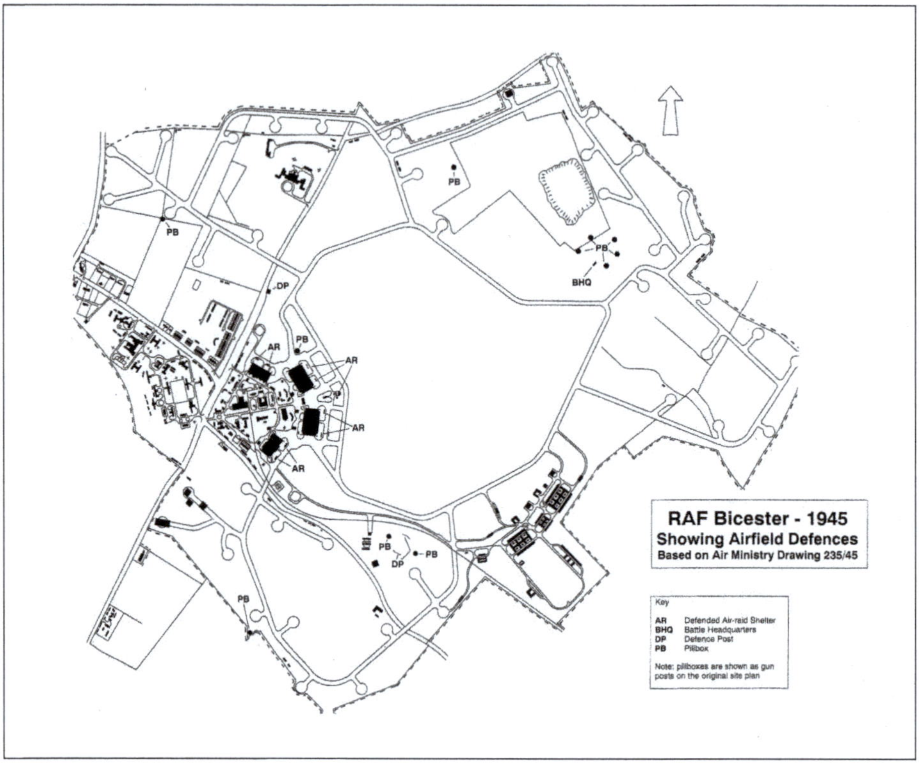

Bicester airfield: a map of the airfield's defences. (*Paul Francis* and *ARG/AiX*)

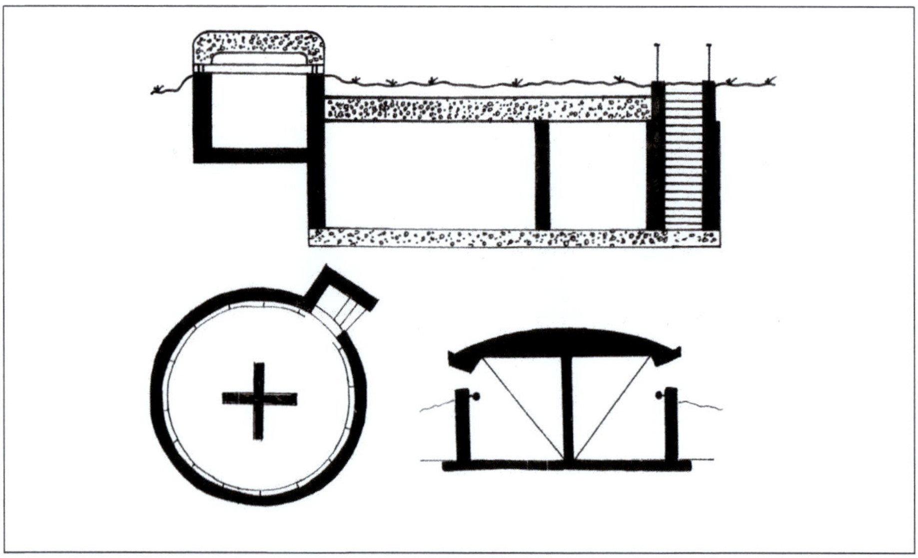

Top: section of the standard Air Ministry Battle HQ (11008/41).
Bottom: plan and elevation of the FC Construction 'Oakington' or 'mushroom' pillbox used only on airfields.

Bicester airfield (SP597239): one of a pair of FC Construction 'mushroom' pillboxes that, along with a pair of seagull trenches, formed a defended locality on the southern edge of the airfield, photographed *c.* 1990.

Bicester airfield: one of the eight loop-holed air-raid shelters, pairs of which stand in front of the four hangars, photographed *c.* 1990.

Akeman Street airfield (SP330139): a prefabricated pillbox, one of two examples there, of a local type also employed at Harwell where a further example, near the school, was only recently destroyed.

Stanton Harcourt airfield (SP415054): two of three fifty-person blast shelters, looking south-west from Halifax Way towards, to the left, surviving hutting now (2022) rehabilitated as housing.

Another structure often seen on airfields was the fifty-man open-topped blast shelter, which doubled as a defence post. Three of these, along with an earth-covered Stanton shelter, have been preserved in the midst of new housing on the green at Stanton Harcourt.

Air Defence

Anti-Aircraft Gun Sites

There were four HAA sites to defend Banbury's industry—Harwell, Astrop, Bloxham, and Wroxham—but there was no sign of them ever being armed as all four were recorded as unarmed in June 1942. There were five HAA sites scheduled for the Oxford GDA but, again, only two were recorded as being armed in June 1942. Those at Marston (SP531092) and Hinksey Hill (SP499039) were each armed with four mobile 3.7-inch HAA guns but only Marston was equipped with gun-laying radar. Adrian Armishaw has located the arcs of four gun pits at Bloxham and Marston from aerial photographs. Three AA guns were reported in the field beyond Watch Hill, protecting Slade Camp, on the eastern edge of Oxford.

Some VPs were given LAA protection as potential targets. Banbury's Aluminium Works (VP422) was initially provided with twenty Lewis guns, but this protection had been upgraded to four 40-mm Bofors LAA guns by May 1943. Airfields were given Lewis guns early in the war: eight at Bicester, Upper Heyford, and Benson; four at Brize Norton replaced by June 1941 by four platform-mounted 40-mm Bofors. A building alongside the Bicester–Buckingham road on the western perimeter of RAF Bicester has recently been identified as an ammunition store with a mounting for an LAA machine gun. Cowley with its Morris Works and the Civilian (Aircraft) Repair Unit along with other industrial targets, had eight sites armed with four platform-mounted 40-mm Bofors and twelve Lewis guns by June 1941. By 1942, the ZAA unrotated projectile launchers, or rocket batteries, had come on stream and these were crewed by the Home Guard of 19 AA Regiment, Home Guard, with its HQ in Oxford. It had four batteries under command in the region including 111 (101 Oxfordshire) Home Guard, AA Rocket Battery, established in November 1942 in Cowley and administered by the 6th (Oxford City) Battalion. Rocket batteries, known as ZAA, were equipped with clusters of 3-inch unrotated projectiles (UP), each one packing the punch of a 3.7-inch HE shell. Salvoes of up to thirty-six rockets were fired, largely intended to distract rather than destroy enemy bombers. Additionally, the Home Guard took on responsibility for the defence of industrial and infrastructure targets. There were LAA guns of various types manned by three Home Guard independent troops: Nos 308 and 309 at the GWR works in Oxford and Didcot; and No. 312 at the

Northern Aluminium Co. Ltd in Banbury under the 1st (Banbury) Battalion. Deddington's Foresters' Hall hosted an exhibition in October 1941 featuring the work of the ATS with a particular focus on driving and the operation of range-finding equipment on mixed AA sites. Nationally the ATS was seeking to recruit 200,000 women to release men for frontline service overseas.

Searchlights

Following plans laid down during the Munich Crisis, early in the war, searchlights were placed in semi-permanent sites at 3-mile (5-km) intervals forming a grid across the country. In 1939, the arrangements were implemented and 35 AA Battalion RE with its four searchlight batteries, each with twenty-four lights, moved into an area spanning parts of Oxfordshire, Berkshire, and Buckinghamshire. Battalion HQ was at Marlow with Battery HQs at Gerrards Cross, Hurley, Woodcote, and Thame, the latter two locations falling in Oxfordshire. Half of Woodcote's sites, controlled from the village hall, and half of Thame's sites lay in the county. Experience would show that this method of deployment was neither efficient nor effective and searchlights were then grouped into clusters of three. This arrangement was later refined to establish belts of searchlights placed to assist the carefully segregated fighter and AA gun zones.

Bombing Decoys (see Appendix X)

One way of deflecting hostile bombers from their intended objectives was to present them with plausible but fake alternative targets. Daylight 'K' sites were mock-ups of real airfields equipped with dummy aircraft, often constructed by technicians from film studios, moved around by a small RAF ground crew to imply lifelike activity leaving tracks and enhanced green grass areas. Night-time 'Q' sites relied entirely on lighting. From a hardened bunker, the ground crew controlled simulated landing lights and a revolving Chance light, which mimicked the movements of aircraft on the ground. Landing lights were lit as soon as approaching aircraft were heard when they were extinguished a few seconds later, giving the bombers just enough time to spot them. When the bomber offensive shifted from airfields to urban infrastructure and industrial targets, new types of decoy were developed. These would either simulate the fiery impact of enemy pathfinders on residential areas, producing phased explosions and fires, or else on the lit activities of specific targets such as railway marshalling yards (MY) with their glowing locomotive fireboxes or the apparently inadequate blackout of factories (QL). Urban decoys were known as SF (special fires) informally referred to as 'Starfish' sites, generally intended to divert bombers from residential and industrial areas.

Seven RAF airfields were provided with decoys in 1940: Bicester and Benson with 'Q/K' decoys, and the rest with 'Q' ones. Kidlington was alone in having three decoys, the general location of one of which, Enstone, would later become a real airfield. Pyrton's 'Q/K' decoy was reckoned to provide cover for both Abingdon and Benson. These airfield decoys had been mostly phased out by 1942. Other sites so protected included the Didcot COD with a 'QL/QF' decoy at Moulsford. Two decoys at Denton and Sandford shielded the Morris Works at Cowley, beginning as 'QL' sites in the 'C' (Civil) Series but later upgraded as permanent 'Starfish' sites in 1942 with Denton equipped as simulated railway sidings (MY) and Sandford as a factory (QL). Banbury's decoy site at Tadmarton originated as a 'QL/QF' site but was later lit as simulated railway sidings (MY) for the GWR marshalling yards. Possibly as a response to the Baedeker raids on other historic cities in the spring of 1942, Oxford had a temporary 'Starfish' site at Cumnor, now submerged under Farmoor Reservoir. It is clearly never possible to quantify the extent to which decoys were successful in their protective function but many decoy sites could claim to have been bombed at some time. The bomb maps produced by the Soldiers of Oxfordshire Museum at Woodstock interestingly show that although most of the county's airfields were bombed, generally in 1940, as many bombs were dropped on Brize Norton's decoy at Chimney as on the actual airfield. The airfield at Weston on the Green became the most bombed location in Oxfordshire owing to its presence beneath the return routes of German bombers, eager to release their unused bombs on any convenient target.

The Royal Observer Corps

Oxford remained the HQ of No. 4 Group throughout the war but moved its reporting centre from Pembroke Street to the New Bodleian Library from 1941–45. During 1940 and 1941, Oxfordshire's existing thirteen ROC posts were supplemented by a further half-dozen. The final new post came about through private enterprise. Lord Esher of Watlington Park set up his own post 750 feet (230 metres) up in the Chilterns in June 1940. He wrote to the Air Ministry to explain the situation: he had built a small hut; connected the telephone; and recruited fourteen men who would man the post on a rota, one night in seven, there always being two men present between 3 and 6 a.m. Lord Esher wanted his post to become official as his men were nervous about their status as possible *francs tireurs* outside the protection of the Geneva Convention. As it happened, this post covered a blind spot in ROC coverage and his lordship's enterprise was welcomed, so Watlington became an official ROC post linked to those at Stradhampton, Thame, and Princes Risborough (Buckinghamshire), all three of which dated back to 1935. Training of the ROC within the context of the entire air defence system continued throughout the war. The range of training activities started with informal local aircraft-spotting competitions and finished with full-scale exercises known as 'Bullseyes' in which bombers were flown along a course starting at Abingdon and running through to Warwickshire, bringing the spotting, co-ordination, and interception operations into play. From 1942, the reporting system was reorganised to take into account the contribution of the new ground-controlled interception (GCI) radar stations. Oxford was linked to the GCI stations at Cricklade (31G) in Wiltshire, and Easthill/Boars Croft (18G) at Dunstable in Bedfordshire. In 1943, a system for warning pilots that they were approaching high ground was developed. This was Granite, a shower of red flares, which was installed in the Shipton-under-Wychwood and Swalcliffe ROC posts.

Training the Armies

The county hosted numerous army camps, built to accommodate the large numbers of troops in training for the scattered theatres of war and, especially, for the 'Second Front'. The demand had increased dramatically with the commencement of Operation Bolero in 1942, bringing US Army units initially into Northern Ireland and South West England. Camps would often change their function over the course of the war years. Checkendon Camp (SU662845) was first a home to RAF No. 70 MU based at RAF Woodcote; next to US Army 440th AAA Battalion; then as an Italian POW camp; and, finally, as a Polish resettlement camp. As the need for camps increased, many country houses with their associated parklands were requisitioned by the War Office, with all sorts of other buildings being improvised as military establishments. The CODs at Bicester and Didcot also absorbed some US Army camps and stores depots, some of which would become POW camps after D-Day.

Checkendon camp: a British Concrete Federation hut, tested for blast-worthiness and used in a variety of settings from airfields and gun sites to POW camps.

By 1943, large-scale training exercises would be held in preparation for overseas adventures. Burford provided the focus for such an event when the 42nd Armoured Division advanced along the line of the A40 road from Gloucestershire during Operation Spartan. In earlier years, however, training was much more piecemeal. By the late 1930s, the Victorian Cowley Barracks in Oxford was proving unable to handle the number of recruits and the advances in training to which they were subjected. The Slade TA Centre had opened in 1938 with its adjacent hutted militia camp added soon after. The first intake of militia conscripts began their compulsory six months' training early in 1939 but were overtaken by events and both they and the existing TA units would be subsumed into the Regular Army on the outbreak of war. Slade Camp lay on the eastern side of Oxford between The Slade and The Ridings, an area now bisected by the A4142 Oxford Ring Road. It started as the principal recruit reception and training camp for the OBLI and soon became No. 16 ITC. After the 1942 rationalisation of infantry training, it became No. 16 Primary Training Centre for both the OBLI and the Hampshire Regiment. Traces of concrete roads and hut bases are still visible in the woodland between The Ridings and the ring road. The training ground also provided testing conditions for tanks built at the Morris Works in Cowley. The Home Guard UTP set up a bridging camp at Pangbourne, training sappers to build pontoons. The Royal Artillery camp at Nettlebed was subsequently assigned to US forces.

Several officer training facilities opened in the county. The Ordnance Service Training School ran alongside the RAOC HQ at Middleton Stoney Hall. Oriel and Pembroke Colleges housed an officers' training wing of the Intelligence Corps. Brasenose College was first requisitioned by the War Office in September 1939, for use as a liaison officers' school from October 1940 to December 1941; then a junior staff officers' school until November 1942; and then a senior officers' school until April 1944. It had also housed RAF Bomber Command's Regional (flying) Control School prior to its removal to Watchfield in December 1941. The college was subsequently assigned to the RAMC from June 1944 with residential facilities for nurses, with its cellars adapted as bomb shelters.

US Army Camps

The US Army units stationed in Oxfordshire prior to the D-Day landings were based in a variety of settings. These ranged from Trinity Hall in Henley-upon-Thames where hammocks were slung from the rafters; to tents in the grounds of Phyllis Court and Henley Football Club; to more capacious grounds as the parks at Ashdown, Kirtlington, Standlake, Middleton, and Bruern were commandeered. The whole range of the US Army's resources were represented including combat formations such as elements of US 87 and 696 Armoured Field Artillery Battalions at Banbury; the 50th Armoured Infantry Battalion at Burford; and the 157th and the 61st and 208th Engineer Combat Battalions at, respectively, Chipping Norton and Besselsleigh. Ramsden was home to the HQ 6th Armoured Division Artillery, with 128th, 212th, and 231st Armoured Field Artillery Battalions. Support services were represented by military police units; auto and ordnance maintenance companies; quartermaster truck companies; and firefighting, salvage, and repair companies.

In 1942, the Shrivenham AA training school was leased to the US Army for use as an officer candidate school, the only such school outside the USA. It operated as such for eighteen months, also training various categories of supply specialists for the SOS, with Beckett House as the officers' mess. From December 1943, the ETOUSA Civil Affairs Center was activated preparing both officers and enlisted men for operating in the armies of occupation administering post-D-Day Europe. From 1,000 candidates in each cohort, complete detachments of varying make-up were prepared for service in major cities as well as smaller urban and rural communities, in France and, in greater numbers, in Germany. Some 343 detachments in all were planned, ranging in size from forty-three personnel in the big city groups, down to ten in those assigned to remote rural areas. Training was a mixture of languages, physical conditioning, and military drill. With trainees' average age of forty, and a top age of sixty, in the context of British weather, lack of recreational facilities, spartan accommodation, and much of the six-week course being a repeat of previous training, much of this experience was not appreciated. Many believed that they were being immunised against the frustrations they would face if they ever reached the field. In the absence of any supporting organisation, the European Civil Affairs Department (ECAD) was set up with military police and medical units to operate alongside the Civil Affairs detachments, ensuring their independence from the tactical formations to which they were notionally attached. In October 1944, the ECAD HQ moved to Troyes to occupy a former Daimler-Benz automotive factory, from which its detachments dispersed to do the work for which they had been so comprehensively prepared. Some preparation for D-Day were also carried out onsite at Shrivenham using landing craft on the Beckett Lake.

The Secret War

Lying so close to the Bedford Triangle, which included Bletchley Park, it was inevitable that Oxfordshire would attract representation from those organisations operating in the field of clandestine warfare and the collection of intelligence material. RAF Bampton Castle (SP313017) was established in 1939 by Nos 2 and 81 Signals Units, Royal Signals, for high-frequency signals communications, and the BBC maintained wartime offices at Woodeaton Manor as part of its emergency decentralisation operation.

The Special Operations Executive (SOE)

Thame Park began life as SOE Special Training School (STS) 52, a holding school that trained agents for operations on the continent. The training curriculum included wireless; escape and evasion; intelligence gathering; cryptography; weapons handling; and shooting practice. Support services, often provided by FANYs, included the maintenance of radio communications. This entailed having operators on permanent standby in case a message should come through from an agent in the field. In 1941, Thame Park was transferred to the SOE Signals Directorate carrying out only wireless security training and also operating as its Signals HQ. Water Eaton Manor was another SOE Operational Holding School, STS 44. Straddling the Buckinghamshire border outside Bicester, Poundon was the receiving station for MI6 agents in Belgium, Holland, Denmark, and Algeria; a listening station; and a receiving site and training centre for the US Office of Strategic Services (OSS) Station 53c. Poundon House, with a receiver, was SOE Station 53b for W/T Signals training, with a transmitter at Goddington. Fawley Court at Henley-on-Thames was from 1940, SOE Station 41, but from December 1941, it was transferred to the Signals Directorate as a training school for wireless operators: SOE STS 54a. It carried out basic training of radio operators who then went for further training at Belhaven School, STS 54b, in Dunbar in Scotland, perfecting their technique by messaging their instructors back at Fawley Court. SOE also maintained a logistics section in Henley-on-Thames. Incidentally, The Firs, which housed the residue of MIRc (Research), evacuated from London and responsible for producing explosive devices for clandestine use, is located in Whitchurch in Buckinghamshire, not Whitchurch in Oxfordshire as is sometimes reported.

Thame Park was initially SOE Special Training School (STS) 52, a holding school training agents for operations on the continent, transferred in 1941 to the SOE Signals Directorate operating as its Signals HQ alongside wireless security training.

Intelligence Gathering and Handling

Following the bombing of Wormwood Scrubs prison, MI5's temporary evacuation refuge, along with other of the security services, it moved out of London to Blenheim Palace in 1940. Its staff were billeted in sites including Kirtlington Park and Cornbury Park, with women clerks put up in Keble College, Oxford, for the duration. Oriel College hosted SIS/MI6 training courses from 1941. The Ministry of Works and Buildings requisitioned Harris Manchester College in 1941 for the Naval Intelligence Department of the Admiralty (NID) and the Inter-Service Topographic Department (ISTD). By the end of the war, the ISTD employed over 300 personnel with a further 400 scattered across the globe. Two geologists were commissioned into the RE in 1943, soon to be joined in the ISTD, by a petroleum engineer, a soil scientist, a sedimentologist, and a mining engineer. The NID was responsible for the compilation and production of the fifty-eight volumes of Admiralty geographical handbooks. These data, and other visual materials, were stored in the New Bodleian Library, and together with the assembled technical expertise of the ISTD, were put to good use informing the planning of the D-Day operations.

In conjunction with the Oxford University Press (OUP), forty members of GC&CS staff from Bletchley Park, largely civilian women known as the 'Construction Section', were moved into Mansfield College to work on the production of codes and ciphers for mainly naval use. Alan Turing at Bletchley Park developed a way of cracking codes by differentiating between random strings of letters and actual sentences. This analysis involved punching messages onto thin cards which were then overlaid to highlight character frequency. These cards were printed in Banbury and became known as 'banburies' and the procedure as 'Banburismus'. In 2015, quantities of these cards, along with handwritten workings out, were discovered stuffed into the ceilings and walls of Hut 6, one of the code-breaking huts, at the time used by Extra Technology, the current tenant. This use of old cards was apparently an attempt to improve the insulation of the unheated hut and was as good a solution as any of destroying sensitive material as the regulations demanded. Oriel and Pembroke Colleges together accommodated the HQ and Officers' Training Wing for the Intelligence Corps at the time of its formation in 1940. A temporary regimental depot was recorded at Manchester College, prior to its move to Wentworth Woodhouse in Yorkshire.

Photographic Reconnaissance and Interpretation

The RAF's photo-reconnaissance activities began at RAF Heston in west London when private companies such as Aerofilms were taken over by the AM in 1940, and No. 1 Photographic Reconnaissance Unit (PRU) was moved to RAF Benson after their Wembley premises were bombed. As techniques became better developed and faster aircraft came into service, vast amounts of product needed rapid interpretation. Danesfield House, a large country house across the river from

Henley, was requisitioned, becoming the Photographic Interpretation Unit (PIU), RAF Medmenham. Nissen huts were put up in the grounds to accommodate the large workforce and Phyllis Court in Henley served as the WAAF officers' mess, briefly joined by the PIU Modelling Section which soon returned to Medmenham. Nuneham Park was requisitioned as the RAF School of Photographic Interpretation in 1941, moving there from Medmenham, and also serving as the unit standby in case of damage. In 1944, the PRU, by now equipped with two Spitfire and two Mosquito squadrons achieved higher status becoming RAF No. 106 (Photo Reconnaissance) Group. The Old Mansion in Ewelme also provided interpretation facilities and some accommodation for PIU staff during 1943. Fyfield Manor was the base for the Joint Photographic Intelligence Committee. Since 1942, one squadron had worked for the Army Photographic Interpretation section. Flying out of Mount Farm, it had been tasked with ensuring that all photographs of the continental coastline from Holland to the Spanish border were examined to record coastal defences as part of the planning for the Second Front. Part of Phyllis Court in Henley became a workshop for the construction of photographic mosaics and models of the D-Day beaches. Mount Farm took over Benson's workload while concrete runways were being laid in 1942. The next year, the VIIIth USAAF Reconnaissance Wing arrived to provide photographic back-up for the bombers. By late 1943, there were four squadrons forming the USAAF 7th Photograph Group (Reconnaissance). The first operational IXth USAAF unit to arrive at Chalgrove was the 30th PR Squadron flying P-38 Lightnings, gradually expanded to become the 10th PR Group and the US Photographic Laboratory.

Beam-Bending

Once it had become apparent that German bombers were using fixed radio beams emanating initially from transmitters in northern Germany, but later from France as well, British scientists found ways of fooling them. This process of radio counter measures was informally referred to in the trade as beam-bending and its operation was entrusted to RAF No. 80 (Signals) Wing. Given that the German beam caused British scientists a 'Headache', the antidote, in the form of a jammer, was codenamed 'Aspirin'. These were installed across the country, and that at Henley-on-Thames, like twelve other such installations, was set up in the town's police station. No. 80 Wing was also involved in the location of bombing decoys (see above) in order to co-ordinate deception operations. RAF units such as those at Watchfield and Upper Heyford flew the missions to determine the extent of the various beams' coverage and to monitor their use and effectiveness as well as the effect of Allied countermeasures.

T-Force

At the very end of the war, two companies of the Buckinghamshire Battalion of the OBLI were assigned to T-Force, charged with capturing German scientists, technologists, and any documentary or physical evidence relating to industrial, technological, or scientific research and development. Effectively in competition with Russian troops on a similar mission, they were centred on the Hanover/Bremen/Hamburg region and spread into the Ruhr after the cessation of hostilities. Individuals prominent in German industry and academia were brought back to Britain for interrogation to benefit British industrial and commercial concerns. A secondary task was to prevent further damage to German infrastructure.

Secret Weapons

As both a last-ditch defence and a deterrent to enemy first-use, the manufacture of chemical weapons had continued in Britain after the end of the First World War with production increased from the late 1930s into the early years of the Second World War. However, there was a new development which would largely replace this inefficient, and generally perceived as inhumane, way of waging war. By 1942, the project to develop an atomic bomb under the codename 'Tube Alloys', overseen by the government's Department of Scientific and Industrial Research, was ready to upscale its experimentation. The Clarendon Laboratory in Oxford had hosted research into a nuclear chain reaction from 1935, carried out by scientists such as Leo Szilard, a friend of Einstein. Its director, Professor Lindemann, utilising funding from ICI, recruited from Germany, particularly Jewish, experimental physicists such as Kurt Mendelssohn and Franz Simon in 1933 to bolster his rivalry with Rutherford's Cavendish Laboratory in Cambridge. Once war had broken out, Lindemann, now Churchill's scientific adviser, was committed to any work which was seen as having a contribution to the successful prosecution of the war. Projects included RADAR, underwater sound detection, and techniques for the enrichment of uranium. The Clarendon was therefore involved in the consultation which converted buildings at the chemical warfare Valley Works at Rhydymwyn in North Wales into a plant to be run by ICI for Tube Alloys. Szilard had gone to the States in 1940 to work alongside Fermi and ultimately enlist Einstein's help in convincing President Roosevelt of the importance of the work which had begun as Tube Alloys and then migrated to the USA as the Manhattan Project.

Munitions Production

Early in the war as mechanisation took over, the British Army required tens of thousands of vehicles. Morris adapted their 10-hp saloon car into the utility vehicle known as the 'Tilly'. Thousands of these were built with a pick-up load bed behind the front seats. Like Standard's Beaverette and a similar light reconnaissance vehicle built by Humber, Morris built over 2,000 of its own three-man Mk I version, which was used extensively in North Africa, Normandy, and by the RAF Regiment to guard airfields in the Azores, with a Mk II version boasting four-wheel drive. Further marques mounting a 6-pounder A/T gun, the Firefly, and the two-seater turreted Salamander were produced only as prototypes. The self-propelled C9/B consisted of a Bofors LAA gun mounted on a Quad chassis but only around 1,600 were built while over 10,000 of the basic Quad artillery tractors were used to draw the 25-pounder gun and limber. Morris also built more powerful artillery tractors for larger guns. Following on from the A13 Cruiser of 1939, its design was refined to become the Mk IV, of which over 500 were built, and the Mk V Crusader. A later Cruiser model developed and produced by Morris and tested on the Slade Camp proving ground was the Centaur, some of which were fitted out as armoured bulldozers. With a more powerful engine, this became the A24 Cromwell, only a small number of which were produced as they had already become obsolete. Only those Centaurs mounting the 95-mm howitzer went into combat, supporting the Royal Marines in Normandy in the summer of 1944. Some of those Crusader A4 tanks, fitted with a pair of Oerlikon 20-mm LAA cannons, were produced at the Cowley works. John Allen of Cowley, manufacturers of tractors, produced a prototype remote-controlled tracked vehicle called the Rabbit for penetrating enemy fortifications, but it was never used. Possibly like Churchill's trench-cutting Nellie, a smaller version of which was produced by Allens, it was designed to fight a previous, trench-bound war. According to John Bolt's memoirs, Cowley's Neptune was an amphibious carrier designed and built by Morris Motors and tested on the lake at Blenheim.

In 1939, the Morris plant at Cowley had become the HQ of the Civilian Repair Organisation, a network of hundreds of factories and workshops set up to repair military aircraft. Cowley was the HQ 43 (Repair) Group RAF Maintenance Command, and itself hosted a Civilian Repair Unit (CRU) alongside the RAF's No. 2 Salvage Unit which would become RAF No. 50 MU, transporting damaged aircraft and parts to the CRU, and collecting non-repairable parts and scrap for recycling. A manager appointed by Lord Nuffield ran the parallel CRU in Burtonwood (Lancashire) staffed by RAF personnel but to be transferred to the USAAF in June 1942 as No. 1 Base Air Depot performing a similar role for the US VIIIth and IXth Air Forces as did Cowley for the RAF. Queen Mary transporters delivered whole aircraft bodies for repair or aircraft parts for reclamation since the Cowley complex also included one of the two Metal and Produce Recovery Units. This covered 100 acres (40 ha), and returned thousands of tons of aluminium, rubber, and steel to the aircraft factories. Many of them women, the Morris workforce topped 10,000 by the end of the war. Responsible for the MU, the HQ of RAF No. 43 (Salvage) Group merged with the Repair Group and moved from the Morris Works to Magdalen College. Meanwhile, the Ministry of Aircraft Production, under whose control the CRO operated, moved into Merton College with some departments going to Banbury. Morris Motors also became sub-contractors for de Havilland's in 1940, producing Tiger Moth biplane trainers, 3,500 of which had been made by the end of the war. The CRU carried out repairs on Hurricanes, Spitfires, Miles Masters, and Tiger Moths. A record of British war production published by *The Times* in 1945 claims that 75,000 aircraft benefited from the CRO's efforts. Many of these aircraft used the new airfield, adjacent to the Morris Works, whence a branch of the Air Transport Auxiliary (ATA) whose, mainly women, pilots delivered repaired aircraft to operational airfields. Morris Radiators in North Oxford built specialist cooling systems for both fighter and bomber aircraft. For the Admiralty, the Cowley factory again included a Mine Sinker manufacturing facility and, in 1944, a torpedo shop. A satellite site of the Banbury first world war shell-filling factory at Middleton Road, Grimsbury, was reactivated and in 2012, developers unearthed a clutch of A/T self-igniting phosphorous (SIP) grenades.

Witney airfield, by 1930 a civilian flying club, was requisitioned by the Air Ministry in September 1939. The AM's regulations prevented civil aircraft from flying into the country's eastern airspace which contained de Havilland's Hatfield base. This meant that an alternative facility would need to be provided elsewhere for maintenance and repair work. As well as working on their own aircraft, de Havilland's Witney works carried out maintenance and repairs on several marques of military aircraft including over 1,000 Hurricanes and Spitfires as well as Mosquitos. Significant complexes such as Cowley were supplemented by shadow factories such as Dandridge's Mill in East Hanney making Mosquito parts and a plant in nearby Tubney Woods making Bofors LAA gun barrels. The Abingdon MG factory manufactured aircraft components. Underground factories in chalk quarries at Park Place and Warren Row, outside Henley-on-Thames, mainly comprising straight lengths of tunnel, were adapted for the manufacture of aircraft components, notably propellers. The Northern Aluminium Company (later ALCAN) had built a sheet rolling plant in Banbury in 1931 and this was expanded to meet the increasing demands of the aircraft industry. At its peak, it employed 4,000 men and women, and processed reclaimed material from crashed aircraft, sourced from the recycling facility at Adderbury, south of the town. Even small industrial concerns were brought into the munitions effort and a factory in Botley made wooden training rifles and clay pigeons as targets. In the eternal quest for raw materials, there was an Army Salvage Depot in the Abbey Gardens, Abingdon, in 1940. Cottage industries were established to disperse manufacturing away from centres of population. Women in Kingston Blount were employed as outworkers to produce radio location components for Belling & Lee, the manufacturers of electrical connections and interference suppressors based in north London.

Witney: part of the de Havilland aircraft works where RAF fighters as well as their own civil and military aircraft were repaired.

Depots

By the mid-1930s, it was becoming apparent that rearmament would require more depots than the five then in use if a large army was to be equipped and maintained. Graven Hill and Arncott Hill, south-east of Bicester, were chosen as the site for one of several new Central Ordnance Depots (COD), supplementing the few established depots such as Didcot. The area was served by 32 miles (51 km) of roads and was close to the railway links which would ultimately feed the COD's 40 miles (64 km) of track; there was natural camouflage, and the hills would provide protection against low flying aircraft; there was a civilian labour force nearby; and only unproductive land would be used. Work started on the six sites early in 1941. The depot was staffed by No. 4 Section, RAOC, and RAF No. 3 MU who would eventually be responsible for supervising an ATS detachment and 24,000 civilian personnel. The two depot areas together covered 12.5 square miles (32 square km) and included hangarage affording 7 million square feet (670,000 square metres) and additionally, 5 million square feet (480,000 square metres) of open storage. The principal elements on the site were A, B, C, and F Sites at Arncott and D and E Sites at Graven Hill. The depot held small arms, MT spares, armament stores, RE stores, and signals equipment, and it opened for business with its first issue of stores in August 1942. The RAOC also had an ammunition depot at Watlington, near the railway station, remembered for the Canberra bomber which once stood outside much later on. The site subsequently became an antiques centre but is now (2022) being redeveloped for housing with what appears to be the original caretaker's bungalow standing at the Station Road crossroads. The expanding Didcot COD, overseen by No. 4 Section RAOC, and with its own rail network, would eventually see a workforce of 3,000 soldiers and 4,000 civilians, taking in the output of the munitions factories and issuing it to units preparing for action at home or abroad. The RASC maintained Command Supply Depots at Shrivenham and Eynsham.

To keep operational airfields supplied with bombs and SAA, the Air Ministry established a network of Air Ammunition Parks, subsequently supplemented by Forward Ammunition Depots (FAD). Eynsham (not to be confused with the similar USAAF park at Earsham in Norfolk) opened as a FAD in June 1940 and was run by No. 96 MU supplying the OTUs in the south Midlands. FADs had separate storage areas for high explosives, incendiaries, chemical weapons, and pyrotechnics as well as specialist handling facilities and all the normal domestic and administrative offices of an RAF camp. Initially designed to hold 1,000 tons of HE bombs, this was quickly increased tenfold, rendering the original site safety margins meaningless. Eynsham FAD was provided with two four-cell HE groups plus three incendiary magazines, but these storage spaces would often be over-stocked. In 1943, No. 96 MU was one of those units equipped with a Kentford plant enabling the manufacture of supplies of oxygen to be issued to airfields. Facilities for filling large quantities of smoke bombs for issue to

Bicester Central Ordnance Depot: a guardroom on one of the many dispersed sites.

Eynsham: huts remaining (2022) from this RAF forward ammunition depot.

Steventon Depot: one of the dozens of Romney huts with an air-raid shelter alongside.

OTUs were also added at Eynsham. The depot was linked to the GWR line from Witney to Yarnton by a dedicated siding which ran from the railway station on the south of the town. By the approach of the D-Day operations, such was the pressure on storage facilities that munitions were stacked alongside back-roads, sometimes covered by corrugated iron Anderson-type shelters, or even left open to the elements, presenting an enormous temptation to adventurous young lads. RAF Milton, No. 3 MU, UED, continued in use with its satellite depot at Steventon.

From early 1942, the US Army and USAAF also established their own network of service of supply (SOS) depots with its HQ in Cheltenham (Gloucestershire). Kingham (O-670), with a capacity of 25 kilotons, by early 1943 was the largest of the US Army's ordnance depots. Although initially commissioned as a ground force ammunition store, it would become a composite depot storing both bombs and SAA for the air forces with an outstation at Wantage (O-670 & 677). Ordnance Ammunition Battalions were based at Clanfield and in a hutted camp at Faringdon House with other ordnance companies scattered across the county.

Infrastructure: Oil and Railways

As well as bombs and ammunition, the AM also had to ensure that fuel reached the airfields. It therefore established a network of fuel depots that, from 1941, would all connect into a ring-main which ran from Avonmouth to Stanlow, across the Pennines to Misterton, and down to Sandy (Bedfordshire) and Aldermaston (Berkshire) and thence back to Avonmouth. A spur off the Sandy to Aldermaston line led to the Islip Air Force Distribution Depot (AFDD) supplying fuel to Fairford and Southrop, both in Gloucestershire, by rail tankers. This depot with its four tanks can be seen to the north of Islip railway station. The National Benzole Company commandeered Stonor Park as the centre for coordinating the requisitioning of petrol and oil. The brand leader in the 1930s, National Benzole would eventually be absorbed into BP. An icehouse in the grounds, consisting of 25 yards of passages, was adapted as an ARS for employees in the event of a bombing raid on any neighbouring military targets.

Britain's total dependency on the railways for moving personnel and freight is underlined by the hundreds of sidings and depots listed by the relevant ministries as additional to the main rail network. A new Bicester Military Railway opened in 1940 to serve the vast ordnance depot with new stations at Piddington, Ambrosden, and Arncott. Its 40 miles (64 km) of track covered 12.5 square miles (32 square km) and was connected to the LMS Oxford–Cambridge line. A further line with sidings was laid in Oxford's Pool Meadow between Wolvercote Siding and Kennington Junction, while a freight-only spur served Wantage. To facilitate the movement of supplies to military sites, extra sidings had been installed by 1942 at RAF stations including Abingdon, Benson, Upper

Heyford, Weston-on-the-Green, Brize Norton, Barford St John, Shellingford, Chipping Norton, Harwell, Kidlington, and Grove. Sidings were extended to the Islip AFDD; the Ministry of Works Cold Storage Depot on Old Grimsbury Road, Banbury; the ordnance depot at Banbury's Telavox Works; the Milton RAF Depot; and the Morris Works in Cowley. Banbury was one of four control points directing troop trains to dispersed destinations during the Dunkirk evacuation and the town's marshalling yards would subsequently be expanded to allow more flexibility in rerouting. From early 1942, locomotives acquired from the USA were allocated to GWR sheds at Oxford, Didcot, and Banbury. In preparation for the planned D-Day landings, the Didcot to Southampton line was closed for six months from August 1942 for doubling the line in places and for extra loops to be added on this important north–south line linking the depot and the military port. Operation Spartan was an exercise held in 1943, co-ordinated from a control office in Oxford, which saw thousands of troops and their equipment moved across the region in over 200 special trains. Especially after D-Day, hospital trains brought casualties to Oxford and US wounded to Shrivenham for distribution to American hospitals, and Oxford was one of three reception centres for the processing of liberated Allied POWs, brought into Liverpool in February 1945.

Agriculture

The WLA picked up where they had left off in the Great War being reformed in 1939. Timber Corps members, the 'lumberjills' were recruited in Nottinghamshire and brought down to West Hanney from whence they were trucked out daily to the woods around Watchfield and Shrivenham to cut pit-props. Some Land Girls stayed in small numbers on individual farms but in other places, hostels were set up for larger groups. The Manor House at Shrivenham and Sir Stafford Cripps' house near Faringdon were both WLA Hostels.

ARP and Civil Defence

Many explanations, often repeated in memoirs and some of them wilder than others, have been offered for why the historic centre of Oxford was never bombed, but no evidence supports any of them. One might have expected Oxford to be a prime target in the Baedeker raids on heritage cities of 1942, but it escaped. Nevertheless, the county as a whole received a total of almost 4,000 bombs, killing twenty people and causing damage to buildings and infrastructure. In October 1940, a raid on Banbury caused severe damage to the gas works and railway goods yards and resulted in the deaths of six railwaymen when their mess room received a direct hit. Witney was bombed in November 1940 when extensive damage to buildings was recorded. Although there were legitimate targets in the county—airfields, depots, and munitions plants—compared to other parts of the country, the attentions of the *Luftwaffe* were only cursory. Given the fact that Oxford city had become an evacuation centre with official and unofficial evacuees causing a significant increase in the population, this was a source of relief.

Evacuation

London's medical students were moved into colleges along with government departments, and child evacuees were received elsewhere in the county including Bicester. The population of the Wantage area was prepared to see a 50 per cent increase but in the event, it was only 15 per cent. Radley College, already inflated by the arrival of Colet Court from London, then took in Eastbourne College, requisitioned by the Admiralty, with some boys going temporarily to Nuneham Courtenay. King's College and Westfield College from London University moved to St Peter's College, Oxford. Staff were involved in running courses for naval officers, and students contributed to the ARP effort. Government departments evacuated to Oxford were able to tap into the expertise and knowledge of local academics whether it be in physics, psychology, nutrition, or agriculture. They also turned to refugees, once they had managed to conquer the red tape and get them released from internment. As part of the Air Ministry's Plan Yellow to decentralise its London offices, 140 staff from the Planning, Production and Research Department of the Ministry of Aircraft Production (MAP) were evacuated to Oxford and 220 more to Banbury. The Ministry of Food was evacuated to St John's College and then to the Clarendon Hotel in Cornmarket. When MI5 went to Blenheim Palace, it displaced Malvern College which had been invited there by the duke of Marlborough after its Worcestershire buildings had been requisitioned by the Admiralty.

Air-Raid Precautions

Late in 1939, the Oxford Extra-Mural Unit of the Ministry of Home Security (OEMU) was set up when the ministry's Research and Experiments Department, under the overall direction of Solly Zuckerman, commissioned the university's Department of Human Anatomy to research the effects of ground shock waves and blast on human physiology. The results of these experiments informed the design of ARS. Working for the Ministry of Home Security from his home at Hill House, Kingston Blount, and coming at the problem from a different angle and with a totally opposite motivation, Jacob Bronowski used his expertise in statistics to plan for maximum damage to German and Japanese infrastructure and civilian populations, by predicting the effectiveness of varied carpet-bombing patterns.

In the early expectation of being subjected to aerial bombing, precautions had been taken to protect the population. Under the direction of the Civil Defence

Co-ordination No. 10 Region with its HQ in Reading, County ARP, Emergency Civil Defence and Invasion committees were set up and most towns mirrored these structures. In September 1939, conforming to government guidance, ARP training exercises were commenced, and the construction of air-raid shelters (ARS) was started in Oxford. Recent excavations suggest that these shelters were of the covered trench variety, provided to shelter those caught out in the open during air raids or else sited in school playgrounds. Households received either the outdoor Anderson Shelters or the metal cage Morrison Shelters for use indoors. In 1941, the Oxford Volunteer Fire Brigade took to the river with a fire boat and that same year the Oxford Fire Fighters and Watchers group was set up as a business initiative to protect properties from, specifically, incendiary bombs, and to limit disruption from spurious or premature air-raid warnings. Bicester's ARP HQ was set up in Claremont House in London Road and the emergency services recruited and trained personnel, many of them unpaid volunteers. As happened in many other villages, East Hanney's parish council minutes for September 1940 detail the measures to be taken for ARP procedures and the treatment of casualties. The ARP in Deddington used a set of models of buildings to prepare local volunteers for tackling fires or bomb damage. Cornwell village hall, a former school, retains its belfry/air-raid siren.

Medical Provision in the Second World War

Military Hospitals

As had been the case in the Great War, Oxfordshire played host to a variety of medical facilities. Opened in snowy January 1942, amid a flurry of VIPs, Oxford's Churchill Hospital was a 600-bed Emergency Medical Service (EMS) facility housed in hutted accommodation. It had been the intention prior to America's entry into the war that, part-funded with American money, it would be run as a joint US/UK operation; would involve integration of the two nations' medical staff; and would benefit from close cooperation with the city's medical research community. However, once America had joined the war, and Operation Bolero was bringing large numbers of US troops to Britain and Northern Ireland, the US authorities realised that, very soon, demand for dedicated military hospitals would grow. Given the established US presence at the Churchill, Oxford was selected as one of four centres in the US Southern Base Section of its military hospital provision. By July, agreement had been reached for the staff of a 500-bed General Hospital to be sent over from the USA to complement the existing American and British personnel. Instead, the 1,000-strong 2nd US General Hospital arrived, effectively squeezing out the resident staff and requiring an expansion of the accommodation. In May 1944, in preparation for D-Day, the 2nd General Hospital moved out and the 91st took its place. As use increased, the Nissen huts were supplemented by tents. The 91st catered for the everyday medical needs of the VIIIth USAAF HQ, 'Pinetree', at High Wycombe and the USAAF base at Mount Farm as well as battle casualties from France. The Churchill admitted officers needing long-term or specialized care from the 1st General Hospital at North Mimms (Hertfordshire) via the 16th Station Hospital which organised the three-hour trip by ambulance.

The RAMC's hospitals operated at home and abroad. The 16th British General Hospital left Oxford for Boulogne in January 1940 returning in the June. It then served in the Middle East until December 1946. The 26th British General Hospital stayed in Oxford for the first seven months of 1940 prior to overseas service in the Middle East, and the 35th British General Hospital spent from April to June in Oxford and was then despatched to Iraq, Sri Lanka, and Singapore. The 65th British General Hospital formed in Oxford between October 1941 and June 1942 prior to deployment to Palestine and Iraq, serving in Sicily and Naples prior to its disbandment in June 1946. The 107th British General Hospital was raised at Oxford in June 1943, went to Normandy in August 1944, and then to Bangalore where, a year later, it was disbanded in March 1946. Headington Hill Hall housed a military hospital for the duration, and then a rehabilitation centre run by the Red Cross and St John Ambulance until 1953. The building was then taken over by Oxford City Council until 1958 and leased to Robert Maxwell, then running Pergamon Press, who described it as the 'best council house in the country'. St Hugh's College, Oxford, was requisitioned in 1939 as a military hospital treating soldiers with serious head injuries. Huts in the college grounds brought the capacity to 300 beds and the hospital treated 13,000 patients during the war. Pioneering work to develop new surgical techniques greatly reduced mortality rates in patients with brain-penetrating injuries from 90 per cent down to just nine.

On 8 March 1943, the US medical service set up the European Theater Medical Field Service School at Shrivenham in the former British military training facility. This exploited the experience gained by RAMC staff during over three years of practice in the field from which the US medics were keen to learn. Two months later, it was joined by an Army Nurse Corps School where senior nurses, 800 in each eighteen-month course, were subject to a three-week intensive course at the 'Commando School for Nurses'. The school also operated a road show which toured US medical facilities training the trainers. As preparations for the D-Day landings progressed, a US Medical Depot, M-401, was set up at Witney. It would receive the components and medical supplies for 1,000-, 750-, and 400-bed field hospitals and assemble them for eventual transportation to France. As M-401T, it moved to Cherbourg to distribute medical supplies to units in the Cotentin Peninsular, closing down in late August when its work was done.

After D-Day, Shrivenham provided convenient railway sidings for hospital trains delivering wounded to hospitals in the Midlands, with nursing orderlies living in a small camp of Nissen huts next to the tracks. The Georgian Holton Park became the centrepiece of the Wheatley Military Hospital, originally set up for the 57th US Field Hospital, but it was the US 97th General Hospital which had moved in by March 1944 in preparation for receiving D-Day casualties, 1,500 of whom had been treated by August 1944, housed in three neat rows of large huts in the grounds, surrounded by other hospital buildings, and the characteristic water-tower. Following the Normandy landings, Southampton was the port of entry for casualties who were then sent by hospital train through Didcot and Oxford. Holton Park was accessed by hospital trains from Kennington Junction. The 97th left for Germany in May 1945, when the hospital was transferred to No. 21 Company, RAMC, for the treatment of head injuries, staffed by nurses of Queen Alexandra's Imperial Nursing Service (QARANC from 1949).

Other US medical units in the county included the US 317th Station Hospital which had been relocated to Finstock Hospital on Ramsden Heath in October 1944, having left a detachment in Belfast. It later moved to Taunton (Somerset), and the 809th US Army Hospital Centre, which was established in Oxford, in January 1945, too late to become operational. In addition to all these hospitals, large numbers of country houses were adapted for use as auxiliary hospitals and convalescent centres, many of them run by the Red Cross. These included High Wall at Headington, previously used for the same purpose in the Great War; Tusmore Park and Fritwell Manor near Bicester; and Swalcliffe Park near Banbury.

Wartime Medical Research and Development

The hitherto unfulfilled research ambition, integral to the planned operation of the Churchill Hospital, would take time to be realised. The Oxford University's Pathology Department under Professor Howard Florey had been instrumental in discovering penicillin using it to treat septicaemia. Only small amounts ever became available, but soon after Florey had found ways to mass-produce it, he met the 2nd General Hospital's Lt-Col. Schullinger at a university reception. This fortuitous meeting led to the arrangement whereby penicillin would be produced in large quantities in the USA. In May 1943, supplies of this wonder drug were allocated to the Churchill for clinical investigations which would greatly increase survival rates in battle casualties. Scientists such as D. S. Evans and Kurt Mendelssohn, one of a number of eminent researchers fleeing Nazi Germany and attracted to the Clarendon by Lindemann, had begun to apply solutions offered by the study of physics to medical problems. These included the accurate measurement of blood pressure and of radiant heat used in medical therapies. The Nuffield Department of Anaesthetics at Oxford University had been founded in 1937 under Sir Robert Macintosh. Following his attempts at improvisation in the Spanish Civil War, hampered by well-meaning nuns, and in which Golden Syrup tins figured prominently, he soon focused the Department's efforts on more effective battlefield provision. In 1941, the compact, portable Oxford Vaporiser apparatus for delivering temperature-controlled ether anaesthesia, needing only boiling water to operate, was produced for practical use in the field. Published in the *Lancet* in July, it was adopted by British and US army medics alike. Two years later, staff invented a lightweight chloroform vaporiser for use by airborne forces. Staff of the department, under the auspices of the Ministry of Supply, founded the Longworth Scientific Instrument Company in premises in Longworth Road near the Radcliffe Infirmary. They would produce anaesthetic devices, such as the Macintosh laryngoscope, and develop techniques for their use.

US Army Combat Rest Homes or 'Flak Shacks'

American servicemen in Britain could not return home on leave so a network of residential combat rest homes, informally known as 'flak shacks', was established in country houses and hotels requisitioned for the US Army Service Command by the Air Ministry. To create and maintain an unmilitary atmosphere, they were generally staffed by civilian members of the American Red Cross but remained under the command of US Army and Army Air Corps officers. Many of the 87,000 men who passed through the system at the rate of 900 per week, were combat flyers and every effort was made to divert their minds from the dangers they were daily facing. Sports activities, entertainments, a healthy diet, and opportunities just to relax were laid on by the mainly female staff as many of the guests were recuperating or convalescing from illness, injury or combat stress, priority generally being accorded to cases of flying fatigue. Moulsford Manor was one of the first two centres, opened in April 1943, and was followed by Buckland House near Wallingford, Pangbourne House, now Coombe Park in Whitchurch, and Eynsham Hall near Witney which had served, between 1939 and 1941, as a maternity hospital evacuated from Hampstead. Centres such as Moulsford Manor were for enlisted men; Eynsham Hall was for officers; and Pangbourne House was for NCOs, but the quality of provision was consistently maintained across the range. After D-Day planning had been completed, Phyllis Court in Henley became a rest home for twenty-eight guests and the American Red Cross set up its administration centre for all such Rest Homes across the country. In the official unit record, Moulsford and Buckland are listed under VIIIth Air Force Service Command, but the other three were lettered detachments of the 93rd SCSRD (Station Complement Squadron Reinforcement Depot), USSTAFE. In Oxford, the Clarendon Hotel became an American Red Cross Services Club, and The Shrubbery at 72 Woodstock Road was set up as a club for US soldiers by St Hugh's College, the leaseholders.

POW Camps

Oxfordshire was home to around a dozen POW camps, many of which were located in military premises that had been vacated after D-Day, and readied to receive the resulting stream of prisoners. Half a dozen camps occupied former US Army camps and stores within the Bicester COD at Arncott and Graven Hill. Some of these were tented while others used Nissen and Romney huts and timber sheds. Initially a camp of 120 bell tents was set in a fenced compound with watchtowers on what is now the site of the officers' mess at Horgard Barracks, Shrivenham. The Germans worked in the fields and were allowed to drink in the pub so long as they observed their 9 o'clock curfew. Italian submariners were also billeted around the village and they, too, worked on the land. The POWs were guarded, according to the village's history, by military police, but at other camps such as Bicester, prisoners were guarded by troops of the Royal Pioneer Corps. In North Hinksey, Harcourt Hill Camp opened in 1942 as an Italian work camp, with a Headington annexe at Old Road Camp, Wood Farm, in a square, fenced enclosure containing fifteen or so huts. The two, together, held up to 1,200 POWs. In Didcot, the Magazine Camp at Durnell's Farm lay within the COD. Both the North Camp at Nettlebed, built by US Army engineers, and Shotover House were German work camps. Large numbers of POWs were shipped back to Britain in the months following D-Day and once the Tactical Air Forces had moved their bases into France, some communal sites on airfields became available for POWs, an example being Stanton Harcourt. Given the temporary nature of the camp structures, few traces remain. A Nissen and a BCF hut stand at Checkendon which enjoyed an extended life; and some Nissen and timber huts remain in the Aylesbury Road scrapyard at Arncott.

8

The Cold War and Beyond, 1945–2020

At the end of the war, military establishments began to wind down, preparing for a peacetime life or for closure. The Americans established a university in the Shrivenham barracks, whose first two terms of operation, between October 1945 and May 1946, saw almost 7,500 students attending. POWs remained in Britain for several years after the end of the war and people remember those laxer times when POWs were more visibly part of the rural community. There were still, however, restrictions on those German POWs considered to be hardcore Nazis. Headington's Old Road camp operated from 1946–48 as a re-education centre for those 'black' Germans, who were permitted to work, but still under the constant supervision of armed guards. The Germans were finally repatriated in 1948 and the huts converted into housing by Oxford City Council and rented out. Most of these can still be seen in an aerial photograph of 1953 as the new houses of the Wood Farm estate begin to surround them. The huts were demolished in 1956 and Stansfield Place now occupies their site. Several camps, including Nettlebed, became centres for the Polish Resettlement Corps. The medieval chapel at neighbouring Stonor Park contains a sequence of artworks depicting the stations of the cross, carved out of wooden Red Cross boxes, by a Polish Catholic displaced person, Jozef Janas. Checkendon Camp had been first transformed into an Italian POW camp, and then from 1948 as a Polish Resettlement Camp, whose chapel remains, along with some huts. The Slade Camp was adapted as public housing by Oxford City Council and Steventon Depot was squatted, only being officially closed in 1959. In Henley, thirty-four prefab houses had been allocated to the town, but the last of the army huts which had also been squatted had finally been cleared away by 1956.

The RAF and USAF in the Post-War Years

The number of active airfields was drastically reduced from 1945 as the services consolidated their holdings. Some would enjoy only short extensions to their active military operation. From 1946, Kidlington was HQ, RAF No. 42 Group (Ammunition Supply & Storage) and also hosted No. 1 Aircrew Holding Unit, but after the OUAS left in 1959, rapidly switched to civil aviation as Oxford's Airport. Bicester carried on into the 1970s, as a support base for supplying equipment; host of the OUAS until 1975; home to units of the RAF Regiment, to the RAF Gliding and Soaring Association, and No. 9 Petroleum Depot, RASC. The domestic site has been sympathetically converted into attractive housing, and the technical site is being developed under Bicester Heritage as a centre for the preservation of vintage cars and aircraft, retaining buildings dating back to the First World War. The Harwell Atomic Energy Research Establishment, established in 1946 on the RAF airfield, houses Europe's first Nuclear Reactor. Culham Laboratories, occupying the Royal Naval Air Station, and from 1965 the UK Atomic Energy Authority HQ and research station, explores the possibilities of nuclear fusion. Both these establishments are primarily promoters and exploiters of the peaceful use of atomic energy. As of 2022, only Benson and Brize Norton remain as active RAF airfields, while the runway at Abingdon appears to remain viable.

Airfields

Abingdon became HQ, RAF No. 4 Group, Transport Command, which transferred from York in April 1947, but disbanded the following February. The Transport Command Development Unit moved in from Brize Norton in 1949, and the next year, the Parachute Training School arrived from Manchester via Upper Heyford, using Weston-on-the-Green and Watchfield as practice dropping zones. In 1956, the Blackburn Beverley, an enormous transport aircraft with a wingspan of 162 feet (50 metres), which could carry loads of 22 tons along with up to 130 paratroopers, came to Abingdon. Not to be confused with the earlier Admiralty 'F'-type hangars, a new hangar, erected in 1959 for overhauling the Beverleys, being the sixth in Abingdon's arc, was lettered 'F'. It comprises three bays, each measuring 180 by 102 feet (55.4 by 31.4 metres) with a clearance of 46 feet (14.2 metres), its revolutionary construction method leaving the vast interior free from obstructions. When the Belfast came on stream, the hangar was required to be raised by the addition of a dormer roof to accommodate the aircraft's higher tailplane. The airfield continued as a Transport Command hub until 1976 when its principal role was as the RAF's Engineering Wing, servicing, repairing and overhauling Jaguars, Hawks, and Hunters. Former civil VC-10s were stored for future military use. The airfield closed in 1992 and was handed over to the army as Dalton Barracks but the runway remains active for both fixed-wing aircraft and helicopters.

Abingdon: Hangar 'F' was erected in 1959 for overhauling Beverleys, designed in such a way as to leave the interior free from obstruction. To accommodate the Belfast with its higher tailplane, the height was increased by the addition of a dormer roof. Continuing as RAF Transport Command's hub until 1976, its principal role was as the RAF's Engineering Wing.

In 1950, the US Strategic Air Command (SAC) took the decision to station a force of bomber aircraft with nuclear weapon carrying capability in Europe, selecting Upper Heyford and Brize Norton as two of the four chosen airfields, with HQ, IIIrd USAF at Abingdon. In 1951, their B-36s moved from East Anglian airfields to Brize Norton, where modifications included extending the runway from 6,000 feet (1,830 metres) to 9,000 feet (2,745 metres); the erection of secure weapons storage; and the construction of hard standings. Within two years, B-47 bombers were based here and, by 1958, B-52s on three-week rotations were stationed alongside reconnaissance units. SAC's Reflex Alert operations included regular flights over Britain and Western Europe by bombers with atomic weapons on board. SAC also operated converted RB-47 spy-planes from Brize, one of which was lost on a clandestine mission over the Barents Sea. By 1965, the bombers had ceased their operations, and were withdrawn from both Upper Heyford and Brize Norton, the latter being returned to the RAF, while retaining its status as a SAC Forward Operating Base if ever needed. Visits to Brize were made by B2 bombers of SAC during the early 1980s, but the airfield was removed from the list of Co-located Operational Bases in 1983 but still without closing the door completely. In 1965, the base became the RAF's major transport hub. The enormous 'Lacon' cantilevered hangar, capable of holding six aircraft of Britannia, VC-10, or Belfast size, was completed in 1967, measuring over 1,000 feet (310 metres) long with a height of over 50 feet (16 metres). From 1984, VC-10s converted as tankers were flying from Brize, but a need for larger strategic transports saw first Tristars and, from 2001, Globemasters coming into service. As the base expanded to include the

RAF's Hercules fleet, A330 Voyager reconnaissance aircraft, and Airbus Atlas A400s, old buildings were refurbished, and many new ones added. In 2012, the two 1930s Lamella hangars on a detached site were upgraded to accommodate the Aeromedical Evacuation Squadron's store, training facilities, and offices. A maintenance hangar holding three A400 Atlas aircraft was opened in 2018. The station's transport schedule includes regular trips to the Falkland and Ascension Islands and, in 2022, Brize remains the main base for the RAF's transport and airborne refuelling operations.

SAC had taken over Upper Heyford in 1951 with its HQ in the old 1938 armoury building, initially for use by B-47 Stratojets and later by B-52s, for whose nuclear bombs a secure weapons storage facility was constructed. This deployment also necessitated the lengthening of the runway to 8,300 feet (2,530 metres) and the construction of nose-docks for servicing the bombers and their accompanying Boeing tankers. Also flying from here from 1962 were U-2 spy planes. At the same time that SAC pulled its bombers out of Britain in 1965, the 98th Strategic Wing, flying converted Boeing 707s stuffed with electronic sensors, moved from Brize to Upper Heyford, operating there until 1970. Then the HQ, 20th Fighter-Bomber Wing, arrived from Wethersfield (Essex), flying three squadrons of F-111 swing wing bombers and making Upper Heyford the largest base of its type in Europe, its tenants being involved in a nuclear alert in 1973 and later operations in Libya and Iraq. In 1980, eighteen hardened aircraft shelters, designed to withstand a direct hit from a 500-pound (220-kg) conventional

Brize Norton airfield: the enormous, cantilevered 'Lacon' hangar of 1967, designed to accommodate six aircraft of the Britannia, VC-10, or Belfast size.

Upper Heyford airfield: a hardened aircraft shelter (HAS) built in 1977–9 to hold F-111's of the US Air Force's 20th Tactical Fighter Wing.

Upper Heyford airfield: a nose dock enabling large aircraft such as B-47s or B-50s to be worked on under cover.

Benson airfield: the 'side-by-side' air traffic control tower (7378a/55) which remains in operation (2023).

bomb, were built, and the existing pre-Second World War hangars and other buildings continued in use. From 1984, a squadron of electronic warfare EF-111s moved in, tasked with jamming enemy radars. The USAF pulled out in 1993 and the base closed for active use in 1994. It is currently being developed for housing and employment, while retaining many of the original buildings.

Benson's photographic work continued after the war to assess Europe's reconstruction priorities. In 1953, the PR units moved on and RAF Transport Command took over, flying the Argosy twin-boom freighter until its withdrawal from service in 1971. Meanwhile Benson had been home to the Royal Flight. From 1993, the Support Helicopter Force HQ was established and two years later the Queen's Flight relocated to Northolt in north-west London. After fifteen years, the Merlins transferred to the FAA and currently Chinooks and Pumas fly out of Benson. The four pre-war 'C'-type hangars remain, along with a single T2, and one 6,000-foot (1,825-metre) runway which continues in service. Training of helicopter pilots for the RAF, RN, Regular Army, and NATO forces is carried out on six flight simulators, in four computer-based classrooms, and for tactical helicopter operations in a tactical control centre. The airfield also hosts the police, air ambulance, OUAS, and a flying club.

Nuneham Park had operated as a back-up to Medmenham throughout the war, but in 1947, only the model section and print library remained at Medmenham, with JAPIC, the Joint Air Photographic Intelligence Centre becoming JARIC, the Joint Air Reconnaissance Intelligence Centre from 1953, established at Nuneham Park, but moving to RAF Brampton (Cambridgeshire) in 1957.

Depots

No. 3 MU at Milton was wound up in January 1947 having devolved much of its work onto flying stations including Kidlington, Weston-on-the-Green, Chipping Norton, Shellingford, Bicester, Kingston Bagpuize, and Grove, along with the Woodcote depot, but none would operate beyond 1959. Shellingford had continued into 1948 to train pilots, including those from the Netherlands, but then passed to the USAF. Its new function was to provide radar maintenance and materiel support until 1957 for the AAA units protecting the UK's several SAC bases. In 1956, US Appropriations contained a request for over $1 million for running the Islip POL depot. The RAOC reorganised its COD structure in 1959 with a new Stores Organisation HQ moving into the Milton Depot, vacated that year by RAF No. 3 MU. This arrangement appears to have operated until the general reorganisation of the RAOC in the late 1970s. Bicester COD was initially serviced by No. 592 (MT) company, RASC, until its disbandment in 1947. Between 1947 and 1951, two battalions of the RAOC were formed at Vauxhall Barracks, Didcot, with four more forming at Bicester, of which two would take up residence in the new barracks at Arncott prior to their eventual absorption into the RLC. Bicester COD replaced its Nissen hut accommodation when St David's Barracks was built in 1958. From 1961, the depot's role changed to one of providing logistical support for the smaller Regular Army taking on the work of other depots including Didcot's 'General Stores' function, absorbing its MT and technical stores, and taking on the materials handling experimental function. Becoming one of just three CODs in 1965, it would soon benefit from increasing computerisation. Didcot was then run down with closure coming in 1964. Originally dependent on horse transport when it was designed in 1915, by the time it finally closed, Didcot COD's two remaining working horses were given a well-deserved retirement. The site went to the CEGB for a new power station, but Vauxhall Barracks was retained, hosting the ammunition assessment system, and currently (2022) occupied by an Explosive Ordnance Disposal unit of the Royal Logistic Corps. In 1975, Bicester survived a cull and was one of only two CODs, from 1999, becoming the Defence Storage & Distribution Centre employing 850 service personnel and 2,500 civilians. St George's Barracks was established as a bomb disposal/EOD training centre, and St David's Barracks, occupied until 2014 by 23 Pioneer Regiment, currently (2022) houses a Royal Logistic Corps unit. In 2007, the amalgamation of the Defence Logistics organisation and the Defence Procurement Agency produced the Defence Equipment and Support (DE&S) agency, several of whose departments, including Defence Clothing, occupied the Caversfield depot on Skimmingdish Lane on the former RAF Bicester site and now part of the domestic Garden Quarter. Despite a programme of refurbishment in 2000, many of the site's buildings date from the early days of the airfield.

Defence Against Nuclear Attack

Alongside the active defence measures afforded by the nuclear deterrent option of the RAF and USAF bombers, a whole range of passive measures were developed.

Royal Observer Corps (ROC) & UK Warning and Monitoring Organisation (UKWMO)

Once the Soviet Union had developed its own atomic weapons, nuclear attack became a real threat. The ROC was resurrected as an aircraft spotting and reporting network, with Oxford, once again, HQ No. 4 Group, redesignated No. 3 Group, in 1953, in the Southern Area, with fourteen active posts. In 1947, the ROC Group HQ had moved into Elsfield Hall where it stayed for two years before transferring to Woodstock Road, Wolvercote, until 1965. When the ROC posts were reactivated in the early 1950s, it was found that the Boars Hill post had been burned out during the VJ Day celebrations. It was decided to improve the conditions of ROC personnel by providing purpose-built shelters. These were built by ORLIT, a company specialising in prefabricated structures made of concrete panels. This new post consisted of a concrete box 10 feet (3 metres) long, 6 feet 8 inches (2 metres) deep, and about 6 feet (1.8 metres) high. A roof extended over half of it to protect the instruments, with an open section enabling visual spotting. The ORLIT 'A' version stood at ground level and the 'B' version was raised on four concrete pillars 6 feet (1.8 metres) in height and accessed by integral steps. Some posts including Culham and Deddington were still using their wartime posts in 1952, while that at Kidlington was physically transferred to a new site. Boars Hill and Swalcliffe were identified as requiring elevated ORLIT type 'B's, while others such as Enstone and Nettlebed were earmarked for ORLIT 'A's and, at the same time, a structure in local stone was requested for Watlington.

However, it would quickly become obvious that observers could not cope with the increasing speed of modern aircraft and that their meaningful contribution to the early warning process was coming to an end. As it happened, a new need for feedback on any nuclear strike that might take place had arisen and the United Kingdom Warning and Monitoring Organisation (UKWMO) was set up to provide this. With the ROC set-up already in place but given the realisation that the existing posts would be too exposed for their new task, ORLIT was again commissioned to design and supply an underground post. A similarly sized concrete box was designed but this one would be sunk 15 feet (4.5 metres) underground and entered through a hatch and down a vertical ladder. The crew of three was supplied with a desk, a radio, bunks, a chemical toilet, and a few days' food, with power supplied by a car battery. Little was visible on the surface: the concrete cube holding the entry hatch; a ventilator; and the tops of the Bomb Power Indicator and Fixed Survey Meter probe all painted green. A pin-hole camera mounted outside would record the flash of a bomb-blast and give some indication of its intensity and its position, or 'Ground Zero'. Information would be telephoned or radioed into Group HQ for transmission to the SOC. Not all of the aircraft posts were in suitable locations for underground works, so a number were relocated. In 1953, No. 3 Group with its HQ in Oxford moved into a new Southern Area and consisted of fourteen clusters of posts. In 1968, now part of the reorganised Metropolitan Area, eight of the county's posts were closed down, while twelve remained in use. At stand-down in 1991, Oxford's No. 3 Group contained twenty-seven ROC Posts, distributed in five clusters of three, two of four, and with four outliers, eleven of these underground posts lying within the post-1974 boundaries of the county. Several of these are thought to survive, but recent visits showed that not all are visible with only Enstone, Swalcliffe, and Middleton Stoney being easily found in the landscape.

A new Oxford ROC/UKWMO control centre at Cowley Barracks, James Wolfe Road, now Rowan House Annexe, was constructed in a semi-sunken bunker, designated as protected accommodation. It was the last of the thirty-one to be built nationally, being completed in 1965 and remaining in use until 1991. These group controls consisted of a bunker, accessed via a ramp and through airlocks, and surface hutting for administration and training. Given that such a bunker would be expected to survive a nuclear blast, there were kitchen facilities for emergency communal use. The bunker's lower floor contained segregated dormitories, a canteen, generator, and air-conditioning plant rooms, all round a central double-height space which held the control table for plotting the fall of bombs, overlooked by a balcony where incoming information was displayed on transparent panels by mirror-writing personnel. A new office block next door to the bunker was the peacetime unprotected HQ of UKWMO, which would consequently have been evacuated to a bunker in Preston (Lancashire) in the event of war. Part of the old Cowley Barracks site is currently (2022) used as student accommodation by Oxford Brookes University and the underground ROC control bunker survives in a good state of preservation, used for the storage of furniture, with its generators intact and double-height balconied control room extant.

After the nuclear accident at Chernobyl in 1988, the Radioactive Incident Monitoring Network (RIMNET) was set up to monitor levels of background radiation around the country. Some fifty locations in England, including RAF Brize Norton, were chosen to host an automated system based on existing weather stations, many of which were on MOD bases. Its introduction, not, incidentally, as effective as the product of UKWMO, but much cheaper to run, ironically prefigured the stand-down of the ROC in 1991, a victim of the peace dividend.

Middleton Stoney (SP543238): the ROC underground monitoring post in use until 1968 on a site first established as an aircraft spotting post in 1935.

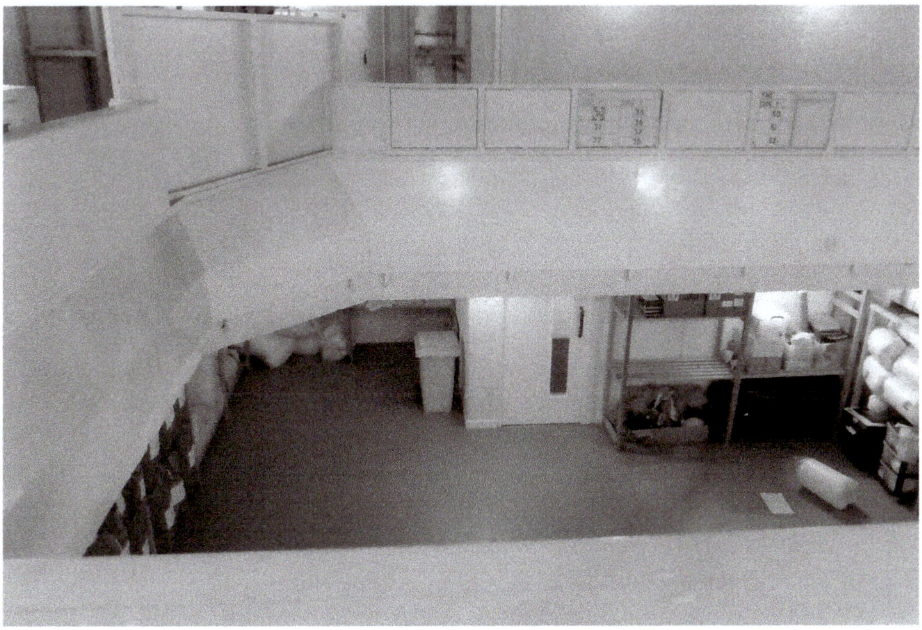

Oxford, James Wolfe Road: the double-height control room of the ROC reporting centre with its balcony overlooking the central well and its plotting table. Formerly set up within the confines of Cowley Barracks, it now provides storage for Oxford Brookes University's residential student accommodation.

Nuclear Bunkers

The UK was divided into regions in the early 1960s, each served by a regional seat of government (RSG) intended, in the event of a nuclear attack (particularly one which had taken out London), to ensure that the functions of government continued. The Southern, No. 6 Region, had its RSG in Warren Row, near Henley-on-Thames, which, as we have seen, had been an underground aircraft components factory during the Second World War. The Warren Row RSG was spread across 1,000 feet (310 metres) of tunnels, which included offices for the regional commissioner and his staff drawn from relevant departments of the Civil Service; offices for the emergency services and the armed forces liaison officers; a studio for the BBC; a GPO telephone exchange; kitchen; and canteen. Stairs led to dormitories on an upper floor for the use of the several hundred personnel who would have been locked down there. Following its sensational exposure by Spies for Peace in 1963, Warren Row was abandoned, although part continued as an army communications centre until 2000.

Those provisions made for national government were replicated at local authority level, and for the public utilities, so bunkers were constructed for the eighty or so personnel who would keep the power on, the water running, and the pumps crewed. Oxfordshire's County Main bunker was dug under Wood Eaton Manor, an LEA special needs school, and accessed via a vertical shaft. The bunker was extensively refurbished in the 1980s when the Thatcher government made money available for what were seen by many as white elephants. The Oxford City Council Emergency Civil Defence control was built in the mid-1950s at 270 Woodstock Road but was stood down in 1968 to be occupied for a time by the commercial radio station, Jack FM. In Banbury, Cherwell

Oxford, Woodstock Road: the emergency bunker built as a base for local administration after a nuclear attack. Since being decommissioned it has been used for a number of purposes including as a radio station.

Council's emergency control centre under the town hall was taken out of service in the mid-1980s and is now a leisure facility. Owing to the height of the water table at Wallingford, the South Oxfordshire Council had to settle for a surface structure added to the existing offices. Decommissioned as part of the peace dividend, the building is now, like so many similar structures, used for storage. A further bunker was constructed in the basement of West Oxfordshire Council's offices on New Yatt Road in Witney.

Communications

RAF Barford St John, whose flying activities had long ceased, became, from 1951, a USAF communications centre for SAC, conveniently close to its four bomber stations at Brize Norton, Upper Heyford, Fairford (Gloucestershire), and Greenham Common (Berkshire). RAF Bampton Castle, originally a Royal Signals communications establishment, was passed to the RAF in 1969 and administered by No. 38 Group's Tactical Communications Wing at Brize Norton. It was wound up by 2006 and is currently a business centre. Beckley radio transmission station opened for BBC use in 1962 with a guyed steel lattice mast 507 feet (154.4 metres) high, surmounted by an UHF TV antenna, helping to launch Radio Oxford in October 1970. As part of the early civil defence preparations, the Home Office set up a network of 'Hilltop' radio stations to ensure secure communication with police chiefs, the military, and other emergency services. In sub-Region 62, the radio station stood at Lockinge Down (SU422834) and is currently recorded as remaining in police ownership.

In the early 1960s, the Backbone network of microwave towers, for disseminating general intelligence and nuclear attack warnings in an emergency, was set up to cover the whole country, its most familiar element being the GPO/BT Tower in London's Tottenham Court Road. Stokenchurch Microwave tower (SU745968) was built in 1963 and is 326 feet (99.4 metres) high, standing at a height above sea level of 1,117 feet (340.5 metres). It was built as a terminal at the crossing of the major east–west and south–north links and as a major hub in Backbone. For aesthetic and environmental reasons, Stokenchurch was one of the seven such towers built in concrete rather than steel lattice. It lies in line of sight of other towers at Bagshot (Surrey), Charwelton (Northamptonshire), Sparsholt Firs (Oxfordshire), and Pimlico (Hertfordshire). The Sparsholt Firs (or Furze) tower (SU340848) near Wantage had been used by 313 Signals Unit as a GEE navigation beacon but had come into GPO use by 1960. The 350-foot-high (107-metre-high) steel lattice tower was shortened but carried horn and dish antennae in 1970, by which time GEE had reached the end of its usefulness. The next link in the westerly chain is the concrete tower at Wotton-under-Edge (Gloucestershire). All these towers' main function currently is the transmission of radio and television programmes.

The MOD's own case study of Marconi's 1970s Integrated Systems network support service for the MOD describes how the 'seamless integration of day-to-day

Sparsholt Firs (SU340848): one of the original chain of microwave towers, built to convey information through the early warning systems in the event of a nuclear attack.

operations with the customers' working practice would ensure the success of its UNITER project'. This system combined many of the disparate communications systems into one that would serve active RAF stations. The equipment was accommodated on each site in a hardened structure designed to withstand missile attack. UNITER bunkers were constructed at forty-six RAF sites, reduced in 2002 to thirty-two, including RAF Benson and RAF Bampton Castle.

Logistics for a Nuclear Emergency

The Ministry of Agriculture, Fisheries and Food (MAFF) set up a national network of depots to store supplies of staple foods including flour, fat, yeast, sugar, and sweet biscuits. This network included pre-existing Second World War-era grain silos such as that at Water Eaton, or Gosford, lying between the A34 and the railway. This example consisted of ten seven-storey-high silos with grain driers and grain handling machinery capable of storing 5,000–6,000 tons of unprocessed wheat, barley, or oats. The structure closed in the late 1980s but was only demolished in 2013 for the construction of Oxford Parkway railway station. Other Oxfordshire depots in Region No. 6, successors to MAFF's wartime buffer depots and managed by the British & Foreign Wharf Co. Ltd, were at Freeland (No. 450); Kidlington (No. 450F); South Leigh, Witney (No. 357); Culham (No. 450G); Kennington (No. 450H); and Grimsbury Road, Banbury (No. 450J). The South Leigh buffer depot was served by a railway siding that had been extended in 1942. It consisted of three adjoining gabled sheds with the clerestory roof, characteristic of these depot buildings. Additionally, to ensure effective distribution, the Home Office administered Supply & Transport Depots in the former RAOC depots in Shirburn Road, Watlington, and at Steventon.

In the event of a nuclear strike, the free movement of troops and supplies would become a priority. While civilian traffic was not banned, it would be confined to side-roads and byways and the resulting gridlock and the early exhaustion of fuel stocks available to the private motorist would quickly bring such unofficial traffic to a complete standstill. The military and the government's supply organisations would use essential service routes (ESR), kept clear of unauthorised traffic by armed troops of the TA, co-ordinated through the hilltop radio stations. The ESRs in Oxfordshire included the A40, M40, A34, A41, A43, and A423 which left few alternatives for anybody else. Additionally, a military road system ensured free movement of military traffic between ports, airfields, army camps, and major conurbations. Named for animals, ELK linked Gloucester to Colchester and the US military port of Felixstowe via the A40, A43, and A41, accessing Luton Airport via BAT up the M1, and then continuing north of London on the A414 to join CAT for its final stages along the A12. In those pre-M25 days, journeys could be just as tortuous, hence the focus on keeping the roads clear for those with the most pressing need to use them.

Gosford: constructed by MAFF between the A34 and the railway, these ten seven-storey-high grain silos could store 5,000–6,000 tons of cereal crops. It was closed in the late 1980s and later demolished for a new railway station. (*Steve Carvell*)

Steventon Depot: the former offices of what had become by the 1960s an emergency transport depot—part of the country's nuclear attack response.

The Army in the Post-War Years

New plans for officer training post-war included the reformation of the Military College of Science which had been dispersed from Woolwich during the war. As soon as the Americans had vacated the Shrivenham buildings in 1946, it assumed the status of a college conferring London University honours degrees. Additionally, courses were mounted for technical staff officers from October 1946, and in 1953, the college became the Royal Military College of Science with its officers' mess in Beckett Hall. RAF Watchfield became Arnhem Camp in 1950 under No. 1 Army Air Supply Organisation, RASC. Resident units included, at different times, Nos 22 and 47 (Air Despatch) Companies RASC and also RAOC units collaborating with the Parachute Training School at RAF Abingdon, on loading aircraft and training air despatchers. Watchfield also carried out parachute training from tethered balloons, and when it closed in 1971, Abingdon's No. 1 Parachute Training School inherited all of its training equipment including jump towers and zipwires.

Following service in Palestine and Germany, the OBLI was reduced to a single battalion in 1948. While serving in Cyprus from 1956–9, the regiment was retitled the 1st Greenjackets, forming, along with the former KRRC and the Rifle Brigade, the Greenjackets Brigade with its depot in Winchester. This rendered Cowley Barracks redundant, although a TA element remained at Slade Barracks in Headington. Service in Borneo and Germany followed until, in 1966, the regiment was involved in an amalgamation which left it as 1st Battalion, The Royal Green Jackets as which it went through several more transitions until in 2007, it emerged as 2nd Battalion, The Rifles, by now one of five regular battalions representing the former county regiments of thirteen shires. While the combat arms of the army underwent numerous reorganisation exercises, so did the combat services which included the transport, ordnance, catering, and pioneer corps, all ending up combining as the Royal Logistic Corps in 1993. Currently (2022) occupying Dalton Barracks, in the former RAF Abingdon, are No. 3 Regiment, RLC, providing logistical support to 1st Armoured Brigade, and No. 4 Regiment, RLC, an integral part of No. 3 (UK) Division. Vauxhall Barracks, Didcot, is currently (2022) home to No. 11 Explosive Ordnance Disposal Regiment, RLC, with other EOD units located in Bicester.

The TA reformed in 1947, with the QOOH being reconstituted in the guise of 387 Field Regiment, RA (TA). Also forming in the county was 1568 Company (Artillery), RASC, at Banbury with a platoon at Bicester but moving to Cowley Barracks the next year. This was part of No. 104 Transport Column RASC (TA) with HQ in Christchurch (Hampshire, now Dorset). Post-war recruitment could be very slow and No. 505 Company, RASC, at Didcot was reduced to a platoon within the larger No. 504 Company at Swindon (Wiltshire) until the creation of the Royal Corps of Transport in 1965. The new Harcourt House

TAC in Marston Road, Oxford, was opened by Earl Alexander of Tunis in 1957 for the QOOH and the OBLI but has lately been converted for use as offices and student accommodation. By 1961, the QOOH had been absorbed, along with similar yeomanry units, into 299 Regiment, RA, (TA), equipped as a close support regiment with 25-pounder gun/howitzers, its 'A' Squadron based at Elsfield Hall, and practising on the ranges at Larkhill (Wiltshire). This regiment was disbanded in 1967 and reduced to a cadre in 1969. From 1975, the regimental name was carried by No. 5 Squadron, 39th (Skinners) Signal Regiment (Volunteers), until 2014 when the unit was transferred to the Royal Logistic Corps as No. 142 (QOOH) Vehicle Squadron based at Banbury, an army reserve constituent of 165 Port and Maritime Regiment, RLC, centred in Plymouth. Since Slade Barracks in Headington closed, 'A' (Royal Greenjackets) Company of 7th Battalion, The Rifles, of the army reserve, has been at Edward Brooks Barracks in the former RAF Abingdon, also home to an army reserve detachment of 202(M) Field Hospital, Army Medical Services. Newspaper reports have suggested that rationalisation of the defence estate will see the closure of Dalton, Vauxhall, and St David's Barracks, Bicester, by the end of the 2020s.

Didcot: Vauxhall Barracks, dating back to the interwar period and currently (2022) housing an explosive ordnance disposal unit of the Royal Logistic Corps.

Oxford: Harcourt House on Marston Road opened in 1957 as a base for the local TA units: the Queen's Own Oxfordshire Hussars Yeomanry and the 4th Battalion, Oxfordshire and Buckinghamshire Light Infantry. It is now student accommodation.

Oxford: Falklands House on Oxpens Road opened in 2000 as a new base for the various branches of the Officer Training Corps recruiting from universities in the Oxford region.

Cadets

With premises since 2000 in Falklands House on Oxpens Road in Oxford, the Oxford University OTC draws students from seven universities across Bedfordshire, Berkshire, Buckinghamshire, Gloucestershire, and Oxfordshire. Also based at Falklands House, drawing from Reading and Oxford's two universities, is the RN Unit, and the OUAS, recruiting from a similar pool, is currently (2022) settled at RAF Benson alongside No. 6 Air Experience Flight, both units flying the Glob Tutor. Schools with CCF units include St Edward's, Magdalen College, and Headington Schools in Oxford, Radley College and Abingdon and Burford Schools, between them providing army, navy, and air force sections. Kingham Hill School CCF, affiliated to the Royal Regiment of Fusiliers, makes membership compulsory for pupils in Years 9 and 10 with the opportunity to continue in subsequent years. ACF units operate on nineteen sites in the county, as do a similar number of ATC units with their HQ at Edward Brooks Barracks. Sea Cadet/ Royal Marine Cadet units include TS *Euryalus* at Donnington Bridge, Oxford; TS *Guardian* at Henley-upon-Thames; and TS *Marlborough* at Abingdon.

Medical Services

As reported in *Hansard* in 1948, Holton Park Hospital, then known as Wheatley Military Hospital, had achieved 300 fully equipped beds towards a planned total of 525 patients. Some of the 190 staff, which included members of Queen Alexandra's Royal Army Nursing Corps (QARANC), could be accommodated in three plasterboard huts. The military hospital closed in 1961 and the site became Wheatley Park School, with the last huts only being removed in 2006. The John Radcliffe Hospital in Oxford currently includes a MoD Hospital Unit. In March 2020, two hangars at Upper Heyford were converted into temporary morgues during the first, unpredictable stage of the COVID-19 pandemic. The successor to the anaesthetics department's Longworth Company, the Penlon Company, is based in Abingdon, and its products have continued to contribute solutions to medical problems and emergencies, right up to COVID-19 in 2020, when it produced 12,000 ESO 2 ventilators in just four months.

APPENDIX I

Prehistoric Forts

Ashbury, Ashdown Park, Alfred's Castle (SU277822) contour fort
Abingdon Vineyard, classified as a valley fort
Badbury Hill (SU261945) contour fort
Binditch or Bozedown Camp, Whitchurch (SU643783) promontory fort
Bladon Heath, Round Castle, Begbrooke (SP457138)
Blewburton Hill Camp (SU546862) contour fort
Burroway (SP308003) valley fort
Cassington Mill Big Ring (SP450100) valley fort
Chadlington, Knoll Bury Camp (SP316230)
Chastleton Burrow Camp (SP259283) contour fort
Checkendon, Castle Grove Camp, Wyfold Wood (SU683810) plateau fort
Cherbury Camp, (SU374963) valley fort
Dorchester, Dyke Hills, (SU570938-577935) valley fort
Eynsham Park Camp (SP394115)
Hardwell Camp, Compton Beauchamp, (SU288867) promontory fort
Idbury Camp, (SP229196) univallate plateau fort
Ilbury (SP437305) camp
Glympton, Hark Wood (SP423200)
Goring Heath, Friarhampstead Wood (SU645807)
Hinton Waldrist, Windmill Hill, (SU379982)
Little Coxwell, Furze Hill fort (SU289928)
Ascott-under-Wychwood, Lyneham, The Roundabout, (SP299213) plateau fort
Madmarston Hill Camp, Swalcliffe, (SP387389) contour fort
Rams Hill (SU314864) camp
Segsbury Camp or Letcombe Castle (SU385844) contour fort
Shutford, Castle Bank (SP407409) plateau fort
Sinodun Camp, Castle Hill, Wittenham Clumps (SU569924)
Tadmarton Heath Camp (SP388356) plateau fort
Uffington Castle, White Horse Hill (SU299863) contour fort

APPENDIX II

Castles, Moated Sites, and Strong Houses

A list of castles published in 1986 by the County Sites and Monuments Record includes thirty examples: nine motte and baileys; six ringworks; two developed or elaborated ringworks; and the rest as fortified manor houses of thirteenth-century date or later.

Castles

Abingdon, Fitzharry's House (SU497976) motte
Ardley (SP539273) ringwork
Ascott under Wychwood, three earthwork castles: Ascott D'Oilly (SP303191); Ascott Earl (SP297184); possible third motte and bailey (*c*SP305193)
Bampton, Ham Court (SP310031), masonry castle, licensed 1315
Bampton Church (SP312034), former Saxon minster, enclosed by a ditch and bank, refurbished as a temporary fortified camp in 1141–2
Banbury, medieval masonry castle (SP457408) and town bars
Brightwell (SU578907) possible siege castle
Broughton (SP418382) moated fortified manor
Chipping Norton (SP311275) earthwork castle
Cholsey (SU585868) possible siege castle
Churchill, The Mount (SP280237) probably a barrow, landscaped in the C18 & C19
Cogges (SP360095) moated fortified house
Crowmarsh Gifford (SU613894) siege castle
Deddington Castle (SP472316) masonry castle
Deddington, Castle House (SP468318) medieval tower house
Faringdon Clump (SU297957) castle of Anarchy destroyed 1145
Greys Court (SU726834) fortified house, licensed 1347
Hinton Waldrist (SU374991) motte and bailey of early twelfth century
Middleton Stoney (SP531233), earthwork castle ordered destroyed in 1216

Minster Lovell (SP325114) fortified house
Mixbury, Beaumont Castle (SP610341) earthwork castle
Oxford Castle (SP509062) masonry Norman castle
Oxford (SP510063) 'Jews Mount' and 'Mount Pelham' possible siege castles
Oxford, Beaumont Palace (*c*SP512064) site only
Radcot, (SU285996) excavated remains of stone keep
Swerford (SP373312) motte and bailey
Shirburn (SU697960) moated castle, licensed 1377
Somerton (SP497289) only moats remain
South Moreton (SU558880) damaged motte on bank of Mill Brook, possible siege castle
South Moreton Manor (SU562884) possible siege castle
Standlake, Gaunt House (SP407033) moated house
Stanton Harcourt (SP417057) fortified house
Stratton Audley (SP609259) rectangular moat of destroyed castle in Court Close
Wallingford (SU608897) earthwork remains of masonry castle
Watlington (SU686948) licensed 1338 to Nicholas de la Beche
Witney (SP357092) bishops' palace of 1137
Woodstock (SP437165) site of earthwork castle; royal palace now under Blenheim Park

Ecclesiastical Establishments with Defensible Features

Abingdon Abbey, precinct wall and gatehouse
Clanfield, preceptory of Knights Hospitaler, moated site, Friars Court
Dorchester Abbey, precinct wall and gatehouse
Eynsham Abbey, Benedictine monastery with precinct wall and gatehouse
Godstow Nunnery, perimeter wall
Oseney Abbey, gatehouse
Oxford, Rewley Abbey, Cistercian monastery, precinct wall and gatehouse
Oxford, St Bernard's Cistercian monastery, now St John's College, gatehouse
Sandford-on-Thames, preceptory of Knights Templar
Stoke Talmage, Stoke Grange Farm, formerly moated grange of Thame Abbey
Thame Park, built around the remains of the Cistercian abbey with solar tower
Thame, Prebendal House
Temple Cowley, preceptory of the Knights Templar

Moated Sites, Fortified Manor Houses, and Strong Houses

Appleton Manor (SP444015), three-sided dry moat
Appleton, Tubney Manor Farm (SP446010), moat

Barford St John (SP439331), irregular, pentagonal moat
Barford St Michael (SP432327), moat
Beckley Park Lodge (SP564113) triple moats of a hunting lodge/castle ('palace' on OS map)
Brightwell-cum-Sotwell (SU578906 & 583905) two moats
Broughton Poggs (SP235038) Manor Farm stands in two arms of a moat
Bucknell (SP563255) moat
Camoys Court, Chiselhampton (SU592986) moated house, licensed in 1318
Chalgrove, Barentin's Manor (SU630970) two islands within thirteenth-century moats
Clanfield, Friars Court (SP285009) moat
Compton Beauchamp, Hardwell Farm (SU284878) moat
Copcourt Manor (SP707009) moat
Cotmore Farm (SP586265) moat
Cuddington (SP411228) Tudor manor-house superseded by Kiddington Manor
Crowmarsh Battle Farm (SU615906) moat on 1:25,000 OS map
Curbridge, Caswell Farm (SP320082) moated house incorporates fifteenth-century fragments including gate-piers, doorways and buttresses
Curbridge, Black Moat (SP320080)
Cuxham, Merton College Manor (SU667952) moated site
Denchworth (SU382917) moat
Ewelme Palace (SU643914) vanished moated site
Eynsham (*c*SP433091) moat, near the site of the abbey
Hanwell (SP436436) brick-built quadrangular mansion of 1490 with corner towers
Holton House (SP599064) moat superseded an earlier moat 303 yards (280 metres) to south-east
Islip (SP430143) moat close to Manor Farm
Kidlington, Moat Cottage (*c*SP497149), foundations of clay and mortar bonded thirteenth-century buildings with slate or tile roofs were found within two remaining sides of a moat.
Kingham, Manor Farm (SP259242) rectangular platform with possible foundations of buildings within three sides of a moat
Kingston Blount, Copcourt (SP707009) moat and medieval tower base possibly indicating the remains of a drawbridge
Kirtlington (SP501197) moat east of school
Lewknor, Moor Court (SU709978) moat
Nether Worton (SP427302) moat north of church
Newnham Murren: no trace of house licensed to Richard English in 1356.
Rycote (SP666046) fourteenth-century manor remodelled as a courtyard house in brick
Shillingford, Rush Court (SU604917) moat

Somerton, Manor Farm (SP496283) moat

Stanford Park Farm (SU362935) moat

Standlake, Gaunt House (SP407033) moated house besieged in the Civil War, rebuilt *c.* 1660

Standlake (SP412034) moat

Sugarswell (SP360440) double moated site

Upholcombe, Great Holcombe (SU610962) licensed 1360, to Richard English

Wytham Abbey (SP474085) fortified house built in 1459 and drastically remodelled in 1809

Yelford Manor (*c*SP359047) fifteenth-century timber-framed house within a moat, built by the Hastings family

APPENDIX III

Licences to Crenellate

Bampton, 1315, to Aymer de Valence
Cassington/Kersington, 1317, to William de Montague
Chiselhampton, 1318, to Richard de Luches
Stanton Harcourt, (SP413059) 1327, to John Wyard
Drayton, 1329 and Wykeham, 1330, to Robert de Ardern
Abingdon Abbey, 1330, to the Abbot and Convent
Watlington, 1338, to Nicholas de la Beche
Rotherfield Greys, 1346 and 1348, to John de Grey
Kingham, 1347, to Gilbert Chasteleyn
Newnham Murren/Upholcombe (SU610962), 1360, to Richard English
Shirburn, 1377, to Warin de Lisle
Oxford, 1381, to the Commonalty of Oxford but revoked
Broughton, 1406, to Thomas Wykeham

APPENDIX IV

Airfields and Other Aviation-Related Sites

NB. Second World War USAAF Station Numbers, where applicable, appear in brackets.

Abingdon: HQ RAF Nos 1 and 2 Groups, RAF Bomber Command, 1936.

Abingdon: HQ No. 6 (Training) Group; then HQ No. 91 (OTU) Group, RAF Bomber Command, from May 1942.

Abingdon, Caldecott House, HQ No. 40 (Maintenance) Group from August 1939 to 1945.

Abingdon opened in 1932 as a bomber airfield; from 1939, it was No. 10 OTU; went to Transport Command 1946, then to Support Command in 1976; it closed in 1992 and is currently Dalton Barracks.

Adderbury, airstrip used by 58th and 87th Armoured Field Artillery Battalions, US Army.

Akeman Street opened in 1940 as a training station until closure in 1947.

Ashdown Park (Station 544) base for 1585th QM Truck Battalion and 17th Special Service Company, IXth USAAF Service Command.

Bampton Castle was in use by RAF No. 2 Signals Unit (Communications) and 81 Signals Unit (Intelligence) from 1969–2006. Now a trading estate.

Banbury (SP430430) was an Automobile Association landing ground in the 1930s with a maximum landing run of 340 yards (315 metres).

Barford St John opened in 1941 as an RLG, upgraded in 1943. It operated as an OTU until 1946. From 1951, it became a USAF communications centre for SAC.

Barton Abbey (SP464248) was No. 28 SLG for Little Rissington (Gloucestershire) and a sub-site for Brize Norton, 1939–45.

Benson commenced building in 1937, initially as an OTU, becoming the centre of photo reconnaissance operations in 1941. It was transferred to RAF

Transport Command in 1953. Since 1992, it has been the base for the RAF Support Helicopter Force, now operating within Joint Helicopter Command.

Besselsleigh, Great Park Farm, RAF firing range for No. 10 OTU.

Bicester was a training depot station from 1917 and was demolished in 1922. From 1925, it was developed as a bomber base and expanded in 1937. It operated through the Second World War initially as an OTU and then as RAF No. 246 MU, supplying equipment to the 2nd Tactical Air Force. It was an equipment disposal depot 1945–1949 and, following varied use, closed in 1976.

Bicester: RAF billets at Bicester House and Market End House, with the WRAF at Brashfield House and Launton Vicarage.

Brize Norton opened in 1937 as a training station and ASU run by No. 6 MU, 1938–51. Its main role was with gliders until 1945. The USAF took over in 1952 staying until 1965. Since then, it has operated as the RAF's primary transport base.

Broadwell opened in 1943 under RAF Transport Command involved in airborne operations, and closed in 1946.

Bruern Abbey (Station 441) HQ 877 Engineer Airborne Command, IXth USAAF Engineer Command.

Bush(y) Barn, Pusey (SU366958), No. 44 SLG for 5 MU RAF Kemble (Wiltshire), 1941–3.

Chalgrove (Station 465) opened late in 1943 for the IXth USAAF No. 10 Photographic Reconnaissance Group and Photographic Laboratory. From 1946, the airfield has been home to the Martin-Baker ejector seat company.

Checkendon Camp (SU662845) hutted camp used by No. 70 MU at RAF Woodcote.

Chilworth near Wheatley (SP640045) Automobile Association landing ground, in the 1930s with a maximum landing run of 550 yards (510 metres).

Chipping Norton was an enhanced RLG used by No. 15 SFTS, closing in 1945.

Chipping Norton, Oldner House was the early HQ for No. 15 SFTS in 1940.

Cokethorpe (Station 423) 926 Aviation Engineer Regiment, IXth USAAF Engineer Command.

Cottisford LG (SP58.31) possible precursor to Croughton (Northants) and RLG for Abingdon from December 1936.

Cowley, Morris Motor Works housed HQ 43 (Repair) Group RAF Maintenance Command, 1940. Cowley airfield was associated with CRU, RAF No. 26 MU.

Culham opened in 1944 as RNAS *Hornbill* to operate as an Aircraft Receipt and Despatch Unit for the Fleet Air Arm (FAA). It was paid off in 1953 but continued as an Admiralty Storage Depot before most of the site was developed by the Atomic Energy Commission. Part of the site is now an industrial estate.

Cumnor (SP45.04) possible LG precursor to Stanton Harcourt, used by Oxford UAS, 1937.

Dorchester (SU583965) LG precursor to Mount Farm, used by No. 1 PRU from June 1940.

Edgehill, known as Shenington, opened in 1941 as a SLG for No. 21 OTU at Moreton-in-Marsh (Gloucestershire) and closed in 1945 when the Gibbs family returned to their farm.

Enstone replaced Edgehill in 1943 as a SLG for No. 21 OTU, ceasing flying in 1946.

Eynsham (SP425084) No. 6 Air Armament Park 1939–51; bomb dump under No. 96 MU at Kidlington.

Goring Heath and Milton Equipment Disposal Depot, No. 70 MU.

Grove (Station 519) planned in 1940 as a reserve RAF bomber station for training, it was handed over to the USAAF in 1943 for US No. 31 Transport Group; 43 & 45 Air Depot Groups; QM Truck Companies. (Aviation); 67 QM Railhead Coy; Ordnance Depot, firefighting, and MP units. It was briefly handed back to the RAF in 1946.

Harwell opened in 1937 as a bomber airfield and spent the war as No. 15 OTU. From 1946, it has operated as the Atomic Energy Research Establishment (AERE).

Haseley Court (Station 401) US 48 Bomb Disposal Squadron which had left by June 1944

Henley on Thames: RFC Equipment Officers' School, 1917.

Henley-on-Thames, Phyllis Court Country Club in Henley was used by RFC in 1917. In 1939, it was requisitioned by MoS with Ballroom as an optical instrument repair facility and rest of the complex taken over by AM to be used as WAAF officers' mess for PRU Interpretation Centre at RAF Medmenham. Then pre-D-Day planning and photo-mosaic construction. HQ, US combat rest homes (Station 494).

Kelmscott (SP005245), RLG in use by No. 2 FTS by February 1939.

Kiddington (Glympton) (SP438230) RLG for No. 15 SFTS from Kidlington until 1945.

Kidlington, opened in 1938 as training airfield by 15 SFTS then by a glider training school. HQ RAF No. 42 Group including No. 96 MU from 1946–1951. Since 1959, it has been Oxford's civil airport.

Kidlington, Campsfield House requisitioned for dormitory accommodation, 1940.

Kingham (Station 543) VIIIth USAAF Service Command, ordnance depot, O-670.

Kingston Bagpuize (Station 403) opened early in 1942 as a RLG for first No. 3 EFTS and then for the gliding school at Thame. Following enlargement works, US No. 4 Tactical Air Depot moved in with HQ IXth USAAF Engineer Command and US No. 2 Air Depot Group with Ordnance Maintenance, Signals, MP, firefighting, and QM Truck Companies. After 1944, the site remained a depot for No. 3 MU until 1954.

Lambert Arms (SU724981 and 723980) were Automobile Association landing grounds in the 1930s with landing runs of, respectively 440 and 500 yards (405 and 460 metres).

Middle Farm (SP609325), No. 3 SLG for Little Rissington (Gloucestershire), but some place the SLG in Shelswell Park to the south at SP60.30.

Milton was RAF No. 3 MU, Universal Equipment Depot (UED) from 1938–72.

Mount Farm (Station 234) opened in 1940, initially as a RLG for Benson and then for Harwell. From March 1943, US No. 7 Photographic Reconnaissance Group took over, accompanied by QM, firefighting, and MP units.

Nuneham Park, Photographic Reconnaissance Interpretation Unit working with Benson from 1942; then Joint Air Reconnaissance Intelligence Centre (JARIC) until 1957.

Otmoor: bombing range for 16 OTU and USAAF.

Oxford: HQ RAF No. 2 Group (South East), 1918.

Oxford (SP563088) was an Automobile Association landing ground in the 1930s with a maximum landing run of 620 yards (570 metres).

Oxford, Brasenose College, Regional Control School, RAF Bomber Command until 1941

Oxford, Jowett Walk, Second World War photographic reconnaissance laboratory in Masters Field.

Oxford, Magdalen College, joint HQ 43 (Salvage) Group merged with 43 (Repair) Group, RAF Maintenance Command, 1941.

Oxford, Merton College: HQ 43 (Repair) Group RAF Maintenance Command, 1940.

Oxford, Port Meadow commenced flying in 1911, becoming a military aerodrome in 1914.

Oxford, No. 15 MU Purgatory Unit (aircraft awaiting assembly and issue).

Shellingford from 1940 housed No. 3 E&RFTS and then glider pilots. After 1945, a later user was a USAF contingent servicing radar sets for bomber units at Brize Norton and Upper Heyford. It closed in 1948.

Slade Farm, Kirtlington, (SP510220) No. 1 SLG for RAF Colerne (Wiltshire).

Starveall Farm, Woodstock, (SP412193) No. 2 SLG for RAF Colerne, Wiltshire).

(Thame was a glider school over the border in Buckinghamshire).

Upper Heyford opened in 1917 for Canadian squadrons. It was resurrected in the 1924 plans, reopening in 1927 as a bomber airfield. It hosted No. 16 OTU through the war. In 1950, the USAF arrived to support SAC. From 1965, it was part of USAFE, continuing as such until 1994. The airfield is now a housing and employment development.

Wallingford (SU643883) Automobile Association landing ground in the 1930s with a maximum landing run of 750 yards (690 metres).

Wallingford, Mongewell Park (now Carmel College), HQ 2nd Tactical Air Force, RAF Bomber Command, from November 1943.

Wantage, airstrip used by 322nd Field Artillery Battalion, 83rd Infantry Division, US Army.

Watchfield opened in 1940 and was a sub-site for Brize Norton, 1940–1, carrying out beam approach training and airfield controller training. After the war, it established the RAF School of Air Traffic Control until 1950 when Arnhem Camp was set up for army parachute training, lasting until closure in 1972.

Weston-on-the-Green opened as No. 28 TDS in July 1918 but soon returned to pasture. In 1939, it reopened as a SLG for Brize Norton switching to Kidlington in late 1940. By the end of 1941, it had No. 2 GTS up and running. Post-war saw Transport Command take over for parachute dropping practice. It still operates as a RAF gliding school.

Witney opened as No. 33 TDS in 1917 and was disbanded two years later. Civil flying resumed in the 1930s and the site was requisitioned in 1939 as a RLG for Brize Norton. From 1940–45, the site functioned as de Havilland's CRU and a RAOC depot.

Woodcote along with Checkendon Camp contained storage administered by No. 70 MU.

APPENDIX V

Drill Halls, TA, and Army Reserve Centres

In 1958, the War Office carried out a census of drill halls and TA centres. This appendix draws on those data along with information from OS maps; local directories; the Oxfordshire and Berkshire CTAs; the South-eastern Reserve Forces and Cadets Association; TA journals; specialist websites; the 1914 Territorial Force List; anecdotal evidence; and previous personal research.

Historical Review of TA Centres, 1958 (TNA: WO32/17253)

Town	1910	1933
Abingdon	1	1
Banbury	1	1
Bicester	1	
Burford	1	
Charlbury	1	1
Chipping Norton	1	1
Culham		1
Faringdon		1
Henley-on-Thames	2	1
Oxford	3	3
Shipton-under-Wychwood	1	
Thame	1	1
Wallingford	1	1
Wantage	1	1
Whitchurch (Goring)	1	
Witney	1	1
Woodstock	1	

Abingdon:	#Old School or Roysses Room, part of Guildhall complex: drill station, 'D' Squadron, Berkshire Yeomanry; base, 'F' Company, 4th Battalion, Royal Berkshire Regiment; #Ock Street: Boys Brigade drill hall; 1908; #Abbey House grounds (now Waitrose), drill hall for 4th Battalion, Royal Berkshire Regiment; ATS training in WWII; later used by Girl Guides; from late 1920s.
Banbury:	#Town Hall (1854): armoury of 2nd Oxfordshire RVC, 1882; #Plough Inn, RVC armoury, 1893; #Calthorpe Street drill hall, base, 'C' and 'G' Companies. 4th Battalion, OBLI, 1911; #Crouch Street drill hall, base, 'D' Squadron, QOOH and 'C' and 'G' Companies. 4th Battalion, OBLI, 1914; #High Street, Red Lion PH, HQ 'D' Squadron, QOOH, 1914; #The Central Exchange Hall, (now HSBC) at 17 Market Place, HQ of 'B' Company, 2nd Volunteer Battalion, OBLI (VF) 1916; # Easington Farm, Oxford Road, drill hall of 400 (Howitzer) Battery, QOOH and 4th Battalion, OBLI, 1938, extended 1950; #Dalton Barracks, Abingdon, ARC: 142 (QOOH) Vehicle Squadron, 165 (Wessex) Port & Maritime Regiment, Royal Logistic Corps, 2022.
Bicester:	#Chapel Street drill hall (vacated by 1933, now Bryan House) drill station, 'B' Squadron' QOOH and 'F' Company, 4th Battalion, OBLI, 1914.
Burford:	drill station, 'D' Squadron, QOOH, 1914; no dedicated premises traced.
Charlbury:	drill station, 'D' Squadron, QOOH, & 'E' Company, 4th Battalion, OBLI, 1914, no dedicated premises traced but the OS map shows the former Town Hall, used as a cinema until 1960.
Chipping Norton:	#Albion Street drill hall, drill station 'D' Squadron, QOOH, and base, 'E' Company, 4th Battalion, OBLI; by 1885 until post-1911, but not post-1919.
Culham:	Culham College drill station 'G' Company, 2nd Volunteer Battalion, OLI, 1895; and 'D' Company, 4th Battalion, OBLI, 1914.
Deddington:	#Town Hall, 6th Corps, Oxfordshire RVC, 1860; 'D' Company, 2nd Volunteer Battalion, OBLI, 1887; drill station 'D' Squadron, QOOH, 1908.

Didcot: drill station, 'D' Squadron, Berkshire Yeomanry in unidentified building hired by Berks CTA, 1908; #Vauxhall Barracks, base for 505/504 Company, RASC (TA), 1947–65.

Eynsham: drill station, 'F' Company, 4th Battalion, OBLI, 1914; NB modern Village Hall, at 46 Back Lane, is now (2022) a cadet centre.

Faringdon: #Southampton Street, Corn Exchange, armoury, 'I' Company, 1st Volunteer Battalion, Royal Berkshire Regiment, 1887; #London Street, ex-Girls' School, drill station 'D' Squadron, Berkshire Yeomanry; later TAC, now dwelling.

Goring on Thames: drill station 'C' Squadron, QOOH, 1914; no dedicated premises traced.

Henley-on-Thames: #Bell Street, Bull PH, Morris Tube range, 'C' Company, 2nd Volunteer Battalion, OLI, 1887 #New Street, St Mary's Hall, a former National school, used by gymnasts of the Henley Volunteers ('C' Company, 2nd Volunteer Battalion, OLI,), 1894, closed 1910, superseded by Royal Gymnasium on Queen Street; #Town Hall, base 'C' Squadron, QOOH & 'D' Company, 4th Battalion, OBLI, 1901, unused; #Northfield End, drill hall, base 'C' Squadron, QOOH, 'D' Company, 4th Battalion, OBLI, and CLB, 1900; possibly the same as Badgemore Lane. #White House, Market Street (Square?), base 'C' Squadron, QOOH, 1911; #Badgemore Lane drill hall, base 'D' Company, 4th Battalion, OLI, 1911; #Friday Street, Queen's Hall, in use from 1930s; ARC/Cadet Centre, 2022

Kingham: drill station 'E' Company, OBLI, 1914; Village Hall marked on 1919 OS map.

Oxford: #New Road, Militia drill hall and armoury, 1854; to Oxfordshire County Constabulary as HQ in 1876; demolished 1969; #32 New Inn Hall Street, former Methodist Meeting House, HQ, QOOH, 1895; #53 St John Street, HQ 2nd Volunteer Battalion, OLI, 1895; #Paradise Street, St Ebbe's, St Thomas House, HQ QOOH, by 1902–1911; #Tidmarsh Lane, Yeomanry Riding School; fire in hay and fodder store, February 1917; #Holywell, former skating rink/racquets court, HQ and A, B, & H Companies,

4th Battalion, OBLI, 1908; demolished late 1959 for St Cross Buildings; #8/9 Alfred Street (now Pusey Street), HQ OUOTC, 1908; #30 Magdalen Street, County Territorial Association office, 1908; #20 Magdalen Street, HQ South Midland Infantry Brigade (TF), 1914; #12 Lonsdale Road, HQ South Midland Mounted Brigade (TF), 1914; #1 Iffley Road, depot, 2nd South Midland Mounted Brigade, third-line Field Ambulance, RAMC (TF), 1914; #High Street, Examinations Schools, HQ 3rd Southern General Hospital + Somerville College; Town Hall; Workhouse; University College & New College; Masonic Buildings; Radcliffe Infirmary and Eye Hospital; #Exeter College, HQ, 2/4th Battalion OBLI, 1914; #New College, HQ 1st Battalion, Oxfordshire Volunteer Regiment (VF), 1916; #Keble College temporary base for 7th Battalion, OBLI, 1914; #20 St Michael's Street, HQ, OUOTC, 1920; #Manor Road, Yeomanry House on Holywell campus, HQ, QOOH and OUOTC by 1929–94; #Elsfield Hall, HQ, 252 HAA Battery, 1938; 'A' Squadron 299 QOOH Field Regiment, 1947; scoring centre for University Examinations Board, 1967; now Myers-Briggs Co; #Slade TAC, OBLI *c.* 1938; redeveloped for housing 2008; #Marston Road, Harcourt House TAC, QOOH & OBLI, 1957–67; now housing; #Oxpens Road, Falklands House, HQ of OUOTC, OUAS and OURN Unit, 2000.

Shipton-under-Wychwood: drill station, 'D' Squadron, QOOH and 'E' Company, OBLI; no dedicated premises traced.

Thame: #Spreadeagle Hotel assembly rooms, drill station 'C' Squadron, QOOH and 'B' Company, OBLI, 1914; #Park Street, Miniature Range on 1921 OS map

Wallingford: #Thames Street drill hall, drill station, 'B' Squadron Berkshire Yeomanry, and 'C' Company, 4th Battalion, Royal Berkshire Regiment, 1914; #Marketplace, HQ 2nd Battalion, Berkshire Volunteer Regiment (VF), 1916.

Wantage: #45 Market Place (now TSB), passage with armoury and instructor's accommodation, base 9th Corps

Berkshire RVC, 'D' Squadron, Berkshire Yeomanry, then 'K' Company, 1st Volunteer Battalion, Berkshire Regiment; #27 Wallingford Street, Yeomanry House, HQ 'D' Squadron Berkshire Yeomanry and 'K' Company, 1st Volunteer Battalion, Berkshire Regiment, until 1908, then 'C' Company, Royal Berkshire Regiment; #Portway, King Alfred's School OTC armoury in former Fire-Engine House, bought 1910; #29 Springfield Road, Alma Drill Hall (1914) opened 9/7/1914 by Lady Wantage.

Watlington: drill station, 'C' Squadron, QOOH, no dedicated premises traced; #Shirburn Street Miniature Rifle Range opposite White Hart PH on 1919 OS map.

Witney: #Marlborough Lane, (Meeting House Lane), ex-Friends' Meeting House, 5th Oxfordshire RVC and OBLI, 1860–1927; #Corn Exchange, base 5th Oxfordshire RVC, 1863–87; 'F' Company, 4th Battalion, OBLI, 1887-1914; drill station, 'C' Troop, 'B' Squadron, QOOH, 1886–1914; #Langdale Hall, drill hall, base 'F' Company, 4th Battalion, OBLI, 1927–39.

Woodstock: #Blenheim Palace likely venue for 'B' Squadron, QOOH; #Oxford Street, Royal Assembly Rooms, extended 1874, possible venue 9th Oxfordshire RVC, 1861; #New Road, drill hall, base 'B' Squadron, QOOH; drill station 'F' Company, 4th Battalion, OBLI, on 1922 OS map.

APPENDIX VI

Barracks, Camps, and Depots

Second World War

British and Commonwealth Barracks and Army Camps

Cornbury Park/Ramsden Heath: army camp
Didcot, Vauxhall Barracks, RAOC
Eynsham Hall: Royal Canadian Army Service Corps, 1939–40
Faringdon, Butts Close, Royal Marine engineers
Letcombe Regis: 4th Battalion, Cheshire Regiment, 1939
Nettlebed Common: Royal Artillery camp
Oxford, Cowley Barracks: OLI then OBLI Depot
Shotover Park: RE training unit, 1943–4
Slade Camp, Oxford; No. 16 Infantry Training Centre (ITC) until 1942, then No. 16 Primary Training Centre (PTC) for OBLI and Hampshire Regiment
Wantage: 53 (Worcestershire Yeomanry) A/T Regiment, RA, 1939
Witney, Marriott's Close hutted camp: RASC, RCASC and RE

US Army Camps

Adderbury: elements of US 87 Armoured Field Artillery Battalion
Ashdown Park: US 466 QM Group with two QM Truck Battalions
Banbury: elements of US 87 & 696 Armoured Field Artillery Battalions
Besselsleigh: US Nos 61 & 208 Engineer Combat Battalions
Bloxham: HQ US 5 Field Artillery Group (Motorized)
Bodicote: US QM units
Bruern Abbey: US Nos 826 & 877 Airborne Engineer Battalions
Burford: US No. 50 Armoured Infantry Battalion
Checkendon: US 440th AAA AW Battalion plus signals and ordnance maintenance units

Chipping Norton: US No. 157 Engineer Combat Battalion

Clanfield: US No. 593 Ordnance Ammunition Company

Cokethorpe Park: US Nos 819, 833, & 850 Engineer Aviation Battalions

Deddington: US No. 215 QM Salvage Repair Company

Henley-on-Thames: HQs US Nos 178–180 Medical Battalions; 582 Ordnance Ammunition Company; 564 & 565 Ambulance Companies (Motorized); HQ No. 1103 Engineer Combat Group

Kirtlington Park: US Army camp

Middle Barton: US MP and QM truck companies

Middleton Park (Middleton Stoney): US Army camp

Kingston Bagpuize: US No. 2 Air Depot Group, repair and supply squadrons; Ordnance Maintenance, Signals, firefighting and QM truck companies

Mount Farm: US No. 7 Photographic Reconnaissance Group; QM, firefighting, and MP units

Nettlebed, US Nos 118, 207, & 411 AAA Gun Battalions, HQ and A–D Batteries plus medical detachments

Over Norton: US No. 163 Engineer Combat Battalion

Oxford: US postal, MP and intelligence units

Pangbourne: US No. 81 Airborne AA Battalion, HQ + six batteries; No. 181 Engineer Heavy Pontoon Battalion

Ramsden: HQ US 6 Armoured Division Artillery; Nos 128, 212, & 231 Armoured Field Artillery Battalions

Shipton-under-Wychwood: US No. 586 Ordnance Ammunition Company; No. 3982 QM Truck Company

Standlake Park: US No. 459 Signal Construction Battalion

Thame: US No. 3419 Ordnance Medium Auto Maintenance Company

Wallingford, Larkstoke Camp: US No. 207 Engineer Combat Battalion; No. 552 AAA AW Battalion; 635 Engineer Camouflage Company

Witney: US No. 25 Ordnance Battalion; M-401 Medical Depot; No. 8 Medical Supply Depot; QM and auto maintenance companies

Headquarters

Abingdon: HQ No. 91 (OTU) Group, formerly 6 (Training) Group RAF Bomber Command from May 1942

Abingdon: HQ 40 (Equipment) Group, RAF Maintenance Command

Middleton Stoney, Middleton Park: HQ RAOC and Ordnance Service training school

Oxford, Morris Motor Works, Cowley: HQ 43 (Repair) Group RAF Maintenance Command, 1940

Oxford, Merton College: HQ 43 (Repair) Group RAF Maintenance Command, then MAP

Oxford, Magdalen College: joint HQ, 43 (Salvage) Group, merged with 43 (Repair) Group RAF Maintenance Command, 1941

Oxford, Shotover House: HQ 31st Independent Infantry Brigade, 1940
Shrivenham: HQ European Civil Affairs Division (ECAD) Supreme HQ Allied Expeditionary Force (SHAEF); US Nos 6901–2 European Civil Affairs (ECA) Regiments
Thame Park: HQ South Midlands District, Southern Command, 1941

Post-Second World War

Abingdon, Edward Brooks Barracks: 'A' Company, 7th Battalion, The Rifles; 'D' Detachment, 202 (M) Field Hospital; The Rifles Band & Bugles, 2021
Abingdon, Dalton Barracks: Nos 3 and 4 Logistic Regiments, Royal Logistic Corps
Bicester, St George's and St David's Barracks, Royal Logistic Corps units
Didcot, Vauxhall Barracks, EOD Unit of the Royal Logistic Corps, 2022
Ramsden Heath: camp for REME other ranks with officers' accommodation and HQ in Cornbury Park, 1946–7
Slade Barracks, Oxford, 2nd Battalion, OBLI, then 7th Battalion, The Rifles, until 2008

APPENDIX VII

Locations of Volunteer Units

Volunteers in the French Wars

1794

Thame troop of yeomanry cavalry (1788); Banbury; Bicester; Bloxham & Banbury Light Horse; Bullingdon Cavalry; Burford; Charlbury Sharpshooters; Cokethorpe; Cuddesdon; Ewelme Hundred; Henley & Binfield; Lewknor & Pirton; Loyal Oxfordshire Cavalry; Loyal Woodstock; Milton; North Wootton; Oxford Cavalry; Oxford Loyal Volunteers; Oxfordshire Langtree; Ploughly; Ploughly Hundred Cavalry; Thame; Watlington County Fencible Cavalry; Wooton North Yeomanry Troop.

1806

Yeomanry Cavalry Troops

In Oxfordshire: Oxford; Watlington; Bullingdon, Dorchester & Thame; Banbury & Bloxham (2); Wootton; Woodstock; and Ploughly & Bicester.

In former Berkshire: 1st Berkshire Cavalry (Abingdon); Faringdon & Shrivenham; Vale of the White Horse.

Regiments of Volunteer Infantry

Oxford, Henley & Binfield; Langtree; Ewelme; Thame; Banbury; Milton & Dorchester; Woodstock; North Wooton; Pyrton; Lewknor; Burford; Cuddesdon & Wheatley; Cokethorpe; the Bicester Independent Company; and in old Berkshire: Abingdon.

Rifle Volunteer Corps (RVC) 1859–1908

Oxfordshire (Oxon)

1st University of Oxford RVC; 2nd Oxon RVC: Oxford; 3rd Oxon RVC: Banbury; 4th Oxon RVC: Henley-on-Thames; 5th Oxon RVC: Witney; 6th Oxon RVC: Deddington; 7th Oxon RVC: Bicester; 8th Oxon RVC: Thame; 9th Oxon RVC: Woodstock.

After 1887, the six companies of the 2nd Volunteer Battalion, Oxfordshire Light Infantry were based in Oxford, Banbury, Henley, Deddington, Thame and Woodstock with three additional companies in 1884 and 1900.

The Oxfordshire Light Horse Volunteers formed in Banbury in 1864 and disbanded in 1870.

Berkshire

4th Berkshire RVC: Abingdon; 8th Berkshire RVC: Faringdon; 9th Berkshire RVC: Wantage. After 1882, 1st Volunteer Battalion, Royal Berkshire Regiment included 'F' Company at Abingdon; 'I' Company at Faringdon; 'K' Company at Wantage; and 'M' Company at Wallingford.

Yeomanry Units 1908–14

HQ and Signal Troop, 2nd South Midland Mounted Brigade, 12 Lonsdale Road, Oxford.

Berkshire Yeomanry: 'D' Squadron, HQ Wantage, with drill stations at Abingdon, Didcot and Faringdon.

Queen's Own Oxfordshire Hussars (drill stations in brackets): HQ and 'A' Squadron, Oxford; 'B' Squadron, Woodstock (Witney and Bicester); 'C' Squadron, Henley-on-Thames (Thame, Watlington, and Goring-on-Thames); 'D' Squadron, Banbury (Deddington, Chipping Norton, Shipton, Charlbury and Burford).

Territorial Force Infantry Units 1908–1920

County Territorial Association office: 30 Magdalen Street, Oxford.

HQ, South Midland Infantry Brigade, 20 Magdalen Street, Oxford.

4th Battalion Oxford & Buckinghamshire Light Infantry (TF): HQ & 'A' Coy: Oxford; 'B' Coy: Oxford with drill station (DS) at Thame; 'C' Coy: Banbury with DS at Brackley (Northants); 'D' Coy: Henley-on-Thames with a DS at Culham; 'E' Coy: Chipping Norton with DS at Kingham, Charlbury, Shipton and Stow-on-the-Wold (Gloucestershire); 'F' Coy: Witney with DS at Woodstock, Burford and Eynsham; 'G' Coy: Banbury with a DS at Bicester; 'H' Coy: Oxford with a DS at Woodburn.

Cadet Corps 1876–1920

Abingdon, Radley College, Junior OTC, 3 infantry companies; Roysse's School, Junior OTC, 1 infantry company; Boys' Brigade, HQ, Ock Street.
Bicester CLB, possibly St Edburg's Hall.
Bloxham School, Junior OTC, 1 infantry company.
Burford GS, TF cadet company.
Cowley, TF cadet company (HQ, 14 Holywell Street).
Henley Royal GS, TF cadet company.
Oxford University Senior OTC; five CLB cadet battalions; Magdalen College School, TF cadet company; St Edward's School, Junior OTC, 1 infantry company.
Thame, Lord William's GS, TF cadet company.
Wantage, King Alfred's School, Junior OTC, 1 infantry company.
Watlington, CLB; Witney, 1st Cadet Corps, Boys' Brigade.
Woodstock, TF cadet company.

Volunteer Training Corps/Volunteer Force in the First World War

VTC Corps 1914–16

Banbury, Bicester, Burford, Chipping Norton, Churchill & Bingham, Didcot, Eynsham, Henley, Oxford, Oxford University, Peppard, Shipston on Stour, Witney (Oxfordshire); Wantage, Abingdon, Faringdon and Brightwell *cum* Sotwell (former Berkshire).

Oxfordshire Volunteer Regiment 1916-18

1st Battalion: HQ New College, Oxford (two HQ Companies), Bicester ('D' Coy), Woodstock Company.

2nd Battalion: HQ 17 Market Place, Banbury ('B' Company) with company/ platoon detachments at Chipping Norton & Churchill, Thame and Standlake.

Berkshire Volunteer Regiment 1916–18

2nd Wallingford Battalion, HQ in Market Place, with detachments in Wantage, Abingdon, Faringdon and Brightwell *cum* Sotwell.

APPENDIX VIII

Second World War Anti-Invasion Defences

GHQ Red Line

Selected examples of Defence Line components:
DFW3/28a A/T emplacements @SU286994; @SP419006 & 419008; @ SU420998 (two); and @SU577935.
DFW3/28 A/T single chamber emplacement near Benson Lock @SU614907.
DFW3/22(s) pillboxes @SU354996; @SU504906; @SU541938; and @SU605797.
Roadblocks at Newbarn Farm @SU554946; and Cholsey @SU589855.

Oxford Canal/River Cherwell Stop Line (South to North)

Oxford, pillboxes recorded @SP492104, 495104, 506107, 489107 all destroyed.
Gosford, DFW3/24 pillbox @SP513133 between River Cherwell and railway.
Kidlington, pillbox on east bank of canal @SP482143; two pillboxes recorded @SP484140 destroyed.
Thrupp, DFW3/24 pillbox @SP484157; DFW3/26 pillbox @SP482157.
Enslow, pillbox recorded @SP483183, destroyed.
Lower Heyford, two A/T Cylinders @SP478248; single A/T Cylinder @ SP483247; pillbox recorded @SP482248, destroyed.
Somerton, two DFW3/24 pillboxes @SP495290.

Nodal Points and VPs

Bicester: loopholes on parapets of railway bridges on A421 road @SP584232; on B4100 road @SP582233; and on by-road @SP593227.

Britwell Salome, loophole in wall at fork in road @SU669929.

Burford, DFW3/24 pillbox @ SP252128.

Charlbury, loopholes in garden wall @SP354196; 4 loopholes in gable-end @ SP354195.

Charney Bassett, spigot mortar base and loophole in wall @SU381944.

Faringdon: non-standard pillbox (with statue on top) on A4095 Radcot road @SU288961; DFW3/22 pillbox and roadblock below Folly Hill on London Road @SU295958; loophole set alongside entrance arch of former police station in Coach Lane @ SU291957.

Islip, three loopholes in wall overlooking bridge @SP528140.

Kidlington, three loopholes in wall @SP504136 (destroyed).

Oxford: Slade Camp, Brasenose Wood, Norcon pillbox on The Ridings @ SP563054.

Steventon Depot, two ROF-type guard-posts @SU450921 and 449920.

Witney, two Norcon pillboxes on Langel Common @SP362097; two loopholes in wall on Mill Road @SP355103; loophole in barn overlooking A4095 road @SP361105.

Airfield Defences

Akeman Street: two circular prefabricated pillboxes @SP329138 & 330139.

Bicester: DL with two 'Mushroom' pillboxes and two Seagull Trenches @ SP597239; non-standard pillbox/loopholed ARS in front of Watch Office; and eight loopholed ARS in front of the four hangars in the Technical Area; single AM-type pillbox on north side of Technical Area.

Harwell, same type as Akeman Street, @SU484859; Benson; and Kidlington (SP478153) were all recorded with pillbox defences, but all have been demolished.

APPENDIX IX

Home Guard Units in Oxfordshire

Oxfordshire Home Guard

1st (Banbury) Battalion; 2nd (Bicester) Battalion; 3rd (Chipping Norton) Battalion.
4th (Bullingdon) Battalion; 5th (Henley-on-Thames) Battalion; 6th (Oxford) Battalion.
7th (Oxford University) Battalion.
Oxford: HQ 19 AA Regiment, Home Guard with four batteries including No. 111 (101 Oxfordshire Home Guard) AA Rocket Battery.
Oxford GWR Works: No. 308 Independent LAA Troop.
Banbury, Northern Aluminium Co. Ltd; No. 312 Independent LAA Troop.
Oxford: HQ South Midland Home Guard Transport Column; Nos 2144 (Motor Transport) and 2147 (Motor Cycle) Companies.

Berkshire Home Guard

1st (Abingdon) Battalion; 4th (Pangbourne) Battalion; 5th (Wantage) Battalion.
Didcot GWR Works: No. 309 Independent LAA Troop.

Examples of Premises used by Home Guard Units

Bicester, Claremont House, then The Garth, The Lodge: HG HQ, 1940; Bell Inn, HG HQ; Chesterton Lodge, HQ, 1943; Bloxham: rifle range; Coleshill House: national HQ & training centre, Auxiliary Units; Combe, Reading Room; Culham, Royal British Legion hall; Deddington Town Hall; Faringdon, Northgate House, London Street, first HQ, Auxiliary Units; Headington, Bury Knowle House; Hifford Manor; Oxford, Cowley Barracks, HQ, 6 (City of Oxford) Battalion, Jackdaw Lane, assault course, and Old Road, grenade range; Radley College boathouse; South Leigh Station; Tetsworth, Swan

PH: HQ 4th (Bullingdon) Battalion, 1941; Wantage Police Station, HQ 5th Berkshire Battalion; West Hanney, Church Farm; Wheatley, Church Road, HQ 4th (Bullingdon) Battalion, 1940 and 'Cranleigh', Battle HQ, 4th (Bullingdon) Battalion, 1943; Witney, Corn Exchange.

APPENDIX X

Air Defence in the Second World War and the Cold War

AA Sites

Banbury area:	HAA sites, all unarmed, June 1942: Harwell (SP469424); Astrop (SP511386); Bloxham (SP531371); Wroxham SP419426).
Oxford gun-defended area:	HAA sites, as of June 1942: Marston (SP531092) four 3.7-inch (mobile) HAA guns; Southfield (SP540057); Cumnor Hill (SP478049); Partridge Pit (SP481132), all unarmed; Hinksey Hill (SP499039) four 3.7-inch (mobile) HAA guns and gun-laying (GL) radar.

Bombing Decoys

Upper Heyford, Otmoor SP581139 'Q'; Bicester, Grendon Underwood SP678198 'Q/K'; Benson, Pyrton SU662982 'Q/K'; Harwell, Beedon SU472779 'Q'; Brize Norton, Chimney SP345006 'Q'; Kidlington, Enstone SP399247 'Q'; Fawler SP378183 'Q'; and Glympton?; Abingdon, Pyrton 'Q'; Watchfield, Kingston Warren SU314842 'Q'; all 1940/1–1942.

'A' Series (Army): Didcot, Moulsford SU539831 'QL/QF'.

'C' Series (Civil): Cowley Denton SP605021 'QL' and Sandford SP548010 'QL'; Banbury, Tadmarton SP401358 'QL/QF'; MY for the GWR sidings, in use into 1943.

Permanent SF (Starfish): Cowley, Denton (Marshalling Yards) & Sandford (Factory Lighting) in use to distract from Morris Works into 1943.

Temporary SF (Starfish): Oxford, Cumnor SP448064, in use in 1942.

ROC Posts

Boars Hill, 1940, SP526029; Orlit B needed for re-site to SP486029, 1948; u/g 1960, still in use 1968.

Culham/Sutton Courtenay 1935, SU514949; Second World War structure in place in 1952; u/g 1960, closed 1968.

Deddington/Bloxham, 1938, SP464319; Second World War structure in place in 1952; re-site to SP451345; still in use 1968.

Edgehill 1939, SP373468; u/g 1963, still in use 1968.

Enstone, 1940, SP372239; structure needed in 1952; u/g 1959; still in use 1968; occasionally open to the public.

Filkins/Carterton, 1936, SP241053; re-site to SP251072, 1959, u/g 1961, in use 1968.

Hailey/Witney, 1940, SP347094, re-site to SP342099, 1942; re-site to SP349131, 1949; re-site to SP347129, 1953; u/g 1959, closed 1968.

Kidlington, 1935, SP498136; re-site to SP502119, 1936; post with Second World War structure re-sited to SP498132, 1953; u/g 1959; closed 1971.

Kidmore End/Shiplake, 1940, SU696800; re-site to SU727779, 1949; re-site to SU688800, 1949; new structure needed in 1952 for re-site to SU695801, 1953; re-site to SU756777, 1957; re-site u/g 1959, to SU759778; still in use 1968.

Longworth, 1935, SU392995; structure needed in 1952 for re-site to SU288996, 1953; re-site to SU413997, 1956; u/g 1959; closed 1968.

Middleton Stoney, 1935, SP543238; structure needed in 1952; u/g 1959; still in use 1968.

Nettlebed/Checkendon, 1935, SU704870; structure needed in 1952 for re-site to SU669862, 1953; u/g 1961; closed 1968.

Shipton-under-Wychwood, 1936, SP287193; *Granite* 1943; structure needed in 1952; u/g 1959; closed 1968.

Stradhampton, 1935, SU601981; structure needed in 1952 for re-site to SU625979, 1956; u/g 1958; closed 1968.

Swalcliffe, 1936, SP374378; *Granite* 1943; Orlit B needed *c*1952; u/g 1962; closed 1968.

Thame, 1935, SP721058; u/g 1959; still in use 1968.

Uffington/Ashbury, 1936, SU306886; Orlit B needed for re-site to SU271847, 1953; u/g 1960; still in use 1968.

Wantage, 1935, SU407870; structure needed in 1952; u/g 1959; still in use 1968.

Watlington, 1941, SU704935; structure needed in 1952 in local stone following re-site to SU711936, 1951; u/g 1959; still in use 1968.

APPENDIX XI

Munitions and Logistics

Abingdon MG factory manufacturing aircraft components, 1939–45

Abingdon, Abbey Gardens: Army Salvage Depot, 1940

Banbury, No. 9 National Filling Factory, 1916

Bicester Depot SU580-600.195-212 established 1941; 20,000 troops & ATS employed there in 1945; 32 miles of roads and 41 miles of railway track; from 1999 name changed to Defence Storage & Distribution Centre employing 850 service personnel and 2,500 civilians. Also, Upper Arncott, Depot SU602-640.162-181

Caversfield, Defence Clothing & Textiles Agency, 1994–2010

Cowley, Hollow Way, Morris Factory extension as Admiralty Mine Sinker Assembly Station, 1917 (building marked on 1925 map but since destroyed)

Didcot Central Ordnance Depot 1915–1964

Eynsham Forward Ammunition Depot (FAD) run by No. 96 MU supplying the south Midlands OTUs.

Faringdon House hutted camp: US Nos 100 & 101 Ordnance Ammunition Battalions; 57th Ordnance Ammunition Company, 1942–5

Islip, AFDD supplying fuel to Fairford & Southrop airfields (both Gloucestershire), *c.* 1938

Kingham: US Ordnance Ammunition Depot O-670; No. 61 Ordnance Ammunition Battalion, 1942–5

Oxford, Marston Road: divisional offices of MAFF, 1939; demolished 2001

Stonor Park: National Benzole Co. (BP) centre for requisitioning of petrol & oil, 1939–45

Tubney Woods: Nuffield Mechanisation & Aero Company's shadow factory manufacturing barrels for Bofors LAA guns.

Wantage: US Ordnance Ammunition Depots O-670 & O-677, 1942–5

Witney: RAOC depot on ex-RFC airfield and de Havilland aircraft repair unit, 1939–45

APPENDIX XII

Military and Auxiliary Hospitals

First World War

Red Cross Auxiliary Hospitals

Abingdon, Burcote House Orthopaedic Hospital
Abingdon, 22 Marcham Road: Tesdale House Red Cross Auxiliary Hospital
Banbury, Grimsbury, West Street Wesleyan Chapel schoolroom: Grimsbury VAD hospital
Bicester Hall VAD hospital
Blenheim Palace military convalescent hospital
Burford, Asthall Manor Auxiliary Hospital
Chipping Norton, Bruern Abbey VAD hospital
Chipping Norton, Cornwell Manor
Chipping Norton, Spring Street: Hill Lodge Auxiliary Hospital
Clanfield, Carter Institute, Clanfield VAD hospital
Didcot Rectory Cottage Red Cross Auxiliary Hospital
Faringdon, Kitemore Auxiliary Red Cross Hospital (SU312942)
Goring on Thames, Battle House VAD Hospital (SU612814)
Henley-on-Thames, Harpsden Court Auxiliary Hospital
Henley-on-Thames, town hall, fifty-two-bed VAD Hospital
Henley-on-Thames, Sywncombe House VAD Hospital
Lower Brailles, Brailles Auxiliary Hospital
(Rotherfield Court, hospital for shell-shocked soldiers, 1921)
Thame, Dorton House Auxiliary Convalescent Hospital
Thame, Old Grammar School: VAD Hospital

Oxford, 3rd (Southern) General Hospital RAMC, TF

Oxford, High Street, Examination Schools
Oxford, New College Shelter
Oxford, behind 49–52 High Street, Masonic Buildings
Oxford, 88–9 High Street, University College, Radcliffe and Durham Buildings
Oxford, Cowley Road, Workhouse (SP532058)
Oxford, Felstead House, 23 Banbury Road, Oxford District Nurses' Hostel, University of Oxford VAD Hospital
Oxford, St Aldate's, town hall
Oxford, Walton Street, Eye Hospital
Oxford, Woodstock Road, Radcliffe Infirmary
Headington, Wingfield Convalescent Home/Orthopaedic Hospital
Headington, Pullens Lane, High Wall Auxiliary Convalescent Hospital
Oxford, Woodstock Road, Somerville College
Oxford, Magdalen College School, Cowley Road
Oxford, Littlemore County Lunatic Asylum, Ashurst War Hospital
Steventon, Milton Hill Sectional Hospital

Second World War

Burcote, The Croft: Red Cross Convalescent Home/Auxiliary Hospital
Banbury, Swalcliffe Park: Red Cross Convalescent Home/Auxiliary Hospital
Bicester, Tusmore Park: Red Cross Convalescent Home/Auxiliary Hospital
Fritwell Manor: convalescent hospital and RAF billets
Goring Heath, Flint House: Red Cross Convalescent Home/Auxiliary Hospital
Headington, High Wall: Red Cross Convalescent Home/Auxiliary Hospital again
Headington Hill Hall, military hospital, 1939–45; then rehabilitation centre run by Red Cross & St John Ambulance until 1953
Henley-on-Thames, Gillotts: Red Cross Convalescent Home/Auxiliary Hospital
Middleton Park: Red Cross Officers' & Nurses' Convalescent Hospital
Oxford, St Hugh's College: Military Hospital for neurological cases
Oxford: 600-bed EMS hospital; then US Southern Base Section General Hospital; US Army 2nd (later 91st General Hospital), 1942, now the Churchill Hospital
Oxford: 809th US Army Hospital Centre established January 1945, non-operational
Ramsden Heath: Cornbury Park, Finstock Hospital, US No. 317 Station Hospital, 1942
Shotover Park (SP557050), Slade Isolation Hospital, US/Canadian camp in hospital grounds
Shrivenham: US European Theater Medical Field Service School, 1943

Stratton Audley Park: Red Cross Convalescent Home/Auxiliary Hospital
Studley Priory: sanatorium for RAF officers
Wheatley Military Hospital; 57th US Field Hospital, then US 97th General Hospital in Holton Park as US No. 347 Station Hospital; later RAMC use
Witney: US Medical Depot M-401, 1944, then to Normandy as M-401(T)

US Combat Rest Homes or 'Flak Shacks' in the Second World War

Henley, Phyllis Court (Station 494), HQ for American Red Cross combat rest homes, 1942. Detachments 'O' & 'X' 93 SCSRD (USSTAFE) combat rest home for twenty-eight NCOs, 1944–5
Moulsford Manor (Station 511) VIIIth USAAF Service Command combat rest home for enlisted men, 1943–5
Wallingford, Buckland House (Station 511a) combat rest home for eighteen enlisted men, 1943–5
Whitchurch, Pangbourne House, now Coombe Park (Station 557). Detachment 'F' 93 SCSRD, USSTAFE, combat rest home for thirty NCOs, 1944–5
Witney, Eynsham Hall (Station 567). Detachment 'L' 93 SCSRD, USSTAFE, combat rest home for sixty-five officers, 1944–5

APPENDIX XIII

POW Camps

First World War

Banbury, Neithrop Workhouse; Charlbury, Cumnor Camp; Deddington, Earls Lane; Enstone, Litchfield Arms PH, German agricultural labour camp; Hook Norton; Watlington Camp

Second World War

Bicester, Blackthorn Old Windmills Camps 632 (SP609206) and 653 (SU608207)
Bicester, Bucknell Road, Italian camp behind Star Inn
Bicester, Graven Hill COD (SP592207 & 588204) centre points for Camps 632/653/657/683
Bicester, Graven Hill COD, Bolero Camp 553, ex-Stores area
Bicester, Graven Hill COD, Camp 657, tented with use of Shed D35, ex-Stores area
Bicester, Graven Hill COD, Camp 683, in Area E3
Bicester, Graven Hill COD, Camp 1011 (SP590197) in Area D30, ex-Stores area
Checkendon Camp (SU662845), Italian POW camp
Didcot, Durnell's Farm (SU514918), Magazine Camp 652/3 (later 693) within COD
East Challow, satellite Italian work camp
Eynsham Hall, Camp 661a; SP395123
Faringdon, Southampton Street
Headington, Old Road Camp, Wood Farm, annexe of Camp 43; fenced hutted compound
Nettlebed, North Camp 246 (SU705868), German work camp, annexe to Basildon House

Nettlebed, South Camp
North Hinksey, Harcourt Hill Camp No.43 (SP488044), 1942, Italian work camp
Shotover House, Camp 687 (SP583067), German work camp
Shrivenham, Horgard Barracks (SU255907) Camp 695
Stanton Harcourt, camp in an airfield Communal Site post-summer, 1945
Watchfield, tented camp alongside Longcott road, now Bower Green military housing

Bibliography

Books and Articles

Adams, M., *The First Kingdom; Britain in the Age of Arthur* (London: Head of Zeus, 2021)

Alexander, C., *Ironside's Line* (Storrington: Historic Military Press, 1999)

Allen, T., *Late Bronze Age and Iron Age: Historic Environment Resource Assessment* for Oxfordshire HER (Oxford: Oxford Archaeology, 2006)

Anderson, I., 'Abingdon, Oxfordshire: Type 'F' Hangar', *Airfield Review* 118 (Thetford: ARG, 2008)

Beckley, R., & Radford, D., *Oxford Archaeological Resource Assessment* (Oxford: Oxford City Council, 2011)

Blair, J. and Steane, J., 'Investigations at Cogges…The Priory and Parish Church', *Oxoniensia* XLVII (Oxford: Oxfordshire Architectural & Historical Society, 1982)

Blair, J., 'Thornbury, Binsey: a Probable Defensive Enclosure associated with St Frideswide', *Oxoniensia* LIII (Oxford: Oxfordshire Architectural & Historical Society, 1988); 'Excavating Anglo-Saxon grid planning: the discovery of a lost layer in the landscape', *British Archaeology* 176 (York: CBA, 2021)

Bond, J., 'Earthen Castles, Outer Enclosure and the Earthworks of Ascott d'Oilly Castle', *Oxoniensia* LXVI (Oxford: Oxfordshire Architectural & Historical Society, 2001); 'The medieval rural landscape', *The Thames Through Time* (English Heritage & Oxford Archaeology South, 2019)

Bowyer, M., *ACTION STATIONS 6: Military airfields of the Cotswolds and the Central Midlands* (Wellingborough: Patrick Stephens, 1983)

Bryan, T., *The Great Western Railway at War 1939–45* (Sparkford: Patrick Stephens, 1995)

Campbell, D., *War Plan UK: the truth about Civil Defence in Britain* (London: Burnett, 1982); *The Unsinkable Aircraft Carrier: American Military Power in Britain* (London: Michael Joseph, 1984)

Carvell, S., 'The Oxford Canal Stop Line', *Loopholes* 39 (Beccles: Pillbox Study Group, 2007); 'RAF Bicester WWII Defences', *Loopholes* 73 (Burgh: Pillbox Study Group, 2018)

Christie, N., 'Creating Defended Communities in Later Saxon Wessex' in Christie, N., & Herold, H., (eds) *Fortified Settlements in Early Medieval Europe* (Oxford: Oxbow, 2016)

Christie, N. & Creighton, O., *Transforming Townscapes from Burh to Borough: the archaeology of Wallingford AD800-1400* Society for Medieval Archaeology Monograph 35 (Oxford: Oxbow, 2013)

Clarke, B., *Four Minute Warning: Britain's Cold War* (Stroud: Tempus, 2005)

Colvin, H., (ed.) *The History of the King's Works, The Middle Ages Volumes I & II* (London: HMSO, 1963)

Creighton, O., and Higham, R., *Medieval Town Walls, an Archaeology and Social History of Urban Defence* (Stroud: Tempus, 2005)

Creighton, O., *et al.*, 'Wallingford', *British Archaeology* 106 (York: CBA, 2009)

Dace, R., 'Outrage at Faringdon', *English Civil War Times* 51 (Leigh-on-Sea: Partizan Press, 1995)

Dawe, N., 'An Anti-tank Ditch Restored', *Loopholes* 5 (Dover: Pillbox Study Group, 1993)

Devaney, R., 'The Excavation of Iron Age, Roman, Medieval and Civil War Features South of the Vineyard, Abingdon', *Oxoniensia* LXXII (Oxford: Oxfordshire Architectural & Historical Society, 2007)

Durham, B., & Halpin, C., *et al.*, 'Oxford's Northern Defences: Archaeological Studies 1971–82', *Oxoniensia* XLVIII (Oxford: Oxfordshire Architectural & Historical Society, 1983)

Eastwood, D., 'Communities, Protest and Police in early Nineteenth-Century Oxfordshire: The Enclosure of Otmoor Reconsidered', *The Agricultural History Review* 44,1, (1996)

Eddershaw, D., *The Story of the Queen's Own Oxfordshire Hussars 1798–1998* (Banbury: Oxfordshire Yeomanry Trust, 1998)

Emery, A., 'Shirburn Castle', *Castle Studies Group Journal* 17 (Daventry: CSG, 2004); 'Greys Court: Castle or Fortified House', *Castle Studies Group Journal* 19 (Daventry: CSG, 2006)

Finstock News, Issue 100, October/November 2016 (online)

Fowler, P., 'Excavations at Tadmarton Camp, Swalcliffe', *Oxoniensia* XXV (Oxford: Oxfordshire Architectural & Historical Society, 1960)

Gee, A., *The British Volunteer Movement 1794–1814* (Oxford: OUP, 2003)

Gordon-Slade, H., 'Broughton Castle', *The Archaeological Journal* 135 (London: Royal Archaeological Institute, 1978)

Goring, J., 'The Military Obligations of the English People 1511–1558' unpublished PhD thesis (London: Queen Mary University of London, 1955)

Guy, N., '*Time Team* at Radcot' in *News* in *Castle Studies Group Journal* 23 (Daventry: CSG, 2009-10); 'Wallingford' in *News* in *Castle Studies Group Journal* 23 (Daventry: CSG, 2009-10); 'A few notes on Bampton Castle' in *Castle Studies Group Journal* 32 (Daventry: CSG, 2018); (editor) 'Castle Studies Group Conference, April 2019' in *CSG Journal* 33, 2019-20; detailed notes on Bampton, Wallingford, Oxford Castle and city walls and Deddington (Daventry: CSG, 2019)

Harrison, J., *et al.*, 'The House of Wessex: a rebuilt early medieval hall', *British Archaeology* 175 (York: CBA, 2020)

Haslam, J., 'The Two Anglo-Saxon Burhs of Oxford', *Oxoniensia* LXXV (Oxford: Oxfordshire Architectural & Historical Society, 2010)

Hassall, T., 'Excavations at Oxford Castle, 1965–73', *Oxoniensia* XLI (Oxford: Oxfordshire Architectural & Historical Society, 1976)

Hinton, D., *Alfred's Kingdom: Wessex and the South 800–1500* (London: JM Dent, 1977)

Historic England Research Records: Bicester Military Railway (1363495); Graven Hill Depot (1411454); POW Camps Nos 553 (1475538), 657 (1475678), and 1011 (1474752)

Hulme, R., reviews of Christie, *et al.*, 'Transforming Townscapes' (Wallingford) qv; and Keats-Rohan, *et al.*, 'Wallingford: the castle and town in context', *Castle Studies Group Journals* 28 pp. 311-13 and 30 pp. 319-21

Hulme, R., 'Siege Warfare in King Stephen's Reign (1135–54)', *CSG Journal* 33, 2019-20 (Daventry: CSG, 2019)

Ivens, R., 'Deddington Castle and the English Honour of Odo of Bayeux', *Oxoniensia* XLIX (Oxford: Oxfordshire Architectural & Historical Society, 1984)

Jenkins, S., *Witney, The Volunteers & The Territorial Army* (unpublished typescript, nd.)

Jope, E., & Threlfall, R., 'The Twelfth-Century Castle at Ascot Doilly: Its History and Excavation', *The Antiquaries Journal* XXXIX, parts 3 & 4 (Oxford: Society of Antiquaries of London, 1959)

Kaye, S., 'Can computerised terrain analysis find Boudica's last battlefield?', *British Archaeology* 114 (York: CBA, 2010)

Keevill, G., *Medieval Palaces, an Archaeology* (Stroud: Tempus, 2000)

Kemp, A., 'The Fortification of Oxford during the Civil War', *Oxoniensia* XLII, (Oxford: Oxfordshire Architectural & Historical Society, 1977)

Laban, G., *et al.*, 'Evidence for a Stephanic Siege Castle at The Street… Crowmarsh Gifford', *Oxoniensia* LXXVIII, (Oxford: Oxfordshire Architectural & Historical Society, 2013)

Liddiard, R., *Castles in Context: Power, Symbolism and Landscape, 1066–1500* (Bollington: Windgather, 2005)

Malim, T., 'Grim's Ditch, Wansdyke, and the Ancient Highways of England: Linear Monuments and Political Control', *Offa's Dyke Journal* 2 (Chester: University of Chester, 2020)

McGlynn, S., *Blood Cries Afar: the forgotten invasion of England, 1216* (Stroud: Spellmount, 2012)

Mortimer, I., *The Greatest Traitor* (London: Vintage, 2003)

Nicol, N., list of POW Camps in WWI (pers. com. during Defence of Britain Project)

Northover, K., *Banbury in the Great War* (Witney: Prospero Publications, 2003

Norton, A., Munby, J., & Poore, D., *Excavations at Oxford Castle, Oxford's Western Quarter from the mid-Saxon period to the late-18th Century* (Oxford Archaeology Monograph, 2011)

Osborne, M., *Sieges & Fortifications of the Civil Wars in Britain* (Leigh-on-Sea: Partizan Press, 2004) *Defending Britain* (Stroud: Tempus, 2004); *Always Ready, the drill halls of Britain's volunteer forces* (Leigh-on-Sea: Partizan Press, 2006); *Pillboxes of Britain and Ireland* (Stroud: Tempus, 2008); *Grandad's Army: Volunteers Defending the British Isles in the First World War* (Stroud: Fonthill Media, 2020)

Palmer, N., 'Excavations on the Outer City Wall of Oxford', *Oxoniensia* XLI, (Oxford: Oxfordshire Architectural & Historical Society, 1976)

Parrott, D., 'The British Civil Wars and the Defence of Oxford', *New College Notes* 11 (Oxford: New College, 2019)

Pitcher, D., 'RFC & RAF Henley-on-Thames', *Airfield Review* 157 (Bedford: ARG, 2017)

Poore, D., and Norton, A., 'Excavations at Oxford Castle's Western Quarter', *Oxoniensia* LXXIV, (Oxford: Oxfordshire Architectural & Historical Society, 2009)

Preston, A., 'A Moated Mound at Abingdon, Berks', *The Antiquaries Journal* XIV (Oxford: OUP, 1934)

Purton, P., 'A lonely gun hole… (Oxford City Wall)', *Castle Studies Group Journal* 34 (Daventry: CSG, 2020)

Rodwell, K., 'Excavations on the Site of Banbury Castle, 1973–4', *Oxoniensia* XLI, (Oxford: Oxfordshire Architectural & Historical Society, 1976)

Rowley, T., 'First Report on the Excavations at Middleton Stoney Castle, 1970–1', *Oxoniensia* XXXVII, (Oxford: Oxfordshire Architectural & Historical Society, 1972)

Salway, P., 'Roman Oxfordshire', Tom Hassall Lecture for 1997, *Oxoniensia* LXIV, (Oxford: Oxfordshire Architectural & Historical Society, 1999)
Shapland, M., 'Buildings of Secular and Religious Lordship: Anglo-Saxon Tower-nave Churches' (London: unpublished PhD thesis, UCL, 2012)
Shapland, M., *Anglo-Saxon Towers of Lordship* (Oxford: OUP, 2019)
Sherwood, J., and Pevsner, N., *Oxfordshire, Buildings of England* (Harmondsworth: Penguin Books, 1974)
Sherwood, R., *The Civil War in the Midlands* (Stroud: Alan Sutton, 1992)
Stevenson, J., and Carter, R., 'The Raid on Chinnor and the Fight at Chalgrove Field, June 17th and 18th, 1643', *Oxoniensia* XXXVIII, (Oxford: Oxfordshire Architectural & Historical Society, 1973)
Spurrell, M., 'Containing Wallingford Castle, 1146–1153', *Oxoniensia* LX, (Oxford: Oxfordshire Architectural & Historical Society, 1995)
Steer, Brigadier F., *To the warrior his arms: The story of the RAOC 1918–93* (Barnsley: Pen & Sword, 2005)
Sutton, J., 'Iron Age Hillforts and some other Earthworks in Oxfordshire', *Oxoniensia* XXXI, (Oxford: Oxfordshire Architectural & Historical Society, 1966)
Thomas, K., *'Flak' Houses Then and Now* (Old Harlow: Battle of Britain International Ltd, 2006)
Thurley, S., *Palaces of Revolution: Life, Death and Art at the Stuart Court* (London: William Collins, 2021)
Williams, T., *Viking Britain* (London: Collins, 2017)
Wright, D., and Creighton, O., *Castles, Siegeworks and Settlements: Surveying the Archaeology of the Twelfth Century* (Archaeopress, 2016)
Young, C., 'The Defences of Roman Alchester', *Oxoniensia* XL, (Oxford: Oxfordshire Architectural & Historical Society, 1975)

Websites

Banbury Museum, www.banburymuseum.org/banburys-role-ww1 on YouTube
Bicester in World War II website
Brennan, N, Hamerow, H., *et al.*, *An Anglo-Saxon Great Hall Complex at Sutton Courtenay/Drayton, Oxfordshire: a royal centre of early Wessex?* ora.ox.ac.uk
british-army-units1945on.co.uk
british-history.ac.uk/vch/oxon
Coggins, G., *Deddington Scrapbooks* www.deddingtonhistory.uk retrieved December 2021
www.controltowers.co.uk
Flintham, V., *Military Airfields in Oxfordshire* www.vicflintham.co.uk retrieved 12/2021
historicengland.org.uk/images-books/publications/Wessex-hillforts-project
Moss, V., *Memories of Shrivenham 1900–1960* www.shrivenhamheritagesociety.co.uk retrieved 7.04.2022.
Norton, S., 'Assessing Iron Age Marsh Forts' (Birmingham: unpublished Ph.D. Thesis University of Birmingham, 2019) etheses.bham.ac.uk
Victoria County History of Oxfordshire, History Online *Ancient Earthworks* <www.british-history.ac.uk/vch/oxon/vol2/pp303-349>
www.gatehouse-gazetteer.info/Indexs/Eng County lists of fortified sites
www.geolsoc.org.uk/Geoscientist/Archive/February-2013/Wartime-Geotechnical-Maps
World War 2 comes to Hanney website

Index